PRELUDE TO ISRAEL'S PAST

PRELUDE TO ISRAEL'S PAST

Background and Beginnings of Israelite History and Identity

NIELS PETER LEMCHE

Translated by E. F. Maniscalco

HENDRICKSON PUBLISHERS

P. O. Box 3473
Peabody, Massachusetts 01961–3473

Printed in the United States of America

English translation by E. F. Maniscalco
Original edition: *Die Vorgeschichte Israels: Von den Anfängen bis zum Ausgang des 13. Jahrhunderts v. Chr.* Biblische Enzyklopädie, Bd. 1. ©Verlag W. Kohlhammer, Stuttgart, Berlin, Köln, 1996.

ISBN 1–56563–343–1

First Printing — November 1998

Library of Congress Cataloging-in-Publication Data

Lemche, Niels Peter.
[Vorgeschichte Israels. English]
Prelude to Israel's past: background and beginnings of Israelite history and identity / Niels Peter Lemche; [English translation by E. F. Maniscalco].
Includes bibliographical references and indexes.
ISBN 1–56563–343–1 (cloth)
1. Jews—History—To 1200 B.C. 2. Bible. O.T. Pentateuch—History of Biblical events. I. Title
DS121.L448 1998
221.9′5—dc21 98–43291
CIP

In memory of Hannes Olivier. There never was a better friend.

TABLE OF CONTENTS

CHRONOLOGICAL TABLE

	3000	2500	2000	1500
Egypt	Early Dynastic Period (ca. 3000–2675)	Old Kingdom (ca. 2675–2310) 1st Intermediate Period (ca. 2310–1980)	Middle Kingdom (ca. 1980–1630) Hyksos (ca. 1630–1520)	New Kingdom (ca. 1520–1075) Amarna Period (ca. 1355–1335) Ramesses II (ca. 1279–1213)
Mesopotamia	Early Dynastic Period I–II (ca. 2900–2600)	Early Dynastic Period III (ca. 2600–2350) Dynasty of Akkad (ca. 2350–2190)	Old Babylonian and Old Assyrian Periods (ca. 2000–1600)	Kassite Dynasty (ca. 1595–1160)
Syria-Palestine	Early Bronze Age (ca. 3200–2200)	Ebla (ca. 2500–2300) Amorites	Middle Bronze Age (ca. 2000–1550) Yamkhad (ca. 1850–1550) Yarim-Lim (ca. 1790–1770)	Late Bronze Age (ca. 1550–1150) Mitanni (ca. 1620–1350) Egyptian Empire (ca. 1525–1200) Ugarit Sea Peoples (ca. 1200)
Anatolia				Hittite Empire (ca. 1450–1200) Suppiluliumas I (ca. 1380–1340)
Aegean			Middle Bronze Age Golden Age of the Minoan Culture (ca. 2000–1400)	Late Bronze Age Mycenean Culture (ca. 1400–1200)

THE ANCIENT NEAR EAST IN THE BRONZE AGE

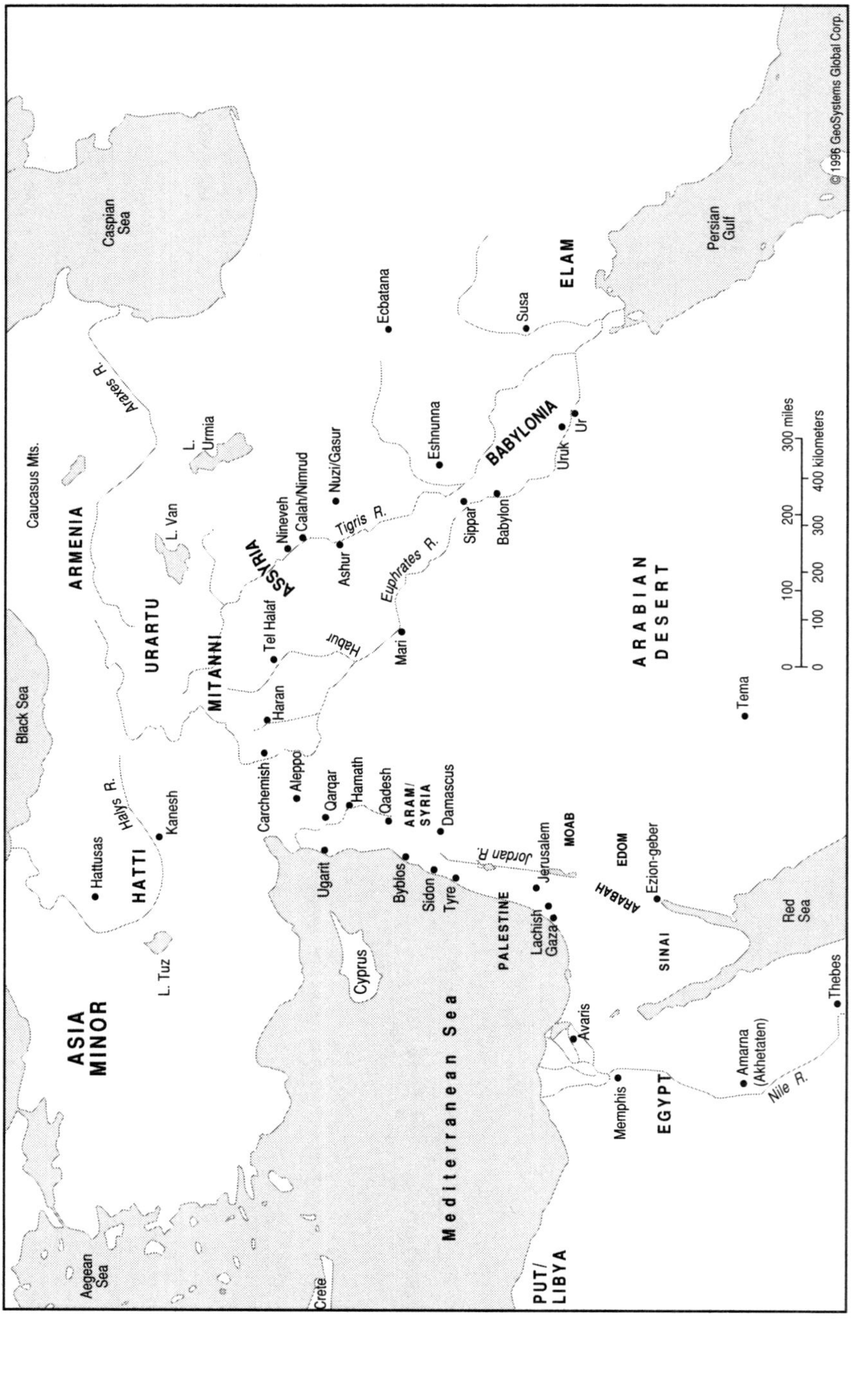

ABBREVIATIONS

ABD	*Anchor Bible Dictionary*. Edited by David Noel Freedman (6 vols.; New York: Doubleday, 1992)
ADPV	Abhandlungen des Deutschen Palästinavereins
AEL	*Ancient Egyptian Literature*. Miriam Lichtheim (3 vols.; Berkeley: University of California Press, 1943)
ANEP	*Ancient Near East in Pictures*. Edited by James B. Pritchard (Princeton: Princeton University Press, 1969)
ANET	*Ancient Near Eastern Texts*. Edited by James B. Pritchard (Princeton: Princeton University Press, 1969)
AOAT	Alter Orient und Altes Testament
BA	*Biblical Archaeologist*
BEvT	Beiträge zur evangelischen Theologie
BHT	Beiträge zur historischen Theologie
BibS(N)	Biblisch-theologische Studien (Neukirchen-Vluyn: Neukirchener Verlag, 1951–)
BJS	Brown Judaic Studies
BN	*Biblische Notizen*
BWANT	Beiträge zur Wissenschaft vom Alten und Neuen Testament
BZAW	Beihefte zur Zeittschrift für die alttestamentliche Wissenschaft
ErFor	Erträge der Forschung
CBQMS	Catholic Biblical Quarterly Monograph Series
COS	*The Context of Scripture*. Edited by W. W. Hallo (3 vols.; Leiden: E. J. Brill, 1997–)
DBAT	*Dielheimer Blätter zum Alten Testament und seiner Rezeption in der Alten Kirche*
Deut	Deuteronomy
EA	El-Amarna tablets, according to *Die El-Amarna-Tafeln*. J. A. Knudtzon (2 vols.; Vorderasiatische Bibliotek 2; Leipzig: J. C. Hinrichs, 1908–1915; reprint, Aalen: O. Zeller, 1964). Supplement in *El-Amarna Tablets*,

	359–379. A. F. Rainey (2d revised ed.; AOAT 8; Kevelaer: Butzon & Bercker; Neukirchen-Vluyn: Neukirchener Verlag, 1978)
Exod	Exodus
FRLANT	Forschungen zur Religion und Literatur des Alten und Neuen Testament
Gen	Genesis
GNT	Grundrisse zum Neuen Testament
Hos	Hosea
HSM	Harvard Semitic Monographs
HSS	Harvard Semitic Studies
Isa	Isaiah
Jer	Jeremiah
JESHO	*Journal of Economic and Social History of the Orient*
JNES	*Journal of Near Eastern Studies*
Josh	Joshua
Judg	Judges
JSOT	*Journal for the Society of the Old Testament*
JSOTSup	Journal for the Society of the Old Testament, Supplement Series
1–2 Kgs	1–2 Kings
KTU	*Die Keilalphabetischen Texte aus Ugarit*. M. Dietrich, O. Loretz, and J. Sanmartín (Neukirchen-Vluyn: Neukirchener Verlag, 1976). Second enlarged edition of *KTU: The Cuneiform Alphabetic Texts from Ugarit, Ras Ibn Hani, and Other Places*. M. Dietrich, O. Loretz, and J. Sanmartín (Münster: Ugarit-Verlag, 1995)
Lev	Leviticus
Num	Numbers
OBO	Orbis biblicus et orientalis
Or	*Orientalia* (Rome)
OrAnt	*Oriens antiquus*
Ps	Psalms
1–2 Sam	1–2 Samuel
SBLSS	Society of Biblical Literature Semeia Series
SBLWAW	Society of Biblical Literature Writings from the Ancient World
SBS	Stuttgarter Bibelstudien
SBT	Studies in Biblical Theology
SHANE	Studies in the History of the Ancient Near East
SJOT	*Scandinavian Journal of the Old Testament*
SOTSMS	Society for Old Testament Study Monograph Series
TZ	*Theologische Zeitschrift*
UF	*Ugarit-Forschungen*
VT	*Vetus Testamentum*

VTSup	Vetus Testamentum, Supplements
VZAGA	Veröffentlichungen des Zentralinstituts für Alte Geschichte und Archäologie der Akademie der Wissenschaften der DDR
WMANT	Wissenschaftliche Monographien zum Alten und Neuen Testament
ZDL	*Zeitschrift für deutsche Literature*
ZTK	*Zeitschrift für Theologie und Kirche*

PREFACE

For some years, a discussion has raged within biblical—particularly Old Testament—studies between a position called "maximalist" and a second position, usually dubbed "minimalist." This controversy is over the amount of historical information that can be found in the pages of the Old Testament: not much, the minimalist would say; a lot more, the maximalist would argue. However, in a normal scholarly environment, neither the minimalist nor the maximalist accepts everything written in the Old Testament as history. The discussion has largely to do with the extent of historical information believed to be present, not with the basic question of why not everything in the Old Testament can be considered history.

Prelude to Israel's Past addresses this question of the historical character of the biblical narrative. I approached the subject by first analyzing the biblical accounts of the patriarchs, the exodus from Egypt, and the sojourn in the desert—in short, the narratives in the books of Genesis through Numbers. After that, I compare the image of the past created by the biblical writers with ancient sources of information from the civilizations of Syria and Palestine in the Bronze Age, which is usually considered as the historical setting of the pentateuchal stories. It will be shown beyond question that there is very little correlation between the biblical portrait of the past and the nonbiblical evidence from actual Bronze Age cultures. We must conclude, however, not that the biblical authors were unsuccessful historians but that they were not at all interested in providing anything like a historical report of the past. They wrote for other reasons, and they used history as the vehicle for their message. When approaching the literature of the Old Testament, people of modern times must realize that the ancient authors did not write primarily for posterity, that is, for us, but for the benefit of their contemporary audience. They followed the moral and aesthetic expectations of their time; they would have had no idea of the rules that govern modern historical studies and interests.

This book was originally the first volume of a twelve-volume project called the *Biblische Enzyklopädie*, initiated by a group of European scholars, including its contributing editor Walter Dietrich from Bern, Switzerland. A common layout was followed for all the volumes in this series: each volume would cover a specific period of the biblical history—from the patriarch Abraham to the apostle Paul in the complete series–and would open with a review of the biblical account of the particular period discussed. The image created by the biblical authors would then be compared with other information about the same period, and a section would follow dealing with the religion and general culture of the period in question. Each volume was expected to end with theological observations and conclusions.

The series was aimed primarily at students of theology and the general reader. The amount of documentation—especially the standard ubiquitous scholarly footnoting—was to be limited as much as possible in order to make the books readable. They were certainly not planned to be dissertations; the contributors involved in the project were all senior scholars who have already shown they could write footnotes!

When preparing this English version, it was decided not to revise the layout of the German original. As a rule, the notes have been left unchanged and their quantity kept small, although some editing has occurred, when, for example, a reference to a German study could be substituted with an appropriate English one. Several extra notes have been added—mostly references to ancient literature or the like—and a number of corrections have been made, making this not only a translation of the German original but also an updated edition. In the conclusion, the discussion about Bible and history has been sharpened or made more precise in comparison to the German *Vorlage.*

I owe a number of people my gratitude for their painstaking work in producing this volume, not least Ed Maniscalco, the original translator of the book. Ed taught me much about English style. The staff at Hendrickson, and especially senior editor John F. Kutsko, was very active in turning my volume into a readable book. John should also be commended for his meticulous reading of the manuscript. It is not least due to his energy and intelligence that several mistakes present in the original volume were identified and eliminated from the manuscript. Any remaining errors are, however, solely my responsibility.

The book is dedicated to the memory of professor J. P. J. Olivier—Hannes, to all his friends—from Stellenbosch in South Africa, who passed away in the spring of 1998 after having put up a long and brave, but hopeless, struggle against the inevitable. From the very beginning, Hannes followed my work with great interest and we shared—in addition to good humor and sympathies—many interests in the direction of our scholarly work.

Gurre, 26 August, 1998

1

THE BIBLICAL PORTRAIT OF THE PERIOD

I.1. THE ACCOUNT

I.1.1. Prologue: The Stories in Genesis through Numbers

Blenkinsopp, Joseph. *The Pentateuch: An Introduction to the First Five Books of the Bible.* The Anchor Bible Reference Library. New York: Doubleday, 1992. **Blum,** Erhard. *Studien zur Komposition des Pentateuch.* BZAW 189. Berlin: de Gruyter, 1990. **Kreuzer,** Siegfried. *Die Frühgeschichte Israels in Bekenntnis und Verkündigung des Alten Testaments.* BZAW 178. Berlin: de Gruyter, 1989. **von Rad,** Gerhard. *Das formgeschichtliche Problem des Hexateuchs.* BWANT 4/26. Stuttgart: Kohlhammer, 1938. Reprinted in *Gesammelte Studien zum Alten Testament.* Vol. 1. Theologische Bücherei 8. Munich: C. Kaiser, 1958. E. T. "The Form-Critical Problem of the Hexateuch." In *The Problem of the Hexateuch and Other Essays.* Pages 1–78. Translated by E. W. Trueman Dicken. New York: McGraw-Hill, 1966. **Rendtorff,** Rolf. *Das überlieferungsgeschichtliche Problem des Pentateuch.* BZAW 147. Berlin: de Gruyter, 1976. E. T. *The Problem of the Process of Transmission in the Pentateuch.* Translated by J. J. Scullion. Sheffield: Sheffield Academic Press, 1990. **Rost,** Leonhard. *Das kleine Credo und andere Studien zum Alten Testament.* Heidelberg: Quelle & Meyer, 1965. **Thompson,** Thomas L. *The Origin Tradition of Ancient Israel, I: The Literary Formation of Genesis and Exodus 1–23.* JSOTSup 5. Sheffield: JSOT Press, 1987. **Whybray,** Roger N. *The Making of the Pentateuch: A Methodological Study.* JSOTSup 53. Sheffield: JSOT Press, 1987.

Just as the Christian message can be summarized in short confessional formulas known as "creeds," the Old Testament contains similar short summaries of Israel's ancient story. We find a striking example of such a creedal formula or "credo" in Deuteronomy 26. In it, the wandering patriarch[1] offers to God the "firstfruits" of his labor. Like any Christian confession that highlights only the most important incidents in Jesus' life, this Old Testament confession avoids expansive recapitulations of Israel's history from its earliest stages to the arrival in Canaan. This and other Old Testament confessions offer only brief snapshots of the history told in the five books of Moses (the Pentateuch). They pay attention to some of the major events in Israel's early history, while other elements of that record remain untold. It is often said that these confessions totally reconfigure the core of the Pentateuch's accounts of the ratification of the covenant and the law. This assumption has spawned many traditio-historical theories that suggest that the unique position of the account of the Israelites at the mountain of God indicates that this report derives from a separate tradition.[2] Later this study will cover that issue in detail. At this point, we merely note that Deut 26:5–6 highlights the significant events for the early Israelites and their families from the moment God chose Abraham and his family until their descendants arrived at Jordan's banks. An idea becomes reality when the Jordan is crossed. At long last, the people have taken possession of their land. Clearly, the creedal snapshot in Deuteronomy 26 mirrors the history about which the Pentateuch speaks.

Deuteronomy 26:5–9

You shall make this response before the LORD your God: "A wandering Aramean was my ancestor; he went down into Egypt and lived there as an alien, few in number; and there he became a great nation, mighty and populous. When the Egyptians treated us harshly and afflicted us, by imposing hard labor on us, we cried to the LORD, the God of our ancestors; the LORD heard our voice and saw our affliction, our toil, and our oppression. The LORD brought us out of Egypt with a mighty hand and an outstretched arm, with a terrifying display of power, and with signs and wonders; and he brought us into this place and gave us this land, a land flowing with milk and honey. So now I bring the first of the fruit of the ground that you, O LORD, have given me." You shall set it down before the LORD your God, and bow down before the LORD your God. Then you, together with the Levites and the aliens who live among you, shall celebrate with all the bounty that the LORD your God has given to you and to your house.

---

[1]Or the miserable, pitiful patriarch. Here the Hebrew word *ʾōbēd* usually means "drifting"; however, it also means "miserable," "pitiful," or even "destroyed."

[2]For a discussion of the principles and methods of traditio-historical analysis, see Douglas A. Knight, "Tradition History," *ABD* 6:633–38.

The Genesis–Numbers narrative complex differs from the credo's literary form in that the latter constructs a tripartite historical flow—first, Israel's ancestors leave Canaan and settle in Egypt; second, Israel endures a period of hard labor in Egypt; and finally, Israel is triumphantly rescued from Egypt and returns to the land of Israel (formerly Canaan). In contrast to the credo's tripartite literary form, the Genesis–Numbers complex offers two story lines. The first, in Genesis 12–50, is rather simple and consists of only two narrative blocks concerning the patriarchs. Israel's ancestors, who have lived under Mesopotamian rule in Ur of the Chaldeans and in Haran, subsequently move to Canaan, the promised land. Eventually, Israel's ancestors travel in stages from Canaan to Egypt. This story is based on the notion that the patriarch Abraham—at that point still called Abram—was compelled to leave his ancestral home. It concludes with Abraham's grandson apparently finding a new home in Egypt. The second story line (in Exodus and Numbers) explains how the people still considered Egypt a foreign land, even though they had lived there for centuries. It could never be a national home for the Israelites. When the relationship between Israel and Egypt disintegrates, the Israelites flee Egypt and return to their own land, Canaan. This story is cut short at the end of the five books of Moses, exactly at the moment when the Israelites are about to realize their goal.[3]

The flow of this tale about the early history of the Israelite people is complicated by a significant and lengthy interruption: the Sinai complex in Exodus–Numbers is a compositional catastrophe that distorts the symmetry between the patriarchal history and the tales of desert wandering. It is therefore necessary to replace the two-part story line in Genesis–Numbers with a more complicated one, consisting of four distinct episodes. The first episode (Gen 12–36) covers the life of Israel's first three patriarchs: Abraham, Isaac, and Jacob. The second (Gen 37–50) describes the fate of Joseph and his brothers. In the third (Exod 1–19; 24), Israel flees Egypt, and Yahweh, Israel's God, greets Israel at Sinai, the mountain of God. Finally, in Numbers 10–36, the narrative recounts the journey from God's Sinai revelation to Canaan's doorstep. The Sinai complex involving the law (Exod 20–23; Exod 25–Num 10) lies between the third and fourth episodes.

---

[3] The symmetry of a movement-code between the two parts of the narrative is marked: this movement leads on the one hand from Mesopotamia through Palestine to Egypt, and on the other hand from Egypt through the desert to Palestine. Ultimately, this symmetry demands that the Israelites must again live in their land. Thus, the tale concerning the taking of the land at the end of the Genesis–Numbers accounts either must be comparable to the one in Joshua or else originally included sections that were at least partially identical with it. This implies that the tale in Joshua was once essential to the conclusion of Numbers.

In all phases of the narrative complex, Israel's wanderings take center stage. First, Abraham, the patriarch of all Israelites, travels from Mesopotamia to Canaan. Second, he moves from Canaan to Egypt with his entire family. Finally, in the third and fourth parts, his descendants wander the Sinai until they almost reach Canaan. The question is whether the story of the settlement of the Israelite tribes in Canaan constitutes a fifth episode or, since it contains little in the way of a journey, should be seen as belonging to the fourth part of the narrative.

In the next section, we will explore individual sections of the four-part narrative complex in Genesis–Numbers described above. Please realize that this is simply a recapitulation of the *biblical* history, rather than a historical assessment of it. That will come later in the chapter.[4]

I.1.2. The Patriarchs of Israel

Abraham

Abram's family originally lived in Ur of the Chaldeans, in the southernmost part of Mesopotamia. From Ur, Abram's father Terah and his family have moved to Haran in northern Mesopotamia (Gen 11:27–32). When God orders Abram to travel to an unknown land, he leaves Haran together with his wife Sarai and his nephew Lot in order to settle in Canaan, while the rest of his family remains in Mesopotamia. From the outset, Abram's future is determined by God's promise (Gen 12:1–2): if Abram travels to the country that God will show him, God will make him the patriarch of a great people. Since the Canaanites still lived in the cities of Shechem, Bethel, and Ai, Abram circumvents them, building altars throughout the countryside: not in Shechem but just outside it; not in Bethel but between Bethel and Ai. Thus he puts his indelible mark on the land. At the end of his journey, he settles in the southern lowland of the Negev.

Soon a famine overtakes Canaan and Abram heads for Egypt (Gen 12:10–20), where he almost loses his wife. Pharaoh brings Sarai into his harem because he thinks she is Abram's sister, not his wife. Only God's intervention prevents Sarai from becoming Pharaoh's wife. When Abram eventually returns to Canaan from Egypt, he is a rich man, thanks to all the great riches Pharaoh has bestowed upon them. However, Abram's family cannot long continue to live together in Canaan: Lot leaves his uncle and settles in the Jordan Valley at Sodom, while Abram remains in Canaan (Gen 13). Almost immediately Abraham must set out to rescue his nephew Lot from four great foreign kings who have joined forces in the Jordanian region (Gen 14) and kidnapped Lot and his family. With his

[4] See below section I.2.

band of 318 men, Abram is able to fight the coalition of great kings and free Lot and his family. Abram gives a tenth of the booty to Melchizedek, the king of Salem (probably Jerusalem) and priest of the highest God (El Elyon), leaving the rest for his allies and the king of Sodom.

Clearly, Canaan now serves as Abram's permanent home; however, the second part of God's promise remains unfulfilled, since Abram has no son. Abram cannot hope to be the patriarch of a great people if he and Sarai remain childless. This new period of Abram's life represents a renewal of God's promise. For the first time, the announcement comes: for four hundred years, Abram's descendants will live in a foreign land (Egypt). God's promise is sealed with a covenant between God and Abram, though Abram and Sarai still remain childless (Gen 15). Now the two of them try to speed up the fulfillment of God's promise: the Egyptian slave and surrogate wife Hagar conceives the son they desire, Ishmael (Gen 16). But it is difficult to circumvent God. First, God renews his association with Abram, renaming him Abraham and his wife Sarah, and the covenant is sealed with the physical sign of circumcision (Gen 17). Although Abraham's attempt to fulfill the promise through Hagar fails miserably, God dismisses the attempt with a blunt admonition: the promise remains solid and Sarah will fulfill it (Gen 17:15–22). Later, the promise of a son is repeated in an emphatic way when three men, one of them apparently representing Yahweh, visit Abraham at Mamre (Gen 18).

When they leave Abraham at Mamre, the two companions (or angels) of God continue to Sodom, where they find lodging for the night at Lot's house (Gen 19). The wanton natives of Sodom conspire to assault Lot's two guests. Although the angels are not physically injured, God determines to destroy Sodom and Gomorrah. His wife is lost, but Lot and his family seek refuge east of the Jordan rather than with their relatives west of the Jordan. In a drunken state, Lot impregnates his daughters, becoming the patriarch of the Moabites and Ammonites (Gen 19:29–38).

Again Abraham settles in the southern region, among the Philistines in Gerar. For a second time Sarah avoids the fate of becoming the wife of a foreign king, this time King Abimelech of Gerar (Gen 20). After these events Sarah finally becomes pregnant, but her pregnancy creates a new problem: What will become of Ishmael, the son of Abraham and Hagar, now that Sarah is pregnant? Can he become the heir to God's promises to Abraham? No, with his mother, he is expelled from his father's house and forced to settle in a foreign land, where he becomes the patriarch of the Ishmaelites (Gen 21:1–21). Meanwhile, in Gerar, hostilities erupt between Abraham's men and the Philistines over the right to use a well. Ultimately, Abraham again must abandon Gerar (Gen 21:22–34).

Obviously, Yahweh fulfilled his promise: Abraham lives in a land promised by God and has a son by his wife Sarah. Logically, the narrative should end here; however, this is not the case. Now God extends a gruesome invitation to Abraham: he must travel to the mountain of Moriah and sacrifice his son to God (Gen 22). Abraham obeys, but at the last possible moment, God intervenes. To preserve his promise, God rescues Isaac.

When Abraham's wife dies during their stay in Hebron (Kiriath-arba), he buys a burial cave in the field of Machpelah from a local Hittite named Ephron (Gen 23). In order to relieve Isaac's bereavement over the loss of his mother, Abraham sends his servant to his family in Haran to find a wife or him (Gen 24). Rebekah, a daughter of Bethuel the Aramean, follows Abraham's servant into Canaan, where she marries Isaac. Thus, Abraham finally fulfills his mission and secures his posterity. All that remains is to recount Abraham's death and funeral (Gen 25).

Isaac

The Old Testament says little about Isaac. His wife is the Aramean Rebekah, Laban's sister, and the mother of Esau and Jacob. Rebekah's story is also rather brief. She, like Sarah her mother-in-law, is sterile. But God pities her, and she becomes pregnant and bears twin brothers, Esau and Jacob (Gen 25:21–26). Furthermore, like Sarah, Rebekah almost marries the Philistine king, Abimelech of Gerar. She is spared from this fate when the king of Gerar discovers that she is already the wife of Isaac (Gen 26:1–11). Another dispute over a well erupts between Isaac's people and those of King Abimelech of Gerar, which leads Isaac to settle in Beer-sheba (Gen 26:12–33).

Jacob

Jacob's story is barely comparable to those of his father and grandfather. First, he is not an only son, but the *younger* of two brothers; therefore, God's promise does not really apply to him. He also marries Laban's two daughters, Leah and Rachel, and he eventually produces not one but twelve sons, from four different wives.

Through an elaborate deception, Jacob steals his naïve brother's birthright. First he bribes his brother with lentil stew (Gen 25:29–34); then, on Rebekah's instruction, he tricks his father into blessing him instead of his brother (Gen 27). Consequently, like Abraham, Jacob must now leave the land. To avoid the consequences of his fraudulent claims, Jacob searches for his mother's family in Haran (Gen 27–28). Along the way, in Bethel, he meets Yahweh in a dream. There Jacob establishes a shrine, and God promises to return him to that land as the heir of his father and the patriarch of a great people (Gen 28:10–22).

In Haran, Jacob meets someone who matches his own shrewdness—his uncle Laban. Jacob's love for Rachel, his true love, is costly, and he endures seven years' labor under Laban's rule. At the conclusion of his toil, Jacob marries Rachel, or so he thinks; in fact, Laban switches daughters on their wedding night. For Rachel's hand, Jacob completes seven more years of service to Laban (Gen 29).

Most of their children are born in Haran. Yet like Sarah and Rebekah, Jacob's beloved wife Rachel is initially infertile. Finally she gives birth to Joseph—the subject of the subsequent narrative. For the time being, Jacob continues to accrue wealth by working for Laban. However, after he cheats his master, he prepares to return to his homeland a rich man along with his wives and children (Gen 30). In a final swindle, Rachel steals Laban's household gods (Gen 31:19–21), though reconciliation ultimately marks his journey home: first, Laban and Jacob (Gen 31:22–54), and then Jacob and his brother Esau make peace (Gen 32:23–33).

One night during the return trip, a fight takes place between Jacob and God at Peniel, east of the Jordan (Gen 32:23–33). As a result of this struggle, Jacob receives a new name: Israel, or "He wrestles with God."[5]

When Jacob returns to Canaan, he settles in Shechem (Gen 33:18–20) where his stay is overshadowed by disaster. It begins when Shechem, the son of the Hivite Hamor, the prince of the land, rapes Jacob's daughter Dinah. Although the sons of Jacob reach a truce with the inhabitants of the city, including a marriage between Dinah and her rapist, two of them, Simeon and Levi, take revenge on the offender and his family and murder the city's entire male population (Gen 34).

Jacob hastily departs Shechem and settles in Bethel, the site of God's earlier promise. During his journey southward, Rachel dies near Bethlehem. There Jacob loses a wife but gains a new son: Benjamin (Gen 35:16–20). Shortly after Rachel's death, Jacob rejoins his father at Mamre in Hebron, and the story of the patriarchs draws to its end. Isaac dies at Mamre and is buried in the tomb of Machpelah alongside his father, his mother, and his wife Rebekah (Gen 35:27–29).

I.1.3. The Joseph Saga

Already in the Jacob stories, but all the more in the Joseph saga, one notices a composing hand that spun a tale with interrelated threads. In comparison, the story of Abraham looks more like a casual collection of anecdotal episodes. The Joseph saga should undoubtedly be viewed as a continuous and coherent narrative: a series of individual scenes or episodes, each presupposing what precedes it. The introduction describes

[5]This is an example of the so-called popular etymologies, which occur throughout the Old Testament. These popular etymologies are not scientifically correct; however, they are descriptive and connected to a particular popular tradition. Scholars still struggle to find a proper explanation for the term Israel.

how Joseph—the second youngest son—and his brothers tend their father's sheep. He is undeniably Jacob's *beloved* son—a circumstance of which Joseph is quite conscious. After all, a dream clearly and precisely ratifies his privileged status. His brothers' envy of his lofty position festers, and their vengeance almost succeeds: they attack their brother when he is away from his father's house, throw him in a well, and finally sell him as a slave to Midianite (or Ishmaelite[6]) merchants. The merchants, in turn, sell Joseph to the Egyptian Potiphar, the commander of Pharaoh's elite guard (Gen 37 and 39). Hiding their dirty deed, Joseph's brothers deceive their father, telling him that wild animals ripped his son apart.

This story might seem to bring Joseph's history to an abrupt halt, but in fact it is the beginning of a marvelous career in Egypt, despite an initial spate of problems: when Joseph rejects the seductive advances of Potiphar's wife, her false accusation lands him in prison (Gen 39). Eventually, his ability to interpret dreams wins his release (Gen 40) and a summons from Pharaoh. Joseph gains fame in Egypt when he successfully interprets Pharaoh's dream about an impending seven-year famine (Gen 41). Joseph then rises to the highest position in Egypt when Pharaoh asks him to prepare Egypt for the approaching famine. Adding prestige to fame, he marries the daughter of the priest of On and becomes a bona fide Egyptian. Consequently, Jacob unknowingly faces a legitimate threat: the loss of his son for a second time. Now, however, the stakes are higher since Joseph is about to lose his Israelite identity.

It is ironic that Joseph's brothers, who are responsible for his being sold to Egypt, should also save him from becoming an Egyptian. Thanks to Joseph, during the famine Egypt fares much better than Canaan. Since Egypt's supplies remain abundant and Canaan's dwindle, Joseph's father urges his sons to travel to Egypt to buy grain and secure their survival (Gen 42). However, Jacob prohibits his younger son, Benjamin, from making the journey with his ten brothers. Upon their arrival in Egypt, the grain manager (i.e., Joseph) welcomes them. Joseph recognizes his brothers, but they do not recognize him. Thus, the narrative has all the

---

[6]The story in Gen 37:23–36 does not differentiate between the Ishmaelites and the Midianites, although these are clearly two distinct ethnic groups of eastern Jordan and the Sinai peninsula. The finest surveys of both groups are by Ernst Axel Knauf, *Ismael: Untersuchungen zur Geschichte Palästinas und Nordarabiens im 1. Jahrtausend v. Chr.* (ADPV; 2d ed.; Wiesbaden: O. Harrassowitz, 1989), and *Midian: Untersuchungen zur Geschichte Palästinas und Nordarabiens am Ende des 2. Jahrtausends v. Chr.* (ADPV; Wiesbaden: O. Harrassowitz, 1988). In this tale, the author shows no concern for or knowledge of the distinction between Ishmaelites and Midianites. See also Walter Dietrich's alternative explanation that this represents a second stratum of the Joseph saga in *Die Josephserzählung als Novelle und Geschichtsschreibung: Zugleich ein Beitrag zur Pentateuchfrage,* (BibS[N] 14; Neukirchen-Vluyn: Neukirchener Verlag, 1989).

elements of a classic "recognition drama"; that is, a key figure observes the right connection and can turn the ignorance of others to his own advantage.[7] Therefore, Joseph's brothers cannot penetrate his manipulative scheming. Little do they know that their current adversary is their long-lost brother. On Joseph's orders, against Jacob's wishes, Benjamin is brought to Egypt, where he is accused of theft. After baiting his brothers further, Joseph finally reveals his true identity. He neither condemns nor penalizes his surprised brothers; rather, he invites them to bring also their father to Egypt. Thus, with his family and belongings, Israel comes to Egypt (Gen 45–46). However, Jacob/Israel never becomes Egyptian. This is shown by the fact that Jacob instructs his family to return his body to Canaan upon his death for burial in the family tomb. The entire family follows Jacob on his final journey: Joseph, his sons, and his brothers, accompanied by many Egyptian officials. After the burial, the tears subside, and they all return to Egypt. This time the Israelites will not return to their homeland; every member of Jacob's family will live and die in Egypt.

I.1.4. Egypt and Exodus: The Desert Wanderings

Egypt could never be Israel's homeland. The apparently harmonious coexistence of the Israelites and the Egyptians at the end of Genesis soon takes a turn for the worse. Before long the relationship between the two peoples erupts into hatred and hostility. From an Israelite or Jewish perspective, the Israelites' ill-conceived decision to stay in Egypt must necessarily lead to a crisis between the Israelites and Egyptians. Exodus, the second book of Moses, begins with that theme.

The Egyptians soon forget Joseph. They know only that the Israelites have multiplied rapidly (Exod 1). Thus, the Israelites become a work force for the construction of Pharaoh's two store cities: Pithom and Rameses. At the same time, every male Israelite child is killed to prevent the conception of further descendants. Following this bitter prelude, a story about Israel's liberation is sketched from a series of narrative fragments. Yet the composite narrative is hardly comparable to that of the

---

[7] To modern people like us, this type of story may seem odd; however, in antiquity, people identified things quite differently. Mario Liverani raises the issue in his essay, "Segni arcaici di individuazione personale: A proposito del motivo del riconoscimento nei tragici Greci": *Rivista di filologia e istruzione Classica* 105 (1977): 106–18. While modern people usually rely on specific information about an individual (i.e., peculiar physical, bodily features), ancient people concentrated on such things as footprints, hair, or clothing. A well-known example of this is the reunion between Orestes and Electra in Aeschylus's play *The Libation-bearers (Choephoroi)*. Electra identifies her brother Orestes not by his features but by his footprints, clothing, ring, and cloak.

Joseph saga. First we hear of the birth and marvelous rescue of the heroic liberator, Moses. His mother places him in a straw basket, and Pharaoh's daughter pulls him from the Nile. Predictably, Moses grows up as an Egyptian in Pharaoh's court (Exod 2:1–10). However, his Israelite blood boils within him when he witnesses a struggle between an Egyptian and an Israelite. He kills the Egyptian and flees to Midian. In Midian, the hero Moses lives for a long time in the house of Reuel, the "priest of Midian." Later, Reuel becomes Moses' father-in-law when Moses marries his daughter Zipporah.

The story now takes a critical turn. While living in Midian as a refugee, the hero Moses is still more of an Egyptian than an Israelite. His Israelite heritage is rekindled, however, when the God of his ancestors springs upon the scene. God appears to Moses from the midst of a flaming thornbush and informs him of the impending liberation of Israel from Egypt (Exod 3). God repeats the patriarchal promise to Moses and entrusts Moses with the mission to lead his people out of Egypt and bring them to Canaan. When Moses refuses on the grounds of his speech impediment, he receives help in the person of his brother Aaron, who becomes his spokesman. After that, Moses returns to Egypt.

The next chapters of Exodus (5–11) narrate Moses' attempts to negotiate Israel's liberation. Pharaoh's intransigence unleashes a series of trials and tribulations. After repeated attempts by Moses (and God) to convince Pharaoh, an angel of God kills Egypt's firstborn (Exod 11). Now the Israelites receive permission to leave Egypt. After celebrating the first Passover, the Israelites pull up stakes and head for the land of their ancestors (Exod 12–13). A small family is now a nation of approximately 600,000 men (Exod 12:37), who carry Joseph's bones with them. Yahweh accompanies them daily, directing their every step with a cloud by day and a column of fire by night (Exod 13:17–22). Yet Pharaoh rescinds his original order to liberate the Israelites and sets out after them. Though he sends his army to recapture the presumptuous Israelites, God rescues them again. Yahweh parts the sea, and after the Israelites pass through safely, the troops are engulfed (Exod 14; 15). Now the Israelites continue their journey to Sinai, the mountain of God. Along the way, the rations dwindle and many begin to regret their journey. Should they return to Egypt? This time, through a divine miracle, manna and quails satisfy their hunger and prevent the Israelites' death in the desert (Exod 16). Similarly, Moses quenches their thirst by drawing water from a rock (Exod 17:1–7). On their subsequent journey to Sinai, the Israelites conquer the Amalekites (Exod 17:8–16), and Moses' father-in-law advises him to establish a judicial bureaucracy (Exod 18).

At this point in Exodus, the story is interrupted by the giving of the law at Sinai. The narrative thread continues in the book of Numbers (10:11), where the Israelites resume their wanderings in the Sinai desert. God again sends quails (Num 11) and continues to supply manna, even to the edge of the promised land. In this part of the story, conflicts abound between God and the rebellious Israelites. Yahweh kills several of the primary instigators, including Korah, Dathan, and Abiram (Num 16). For Moses' sister, the penalty is leprosy (Num 12). In some cases, all the people are culpable, as when, for example, they are too easily persuaded to doubt God, convinced that they cannot enter Canaan because the land—according to the scouts—is peopled by giants (Num 13–14). Yahweh punishes their distrust with forty additional years of desert wanderings. God punishes even Moses when he draws water from a rock a second time (Num 20). Moses dies in the desert and never sets foot in the promised land.

Israel moves on. Along the way fights continually erupt with the desert-dwellers (Num 21:1–3) and the inhabitants east of the Jordan (Num 21:10–31; 31). When the magician Balaam the son of Beor threatens to curse the Israelites, Yahweh intervenes and causes Balaam to bless them instead. Finally, the people reach the bank of the Jordan River, at Canaan's threshold—ready to conquer the promised land (Num 25).

I.1.5. Sinai

The Sinai complex clearly interrupts (or at least delays) the progression of the story concerning Israel's journey from Egypt to Canaan. This complex, which generally consists of legal codes, comprises the central portion of the pentateuchal tradition (Exod 19–Num 10).[8] It contains few narrative elements, although it begins with a story about God's revelation and enactment of the covenant—evidently a link to the antecedent parts of the desert-wandering tradition. The first part of the desert journey ends as the Israelites arrive and encamp by the mountain of God (Exod 19).

Moses climbs the mountain and inquires about imminent events. Subsequently, he descends the mountain to retrieve his brother Aaron and then returns again to Yahweh to receive the tablets of the law. Altogether, the revelation includes the Ten Commandments (Exod 20:1–21), the altar regulations (Exod 20:22–26), and the Book of the Covenant (Exod 21:1–23:16). After that, Yahweh again extends a promise: he will personally lead the Israelites through the desert, and he will guarantee the future conquest of Canaan. The ratification of the covenant foreshadows a future when Israel will be Yahweh's people, and Yahweh will be their God (Exod 24:3–8).

The convoluted story that follows describes how Moses ascends the mountain to visit Yahweh. Each time, he brings along guests: Aaron,

---

[8] This is not the only section in the Pentateuch that concerns the law. Additional legislation dots the overall portrayal of the desert wanderings. Finally, Deuteronomy (the fifth book of Moses) includes a very extensive law collection.

Nadab, Abihu, Joshua, and seventy elders of Israel. When Moses lingers on his private journey up the mountain, the people, at Aaron's suggestion, construct a golden calf—a substitute god described as the one who saved Israel and led it from Egypt. When he returns, Moses shatters the tablets of the law and then destroys the golden calf. Subsequently, he reascends the mountain to receive the law again (Exod 32–34). Thus ends the Sinai complex's narrative components. Subsequent chapters of Exodus, all of Leviticus, and the first ten chapters of Numbers concentrate exclusively on the laws that according to tradition Moses proclaimed at Sinai.

I.2. THE INQUIRY

I.2.1. History or Story?

GENERAL: **Clines,** David J. A. *The Theme of the Pentateuch.* JSOTSup 10. Sheffield: JSOT Press, 1978. **Fokkelman,** J. P. *Narrative Art in Genesis: Specimens of Stylistic and Structural Analysis.* 2d ed. The Biblical Seminar 12. Sheffield: JSOT Press, 1991. **Thompson,** Thomas L. *The Origin Tradition of Ancient Israel,* vol. 1, *The Literary Formation of Genesis and Exodus 1–23.* JSOTSup 55. Sheffield: JSOT Press, 1987. Pages 1–59.

CONCERNING FOLK LITERATURE AND THE OLD TESTAMENT: **Assmann,** Jan. *Das Kulturelle Gedächtnis: Schrift, Erinnerung und politische Identität in frühen Hochkulturen.* Munich: C. H. Beck, 1992. **Coats,** George W., ed. *Saga, Legend, Tale, Novella, Fable: Narrative Forms in Old Testament Literature.* JSOTSup 35. Sheffield: JSOT, 1985. **Gunkel,** Hermann. *Das Märchen im Alten Testament.* 1921. Reprint, Frankfurt am Main: Athenäum, 1987. E. T. *The Folktale in the Old Testament.* Translated by M. D. Rutter, with an introduction by J. W. Rogerson. Sheffield: Almond, 1987. **Kirkpatrick,** Patricia G. *The Old Testament and Folklore Study.* JSOTSup 62. Sheffield: JSOT Press, 1988.

No doubt, the ancient storytellers viewed their stories as history, recounting the actual lives of Abraham, Isaac, and Jacob, as well as the early Israelite generations. The question is, did they understand "history" in the modern sense, or with something else in mind? How naïve this question seems to us. After all, those authors composed their stories thousands of years ago. Naturally, they could not write history in the modern sense. They did not possess the technical research methods that are the prerequisites for contemporary historians and their writings. Clearly, we would not expect the Old Testament to be composed like something comparable to a modern history book; however, this does not mean that it or its writers lacked any historical awareness. Ancient narrators undeniably had such an awareness to some extent. For example, the Old Testament's main story line represents a rough chronology from the creation of the world to the fall of Jerusalem in 596 or 587 B.C.E. Therefore, its stories do not appear as isolated episodes detached from the main story line, however abstract that line may be. Furthermore, these reflections come from a universal understanding of the world: the first part of Genesis reflects upon the worldwide, universal, primeval history (Gen 1–11). The story of a unique people, set apart from the world, begins only in the second part—a tale that stretches from the origin of the people to their (temporary) demise.

Yet the Pentateuch's chronological schemes alone do not qualify them as historical writings. In antiquity, other cultures used chronologically arranged collections of information, usually as chronicles (e.g., annual lists that detailed important information about significant events from year-to-year).[9] To this genre belonged the practice, known from Egypt and Mesopotamia, of providing official documents with precise dates; for example, references to well-known events such as great battles, the digging of important canals, or the construction of magnificent temple complexes.

This ancient interest in chronology, however, should not be overrated. Most state documents and almost all private documents from the ancient Near East are undated, and this is especially true of official documents from preclassical Syria and Palestine. Thus the many texts found at Ugarit are hardly ever dated apart from an occasional reference to the name of the ruling king (although without mention of his regnal year).

Furthermore, we must consider carefully the uniqueness of the historical literature of the Old Testament among its ancient Near Eastern neighbors, from whom no comparable literary forms developed. Some skepticism is needed when others suggest that the narratives of the Old Testament are truly history and part of a literary genre common to the ancient Near East. There is no comparable historical literature from Western Asia and Egypt before the Hellenistic period (when history writing became more common in the work of such authors as Berossus, who wrote a Babylonian history; Menander of Ephesus and Philo of Byblos, both of whose area of interest was Phoenician history; and Manetho, whose chronology of the Egyptian pharaohs has remained important even to modern Egyptologists).[10] Based on the unique character of the biblical historical narrative, John Van Seters suggests the influence of Greek historical writing in these Old Testament stories. The similarities warrant our attention; however, substantial differences remain between

---

[9] This chronological literature will be discussed later in sections II.1.2 and III.2.2 below.

[10] None of these histories is preserved except as fragments in the works of other authors, especially Josephus and the church father Eusebius of Caesarea. The fragments of the work of Philo have been collected and edited by H. W. Attridge and R. A. Oden Jr., *Philo of Byblos: The Phoenician History* (CBQMS 9; Washington, D.C.: The Catholic Biblical Association of America, 1981).

the two traditions.[11] The compelling parallels between the biblical and Greek traditions notwithstanding, it does not necessarily follow that the Old Testament writers borrowed from their Greek counterparts. The many dissimilarities between, the Pentateuch and Herodotus's *History*, for example, count against an easy association of the Greek and Hebrew traditions. It is probably better to think of a parallel development within postexilic Jewish society on the one hand and among Greek intellectuals of the classical and postclassical periods (sixth–third centuries B.C.E.) on the other.

In this review of the character of the biblical historical literature, two related terms are used: *Tradition* and *Überlieferung*. Both terms signify narrative segments that the authors used to create a piece of *literature*. Neither an *Überlieferung* nor a *Tradition* need contain any historical information. There is, therefore, no reason to assume in advance that the pentateuchal narrative has anything to do with the real prehistory of the Israelite people. Here *Überlieferung* means simply this: a thematic or stylistic element in the story, probably extracted from the world of folk literature, and injected into the literary forms of the Old Testament for strictly aesthetic purposes. In this sense, one finds neither of the two linchpins of German and Scandinavian Old Testament research: *Überlieferungsgeschichte* or *Traditionsgeschichte*, respectively. *Überlieferungsgeschichte* retraces the *literary* history of transmission, attempting to isolate and assess the story's historical seeds. *Traditionsgeschichte*, the history of tradition, seeks original historical incidents behind the text's *oral* history. These research schemes are unsound and pointless, because they insist upon the historical symbiosis between story and content. After all, a story does not require any historical underpinnings. Thus it can be said that even the patriarchal narratives did not necessarily develop from historical reflection. Rather they could be considered literary masterworks of art.

One can address this problem from another angle: were other ancient Near Eastern literary forms used as sources for the Old Testament's historical narratives? Are there sufficiently compelling similarities to constitute evidence of such dependence? Two ancient and widespread Near Eastern literary forms come to mind: epic literature and purely fictional adventure tales. In this connection, it has to be said that several North American scholars who have attempted to identify an Israelite epic tradition as the source of the Pentateuch (especially the patriarchal narratives) have completely missed the point. Why? Because there are no

---

[11] See John Van Seters, *In Search of History: Historiography in the Ancient World and the Origins of Biblical History* (New Haven: Yale University, 1983; repr., Winona Lake, Ind.: Eisenbrauns, 1997), and his later clarification in *Prologue to History: The Yahwist as Historian in Genesis* (Louisville: Westminster John Knox, 1992).

epic poems in the Old Testament, nothing which can compare with other epic tales: the tales of Aqhat or Kirta (Ugarit), the Gilgamesh Epic (Mesopotamia), or the Homeric epics.[12] This is not to suggest that parts of the Old Testament narratives could not have evolved from epic traditions. It just is not the only or the best explanation.

It remains possible that the Old Testament's historical narratives emerged from other Near Eastern literary forms. This hypothesis is supported by the form and content of the narratives in the book of Genesis, although there is no reason to see any epic tradition behind these. We should rather look for other literary genres that were the sources of both the prose narratives of the Pentateuch and the ancient epic literature. Specifically, we should consider a common tradition among the peoples of the ancient Near East of telling stories, jokes, and fairy tales, which reappear as narrative segments in major literary compositions such as Gilgamesh and Genesis.[13]

The patriarchal narratives in Genesis bring together formerly independent historical elements and settings to relate a single family's three- or four-generation story. That story develops around a recurring literary formula: a good man is pressed to leave his land, taking with him his family and possessions, and head for parts unknown. Two themes that were important in the society that composed this literature dominate this story: first, the acquisition of property and land rights; and second, the begetting of posterity. Obviously, such themes are not at all original; rather, they are universal community problems. But in the biblical saga, insecurity overshadows all other concerns. It simultaneously involves both the appropriation of the land and the begetting of posterity.

The appropriation of the land and the acquisition of wealth are already foreshadowed at the beginning of the Abraham narratives. During the migration through Canaan from Shechem to the Negev, Abraham marks his presence at every significant point along the route. Thus, with his encampments and altars, he outlines the unmistakable boundaries of his country. Yet these borders cannot guarantee Abraham's life

---

[12]William F. Albright remains the primary source for this hypothesis, noteworthy expansions of which include Frank M. Cross, *Canaanite Myth and Hebrew Epic: Essays in the History of the Religion of Israel* (Cambridge, Mass.: Harvard University, 1973) and Ronald S. Hendel, *The Epic of the Patriarch: The Jacob Cycle and the Narrative Traditions of Canaan and Israel* (HSM 42; Atlanta: Scholars Press, 1987). In *History and Prophecy: The Development of Late Judean Literary Traditions* (The Anchor Bible Reference Library; New York: Doubleday, 1993), Brian Peckham again tackles the issue; however, he speaks of an epic that must be viewed exclusively as prose, a terminological impossibility. By definition, epics are composed or written in poetic form. Narrative prose best suits sagas or legends.

[13]This topic will reappear below in section III.2.3.

in Canaan. For soon a famine engulfs the land, forcing him to retreat to Egypt. On his subsequent return to the land, Abraham completes the acquisition of his country as he arrives at his old altar near Bethel (Gen 13:3–4).[14] The subsequent theophany emphasizes Abraham's receiving the land: at Yahweh's behest, Abraham crisscrosses the land God has given to him.

This theme reappears in the Jacob narratives with an intriguing and perhaps inadvertent twist: Jacob must flee his land in the wake of several family squabbles; however, rather than traveling to Egypt, this time he returns to Mesopotamia. Here the sanctuary at Bethel takes on special significance: the sacred pillar serves as a guidepost for the abandonment of and the subsequent return to his homeland (Gen 28:10–22; 35:1–15). In both passages, God appears and guides Jacob.

The Joseph saga presents a critical moment in this theme of the appropriation of the land. Joseph, the firstborn son of Jacob and Rachel, is sold as a slave to foreign merchants, who subsequently cart him off to Egypt. The situation worsens when famine forces his family to follow him to Egypt. This latest departure portends disaster: the very real threat that the land will be forever lost. Not one member of the tribe of Jacob remains in Canaan to claim ownership of his land. Furthermore, the longer this family lives in Egypt, the more likely it will lose its identity and become Egyptian.

The second theme, that of the begetting of posterity, which is threatened by the matriarch's infertility, is present as a red thread from one end of the Abraham narratives to the other. Although it plays a similar role in the Isaac narratives, the beloved wife Rachel is the sole subject of this theme in the Jacob complex. However, an uncharacteristic fertility in the Jacob narratives replaces three generations of relatively childless Israelite wives. Until modern times, Near Eastern tradition has simply affirmed the general verdict that infertility rested squarely on the wife. This affected the wife's social standing enormously. After all, she alone was capable of producing children: she *must* bear sons. Conversely, a man's social standing, not his fertility, determined his prestige. Modern sentiments reject such an arrangement, but formerly a childless woman suffered a social stigma, while the husband could compensate for a childless marriage by adopting a son. His dignity remained intact.

This theme reappears throughout the patriarchal narratives with a particular emphasis: the patriarch's efforts to circumvent the matriarch's infertility, whether by adoption (cf. Gen 15:2) or through a surrogate (cf. Gen 17:15–21), consistently fail. Each attempt produces an

---

[14] The plot of Gen 12 mirrors those of the two parallel stories in Gen 20 and 26. This time, the patriarch does not abandon his land; however, he settles in an area populated by the Philistines.

unwanted son. Only a male sibling conceived by the matriarch attains his father's full heritage and status.

The patriarchs frequently encounter other people in their travels. Generally, these encounters are uneventful. Thus the text mentions no enmity between Abraham's father Terah and the inhabitants of Ur or of Haran that could have caused Abraham's flight to Canaan in the first place. There is no reason to postulate such enmity, since it would also contradict the sense of the story that friendly relations exist between the patriarchs and their relatives who remain in Mesopotamia. One could say that in the patriarchal narratives the Mesopotamians are not a belligerent force.

The patriarchal narratives have nothing to say about Syria's ethnically diverse population, although the patriarchs, their relatives, and even Abraham's servants often traverse its boundaries (either from Mesopotamia to Canaan or vice versa). For narrative purposes, Syria's inhabitants are irrelevant and never mentioned. Once the patriarchs are in Canaan, interest in foreign nations rekindles, and the Canaanites take center stage (Gen 12:6). Other tribes (or in the classical sense, nations) mentioned in this complex include the Perizzites (Gen 13:7), the Kenites, Kadmonites, Kenizzites, Hittites, Rephaim, Amorites, Girgashites, and Jebusites (Gen 15:20–21). None of these play an important role in the narratives except for the Hittite who sells Abraham his tomb at Kiriath-arba (i.e., Hebron) (Gen 23). Finally, there are plenty of references to the Philistines; for example, the implication that they lived in the southern region, near Gerar (Gen 21:32).

Although they intend to build the future on Canaanite land, the patriarchs never develop a rapport with the native people, whom they always treat as strangers. The already tenuous relationship between the patriarchs and the inhabitants of Canaan continues to degenerate because the patriarchs choose their wives from among their Mesopotamian relatives. Thus, one has to characterize Isaac's and Rebekah's marriage in classic ethnographic terms as a truly valid "father-brother-daughter-marriage." Even today, such marriages still retain their prestige in the Near East.[15] According to this form, the bride is always a member of the groom's family. Preferably, the wife is the daughter of the father's brother, although other women in the same family can be classified as "daughters" of the father's brother. A marriage in which husband and wife are not from the same paternal lineage is looked down upon, especially when the mother of the bride is not from the "father-brother-daughter" caste.

---

[15]For this marriage form (elaborately described in the ethnographic literature) and its importance for interrelationships in the Near East, see Niels Peter Lemche, *Early Israel: Anthropological and Historical Studies on the Israelite Society before the Monarchy* (VTSup 37; Leiden: E. J. Brill, 1985), 223–31.

Abraham adheres to social convention when seeking a wife for his son. His servant travels to Haran, Abraham's ancestral home and that of the chosen bride, Rebekah, described here as Bethuel's daughter (Gen 24:15). Genesis 11:29 says that Bethuel is the son of Abraham's brother Nahor and his wife Milcah, who is also from this region. Strictly speaking, Rebekah is not a daughter of the father's brother, but a daughter of the son of the father's brother—but this distinction is insignificant and the marriage between Isaac and Rebekah remains true to the father-brother-daughter-marriage form. This also applies to Jacob's marriages, since he chooses his wives from his mother's family. Actually, Leah and Rachel are daughters of the mother's brother, because their father is Rebekah's brother; thus, they all come from the same family, and their marriages conform to the prevailing custom.

At the beginning of the courting expedition to Haran, the reason for seeking wives in distant locales is explained: Abraham could not abide a marriage between Isaac and a Canaanite (Gen 24:3). Similarly, Esau's marriages to two Hittite women violate family custom (Gen 26:34–35). These misbegotten marriages motivate Jacob's subsequent trip to Haran. He will avoid Esau's mistakes: Jacob will not marry a Hittite or any other local girl. This marriage custom ends with the next generation: all of Jacob's sons marry women not belonging to the patrilineal or matrilineal line; for example, Judah, the elder son, marries a Canaanite (Gen 38:1–2), and the "beloved son" Joseph understandably marries an Egyptian (Gen 41:50).

Thus endogamy survives three generations, although its greatest import remains in the primary marriage. Secondary wives such as Hagar very easily could come from different families. This endogamous marital practice implies that the patriarchs consciously tried to distance themselves from the other inhabitants of Canaan. The proliferation of interracial marriages between patriarchal family members and native Canaanite wives would signify the estrangement of these people from their Israelite heritage. A marvelous narrative portrayal of this gulf between the patriarchs and the Canaanites appears in the purchase of the tomb in Machpelah (Gen 23). The story describes how Abraham *bought* the tomb, emphatically refusing to accept it as a gift. Through the sale of the cave, Ephron the Hittite irrefutably loses ownership of this property to Abraham. The patriarch's behavior suggests that Abraham is not beholden to Canaanite charity: rather, he is a landowner amidst the indigenous population. In subsequent narratives, his claim to the land is reinforced when his wife, he himself, his son, and his grandson are all buried in the same cave.

Although the patriarchal narratives speak of this gulf between the patriarchs and the rest of the population of Canaan, they only once mention a clash between the patriarchs and the Canaanites, as a matter of fact, a strife that arose because of a marriage between Jacob's daughter Dinah and young Shechem who had raped her (Gen 34). Apart from this, Israel's ancestors never battled the Canaanites, that is, there are no *references* to such confrontations. This silence is understandable as the inhabitants of Canaan play no independent role; they are there only to *populate* the future homeland of the patriarchs and to show that it is habitable. Only when it is absolutely unavoidable are they allowed to enter into the narrative. Nations such as the Philistines and the Arameans, therefore, play subordinate roles. We hear about the Philistines only when Abraham and Isaac visit the king of Gerar, who clashes with their herdsmen (Gen 21:22–32; 26:12–33). But we must view these conflicts as limited, local phenomena that cannot explain the subsequent enmity between the Israelites and the Philistines. In contrast, Arameans such as Laban are described as the relatives of the patriarch's family. Laban is introduced *before* Jacob's journey to Haran as the *Aramean* Laban (Gen 28:5). Or consider how the peace with the Egyptians continues even after Abraham deceives Pharaoh (Gen 12:10–20).

Clearly the narratives provide very little information regarding the people who inhabited the patriarchs' world. Although they briefly refer to the Mesopotamians, Canaanites, and Egyptians, they remain largely irrelevant to the narrative. Furthermore, the story lines offer scant information regarding their cultures.[16] Similarly, silence reigns regarding the lives of Canaan's city-dwellers in places like Shechem, Bethel, Ai, and Kiriath-arba (Hebron). Here and there, Canaanite kings are mentioned, but only in connection with outlying cities like Sodom and Gerar. One exception is Gen 14:18, which portrays the king of Salem (a possible abbreviation for Jerusalem)[17] as the priest of the supreme God, El Elyon. The narratives describe how the leaders of firmly established, influential families ruled these small Canaanite cities.[18] Noteworthy examples of such cities include Kiriath-arba, where Abraham confers with the elders at the city gate (Gen 23), and Shechem, at whose city gate Jacob strikes deals with its elders (Gen 34:20–24).

Other riddles abound in Genesis's description of the patriarchs themselves. Are they meant to be urbanites or small villagers? The relatives of Rebekah and Rachel live in cities where the residents and visitors

---

[16] In the Joseph saga, Joseph himself provides a noteworthy exception when he says that "every shepherd is an abomination to the Egyptians" (Gen 46:34).

[17] This exception may owe its existence to the probably secondary character of Gen 14 in the Abraham narrative. For a thorough discussion of this issue, see John A. Emerton, "Some False Clues in the Study of Genesis XIV," *VT* 21 (1971): 24–47.

[18] The Hebrew title *zāqēn* and the Roman title "senator" are analogous in that they serve as both honorary and functional designations, but despite their etymology indicate nothing about the recipients' age. Although it is presumed that young persons will not obtain these high positions, compare 1 Kgs 12:6–11.

regularly meet "at the well"; however, these "cities" show no evidence of being protected by walls. Apparently, the patriarchs' Mesopotamian relatives are breeders of sheep and goats; they are neither farmers nor artisans. On their journey to Canaan, the patriarchs bring their animals and belongings with them. Once in Canaan, Abraham, Isaac, and Jacob live in tents and breed sheep and goats. Nevertheless, one gets the impression that the patriarchs live in fixed locations, and shepherds normally manage their animals. Household possessions include both cows and camels (Gen 12:16; 24). Conversely, Abraham's nephew Lot is described as a city-dweller after he settles in Sodom.

There is as little solid information about the country as about the social situation of the patriarchs. Several times the patriarchs travel between Haran and Canaan, but we only once hear anything about how they prepare provisions for the journey. It always appears that the travelers reach their destination the very next day; thus, the narrative ignores the predictable trials and tribulations associated with such journeys. One exception is Jacob's adventures during his return from Haran. He encounters and reconciles with first his father-in-law (Gen 31:22–54) and then his brother (Gen 32–33), and he battles in the night with God (Gen 32:23–32).

The journeys have only one aim, namely, to connect the patriarchs with either their home station or the goal of their traveling. The narrator is not at all interested in geographical details. The same is true when the patriarchs travel in Canaanite territory. Only a few cities are mentioned repeatedly: Shechem, Bethel/Ai, Mamre, Kiriath-arba (Hebron), and Beer-sheba. Then come the geographical bookends: Sodom at the eastern frontier and Gerar at the western frontier. Jerusalem is mentioned only once (Gen 14:18), and in a way that raises various problems. Only one area is described in detail: the fertile plain of Jordan around Sodom (Gen 13). Yet, for the author of this narrative, in the wake of its destruction (Gen 19), this area is a barren waste—a stark contrast to its earlier opulence.

Similar observations apply to the Joseph saga, which provides sketchy information coupled with occasionally exotic information about Egypt. Joseph's brothers actively herd their father's animals at Shechem (or Dothan), while their father lives in Canaan (Gen 37:1). More precise information follows: Jacob lives in Hebron (Gen 37:14), not Beer-sheba, the latter being his final stop before departing for Egypt (Gen 46:5).

Joseph's brothers sell him to Ishmaelite or Midianite merchants on their way to Egypt. They are accompanied by their heavily burdened camels. In Egypt, Joseph begins his association with high-powered national figures by serving Potiphar, the commander of Pharaoh's bodyguard. During his subsequent imprisonment, Joseph shares a cell with Pharaoh's cupbearer and baker. On the cupbearer's recommendation and Pharaoh's personal command, Joseph is finally released from prison.

Soon Joseph rises to Egypt's highest ranks and marries the daughter of the priest of On: undoubtedly the highest of all Egyptian clergy.

In the Joseph saga, his intimate relationship with the Egyptians is certainly essential. By the time his brothers come to Egypt, he is already its preeminent official. When Joseph, as grain manager, aids his brothers, their relationship takes center stage in the narrative: Egypt and the Egyptians are nowhere to be found. When ordinary Egyptians enter the narrative, they do not play critical roles but remain shadowy figures; but when Jacob arrives, he immediately goes before Pharaoh (Gen 47:7–10). The narrative refers to Pharaoh's courtier and servants, but they remain almost totally obscure. Common folk are mentioned only when Joseph purchases their property for Pharaoh (Gen 47:13–26).

The preceding observations raise a basic question. Is it possible to regard the patriarchal narratives (including the Joseph saga) as historical portrayals? First we must try to determine more precisely the type of stories with which we are dealing, where they originated, and the reason for their composition. Finally, can we glean anything about the early history of Israel from these stories?

First it has to be stressed that most of the redactional problems of the Pentateuch belong in another context. They are part of Israel's later history and as such have little relevance to the question of the historicity of the patriarchs.[19] It also has to be said that the narratives were written down in a period that was removed from the historical era of the patriarchs (if such a historical period really existed) and that there is hardly any historical relation between the narratives and the time of the patriarchs. This remains true if we posit a phase of oral tradition for these narratives that extended for more than a very short time. It is

---

[19] In discussing the date of the Pentateuch, one must note carefully that the most ancient text level of the Pentateuch (identified with the Yahwistic stratum, according to the most general understanding) cannot possibly predate the tenth century B.C.E. If the stratum were that ancient, the time span between the period within which the Yahwist wrote and the time of the patriarchs would still cover 1,200 to 1,300 years—an evaluation based solely on Old Testament chronological information. Even if we revise the biblical chronology and move the patriarchs from the Early Bronze Age (the end of the third millennium B.C.E.) to the Middle Bronze Age (the beginning of the second millennium B.C.E.), or even to the Late Bronze Age (the last half of the second millennium B.C.E.), there is still a 150-year span between the patriarchs and the so-called Yahwist. In either case there is still no reason to speak of historical recollections that were faithfully preserved in oral tradition. Amid the vast literature on this subject, note especially the following volumes: Joseph Blenkinsopp, *The Pentateuch: An Introduction to the First Five Books of the Bible;* Rolf Rendtorff, *The Problem of the Process of Transmission in the Pentateuch*; and John Van Seters, *Prologue to History: The Yahwist as Historian in Genesis*, and his *The Life of Moses: The Yahwist as Historian in Exodus–Numbers* (Kampen: Kok Pharos, 1994).

accordingly difficult to find here any evidence of early Israelite history.[20] We can reckon that the patriarchal narratives contain historical information only to the degree that they present a historical scenario pertinent to the time when the patriarchs supposedly lived. And in fact, the narrratives contain no concrete information to indicate that they are based on historical recollections from the past. Ultimately, the narratives provide information of no historical value but are dominated by vague recollections of the countryside. They mention only a few reference points and places: the names of various Canaanite populations, or places the patriarchs allegedly visited. These names and places provide the necessary setting for the patriarch's wanderings and the widening gulf between the Israelites and the foreign nations of Canaan. Clearly, rather than concerning themselves with historical actualities, the narrators are determined to tell lively and engaging stories. These tales present generally recognizable geographical backdrops—such as Haran or Canaan—while the exact contours remain obscure. Even the chronological setting depends on generalities: it is "once upon a time" with only the approximate time frame within which the patriarchs lived. Thus, the setting becomes an artistic stage for the choreography of the patriarchal narratives; it is well designed for the script relating their wanderings to and from Canaan, Mesopotamia, or Egypt. According to this script, the patriarchs sometimes leave on the command of God, sometimes contrary to the will of God, whereupon God himself has to intervene in the narrative. In this way, the patriarchs act like a kind of representative *(Stellvertreter)* for the later Israel. The center of the narrative is the land called Canaan, and the narrative ends only when the patriarchs finally settle in the country, never to leave it again. It is an ironic feature of the narrative that this settlement can occur only when the patriarch dies and is buried in Canaan.

The script can be condensed as follows. Abraham journeys first from Mesopotamia to Canaan, then from Canaan to Egypt, and finally dies upon his return to Canaan, where he is buried. Isaac lives all his life in Canaan and never leaves it. Conversely, Jacob must leave the land twice, first to find his wives and then to visit Joseph in Egypt. Initially, it appears that Jacob will remain in Egypt; however, when he dies his body is returned to Canaan and buried in the ancestral tomb. Here Canaan is a literary stage between Mesopotamia and Egypt, both of which become important ports of call when the fathers seek brides or meet with famine.

---

[20] See Patricia G. Kirkpatrick, *The Old Testament and Folklore Study* (JSOTSup 62; Sheffield: JSOT Press, 1988), 113–14. Based upon modern data, she suggests such oral traditions cannot survive for more than 150 years. Scholars who study oral traditions often employ the "law of three generations." It suggests that with the death of the grandfather, the grandson's recollection of the great-grandfather fades.

They never settle for long, however, since troubles would arise should they stay for good in a foreign country.

First, Abraham has to leave Haran on God's order and move to Canaan. He will never return to Haran; only his servant will make a short visit there in order to find a bride for Isaac and bring her back to Canaan. When Rebekah leaves Haran, no problems have arisen. Jacob, however, must live and work with Laban for two seven-year commitments in his quest for a bride. The harsh demands of his father-in-law complicate his escape—Jacob's only hope for freedom. Furthermore, strife erupts when Rachel steals Laban's household gods. Abraham's brief stays in Egypt produce similar problems; he barely retains both his wife and the promise to his descendants. Ultimately, he returns from Egypt with his wife safe and wealth intact.

Joseph's fate seemingly contrasts that of Abraham. He is sold to Egypt and has to remain there. The result is clear: Joseph becomes an Egyptian, a fact which is not changed by the subsequent arrival of his family in Egypt. When he dies, his body is embalmed according to Egyptian customs and placed in a sarcophagus.

The sparse chronological indications that are present in the patriarchal narratives have nothing to do with the scripted time line that was added very late in the process of redaction. This time line is a construct connected with the building of Solomon's temple, which is a pivotal point for Old Testament chronology. This overarching chronological framework is best expressed by the presence of the so-called *toledot* structure, namely, the genealogical system of the book of Genesis.[21] These genealogies or genealogical sketches are compact units that are inserted into the narrative script to help provide structure. For example, the genealogy of Terah in Gen 11:27–32 introduces the cycle of Abraham narratives that run until Gen 25:11, where two new genealogies appear: that of Ishmael (Gen 25:12–18) and that of Isaac (Gen 25:19–26). Next, at the conclusion of the Jacob cycle, there appears a full-blown listing of Esau's descendants (Gen 36), followed by updated information from the *toledot* of Jacob: Joseph has joined the clan (Gen 37:2). We cannot know exactly when this *toledot* structure first became part of the patriarchal history; we can only say that it provides a chronological framework for the narratives.

---

[21] Here the Hebrew *tôlēdôt* refers to a "genealogical tradition." For discussions of this structure, see Thomas L. Thompson, *The Origin Tradition of Ancient Israel*, vol. 1, *The Literary Formation of Genesis and Exodus 1–23* (JSOTSup 55; Sheffield: JSOT Press, 1987), esp. 61–131, and Joseph Blenkinsopp, *The Pentateuch: An Introduction to the First Five Books of the Bible*, 58–59, 99–100; see also Sven Tengström, *Die Toledotformel und die literarische Struktur der priesterlichen Erweiterungsschicht im Pentateuch* (Coniectanea biblica: Old Testament Series 17; Lund: Gleerup, 1982), although he limits his analysis to Gen 1–11.

The genealogies that are scattered throughout the book of Genesis and continue somewhat in the subsequent Mosaic texts correspond with formulae commonly found in other traditional (and not at all "primitive") societies. Such formulae contain long patriarchal lists that refer either to entire races or to individual families. As in the lists in Genesis, man A procreates son B, who in turn procreates son C, etc. These lists highlight the familial relationships of the race or family in question. For example, they can prove conclusively whether an individual is a relative or an alien. Since members of the same family or society are supposed to assist each other, it is important to know whether a certain person in distress is a relative. Similarly, they can clarify social status: someone belonging to a collateral branch of the family may have to accept a lower station, while someone from the main branch of the family may seek a higher station. For societies that make no professional distinctions, these lists are indispensable tools. They can designate people as either "aristocratic" or "plebeian" and place them in their corresponding social position. These functions recall the results of ethnographic research: genealogies vary in content because they reflect the constant social and economic changes in traditional societies. Contemporary ethnographers call this phenomenon "genealogical manipulation," such as when formerly undocumented familial relations find their way into the written genealogy. Political or social agendas can inspire such manipulations. For example, by way of genealogical manipulation, people who previously enjoyed no social status whatsoever can be added later to existing lists and gain new standing in that society.

Clearly, Israelite-Jewish genealogies are no exception to this rule. Emended lists appear throughout the Old Testament: in the Pentateuch, Chronicles, Ezra, and Nehemiah. In Ezra 10, foreign wives are expunged from the society—a process which nowadays would be labeled "ethnic cleansing." Such conventions served to both unify the Jews and to segregate them from foreign elements in the land. Similarly, Genesis's *toledot* lists emphasize proper breeding. Such collections are neither random nor speculative. They superimpose present-day realities onto stories of and from antiquity, but from the compiler's perspective, they are completely positive declarations regarding bona fide Israelite identity.

The preceding remarks underscore an important point, namely, that the two decisive factors—time and space—are literary devices that help structure the patriarchal narratives. The chronological and geographical information contained within those narratives is meaningless except as part of the narrative complex. Those narratives clearly do not contain any viable information regarding the early history of the Israelite people because their spatiotemporal framework reflects a much later period. They are not eyewitness accounts or authentic recollections; rather, they are historical novels with clearly defined agendas. For the authors of the Pentateuch, the narratives are idyllic portrayals of the patriarchs that reflect their own times and situations. The patriarchal narratives relate the fourfold story of Israel's estrangement from Canaan, warnings not lost on their authors' contemporaries, who like their forebears were experiencing life in exile. Those distant events struck close to home. Again, the historical details of these stories contain no probative use; however, they provide important clues for redaction-critical exploration of the Pentateuch.[22]

We therefore have to consider even elements of the narrative structure of Genesis to have been created by the redactors. There is, then, no reason to make a distinction between individual episodes and their redactional context, namely, the larger complex of patriarchal narratives. The main plot is not history but the literary work of a redactor, and this plot belongs to a kind of "never-never land." Its elements are literary elaborations of motifs belonging to the realm of folktales. We are moving in a world of fairy tales and sagas where mythical motifs are blended with legend. In this world, every single narrative component possesses its own meaning and importance; it cannot be removed from the narrative plot, nor will it provide information when separated from its narrative context. The redacted patriarchal narratives are therefore not "folktales," which belong to a period defined only as "once upon a time."[23] The *toledot* structure and the other chronological and geographical information that is incorporated into the narrative prevent it from being seen as a fairy tale. The patriarchal narratives are related to the genre of folk literature but are far more advanced than the ordinary folktale.

This does not imply that there never was a period of the patriarchs. Although the producers of the patriarchal narratives employed literary conventions, a period of the patriarchs might be feasible. Oddly, such rash denials of this possibility continue to flourish among German and Scandinavian scholars, though it is quite inconsistent to deny the historicity of a patriarchal period while simultaneously isolating individual elements in the patriarchal narratives for historical reconstruction. Yet this is the precise "method" of some Genesis scholars: a rationalistic paraphrase that expunges all disquieting improbabilities from the investigative process.[24]

---

[22]See John Van Seters, *Israel in History and Tradition* (New Haven: Yale University Press, 1975), who argues that the entire Abraham complex is contrived and fabricated, the product of the Babylonian exile.

[23]An example of the latter genre would be the book of Job, where the first verse ("There was a man in the land of Uz") should really be translated, "Once upon a time there lived a man in the land of Uz."

[24]Early in the twentieth century, Eduard Meyer denounced this method. See his *Die Israeliten und ihre Nachbarstämme: Alttestamentliche Untersuchungen* (1906; repr., Darmstadt: Wissenschaftliche Buchgesellschaft, 1967), 50. For detailed criticism of the use of genealogical information for historical reconstructions of the patriarchal narratives, see Niels Peter Lemche, "Rachel and Lea. Or:

Another view suggests that the narratives *do* depend on historical recollections. Several examples come from the narratives about the adventurous exploits of historical individuals (especially kings) from the ancient Near East. One such story concerns Sargon, the mighty king of Agade (ca. 2355–2279 B.C.E.), whose birth and miraculous rescue seem to foreshadow a similar birth-rescue motif in the Moses narratives. Similarly, the autobiography of King Idrimi (ca. 1500 B.C.E.) of Mukish-Alalakh (which is carved into his statue) describes how this royal son of Aleppo came to control the neighboring state of Mukish-Alalakh.[25] But a literary analysis of the Idrimi inscription quickly proves that it is no historical report; rather, it is a historical novel, an adventure story about a young hero who plunges into the world to secure an empire and a princess.[26]

The use of adventure stories in ancient Near Eastern inscriptions is doubly significant. First, these stories form the backbone of the patriarchal narratives. However, this does not imply that there existed an old tradition of telling stories about the patriarchs. The authors and composers of literature in the ancient world were well equipped to employ motifs and themes from folk literature in their own literary compositions. It was unimportant whether the "hero" was a historical person or an invented literary figure. Second, all narratives incorporating adventure stories are not ipso facto necessarily false. After all, they could describe actual historical personages as well. Yet the reverse cannot be affirmed, namely, that everything happened as told. We still do not know whether the patriarchs ever existed.

I.2.2. The Patriarchs: Was There a Patriarchal Period?

Albertz, Rainer. *A History of Israelite Religion in the Old Testament Period.* Vol. 1, *From the Beginnings to the End of the Monarchy.* Translated by J. Bowden. London: SCM, 1994. Pages 25–39. **Alt,** Albrecht. "The God of the Fathers." In *Essays on Old Testament History and Religion.* Pages 1–77. Translated by R. A. Wilson. Oxford: Blackwell, 1966. Reprint, Sheffield: JSOT Press, 1989. **Blum,** Erhard. *Die Komposition der Vätergeschichte.* WMANT 57. Neukirchen-Vluyn: Neukirchener Verlag, 1984. Esp. pages 459–506. **Dever,** William G., and W. M. **Clark.** "The Patriarchal Traditions." In *Israelite and Judaean History.* Edited by John H. Hayes and J. Maxwell Miller. Pages 70–148. The Old Testament Library. Philadelphia: Westminster,

---

On the Survival of Outdated Paradigms in the Study of the Origin of Israel—I–II," *SJOT* 1 (1987): 127–153; *SJOT* 2 (1988): 39–65.

[25] I will cover both of these narratives later: Moses and Sargon in section I.2.4, and Idrimi in section III.2.2.

[26] Perhaps Idrimi would affix to his autobiography the title of Hans Christian Andersen's *The Adventure of My Life.* For both, life and career certainly are cast in an inseparable combination of reality and adventure, neither of which diminishes the story or the man. Of course, Goethe's *Dichtung und Wahrheit* belongs to the same literary tradition.

1977. **Koch,** Klaus. "Die Götter, denen die Väter dienten." In *Studien zur alttestamentlichen und altorientalischen Religionsgeschichte.* Pages 9–31. Göttingen: Vandenhoeck & Ruprecht, 1988. **Köckert,** Matthias. *Vätergott und Väterverheissungen: Eine Auseinandersetzung mit Albrecht Alt und seinen Erben.* FRLANT 142. Göttingen: Vandenhoeck & Ruprecht, 1988. **Noth,** Martin. *The History of Israel.* Translated by S. Godman. 2d ed. London: A. & C. Black, 1958. **Thompson,** Thomas L. *The Historicity of the Patriarchal Narratives: The Quest for the Historical Abraham.* BZAW 133. Berlin/New York: de Gruyter, 1974. **Van Seters,** John. *Abraham in History and Tradition.* New Haven: Yale University Press, 1975. **Weidmann,** Helmut. *Die Patriarchen und ihre Religion im Lichte der Forschung seit Julius Wellhausen.* FRLANT 94. Göttingen: Vandenhoeck & Ruprecht, 1968. **Westermann,** Claus. *Genesis 12–50.* Translated by J. J. Scullion. Minneapolis: Augsburg, 1986. **Worschech,** Udo. *Abraham: Eine sozialgeschichtliche Studie.* Europäische Hochschulschriften 23: Theologie 225. Frankfurt am Main/New York: Peter Lang, 1983.

Many scholars have staunchly defended the historicity of the Bible's patriarchal narratives. While four arguments stand out above the rest, all fundamentally affirm the same basic premise: those narratives are authentic reflections of antiquity.[27]

The first argument involves personal names, place names, and the names of nations mentioned in the narratives: the Amorites, Canaanites, etc. The second argument specifically involves the nomadic patriarchal lifestyle that apparently reflects an early stage of human existence. Thus, the wandering patriarchs represent this early phase of Israelite history prior to occupying the land, a dream that would remain unrealized for many generations. The third argument involves the special lifestyle as well as the mundane customs in the patriarchal narratives, apparently very similar to living conditions elsewhere in the ancient Near East in pre-Israelite times. The final argument involves the religion of the patriarchs as described in Genesis. This religion always takes center stage in the debate over Israel's early history. Albrecht Alt, who is principally associated with this argument, focused his studies on the nature of the patriarchs' belief in the so-called God of the Fathers, a religion based on a specific socioeconomic relationship between God and the desert wanderers. Alt's students first appropriated and then expanded this idea. The patriarchs' religion proved either that they lived a nomadic existence or that the patriarchal wandering tradition originated among nomadic peoples. The erection of sanctuaries throughout Canaan suggests that their way of life and their religion became part of the very landscape. Thus, Alt and his

---

[27] Among these scholars belong the circle of William F. Albright. The major work of this group or school is Albright's book, *From the Stone Age to Christianity* (2d ed.; Baltimore: Johns Hopkins, 1967). The most important description of the time of the patriarchs from this circle is, however, John Bright, *A History of Israel* (Westminster Aids to the Study of the Scriptures; 1st ed.; Philadelphia: Westminster, 1959 [now in a 3d revised ed., 1981]).

circle could affirm that the patriarchs' religious practices constituted an early form of or precursor to later Israelite religion.[28]

If we consider the foregoing items to be decisive arguments for the historicity of the patriarchal period, then certain conclusions must follow: (1) individual customs belong within clearly defined, specific time frames; and (2) those customs do not conform to a generic Near Eastern milieu. Furthermore, a biblical reference to a site known to be present around 1800 B.C.E. but settled in socioeconomic terms only in the fourteenth century B.C.E., does not prove the patriarchs were historical persons. To verify an authentic patriarchal period, we must verify a cohesion between the narratives and a specific historic milieu.

The results are compelling: the individual pieces of information in the patriarchal narratives do not yield a viable period that supports their historicity. In this century, scholars have proposed many and varied theories regarding the exact period of the patriarchs by stretching them over a thousand years. If we use the biblical chronology as our start, the search for the historical patriarchs begins at the end of the Early Bronze Age (ca. 3200–2200 B.C.E.).[29] In that case it would be possible to build a bridge between the patriarchs and the so-called Amorite (or *Amurrite*) transmigration that many previously dated around 2000 B.C.E. Of course, this formerly accepted link to Amorite wanderings no longer retains its currency since these wanderings are now generally believed not to have taken place. Some scholars argue that the nomadic life of the patriarchs began in Mesopotamia and continued on foreign soil. They look for a period when a large number of people left the settled way of life to become nomads. In this case, the archaeological evidence points to the beginning of the Middle Bronze Age (ca. 2000–1800 B.C.E.): a time of urban flight throughout the Near East. In light of the excavations at Tell el-Hariri (ancient Mari) in 1929, which unearthed a comprehensive palatial archive, many scholars place the patriarchs in this period. The results of that dig provide important insights into Syrian and upper Mesopotamian nomadic groups of that time. Included among those groups or tribes is the *Binu-Yamina* (i.e., "Sons of the South"), or Benjamin.[30] Finally, others place the patriarchs in the Late Bronze Age (ca.

---

[28] See Albrecht Alt, "The God of the Fathers"; and also the beginning of the introduction of Siegfried Herrmann, *A History of Israel in Old Testament Times* (trans. J. Bowden; revised and enlarged ed.; Philadelphia: Fortress, 1981), 48–49. We will discuss this form of religion later.

[29] Here we follow the chronological data of Helga Weippert's *Palästina in vorhellenistischer Zeit* (Handbuch der Archäologie 2/1; Munich: C. H. Beck, 1988). But we must emphasize that this suggestion is only one among many.

[30] John Bright championed this theory (*A History of Israel*, 69–78), dating the patriarchs at the beginning of the second millennium B.C.E. Formerly, most scholars did not think that the *Binu-Yamina* bore the same name as the biblical

1550–1150 B.C.E.). This date is based on juridical customs shared by the documents from ancient Nuzi in northeastern Mesopotamia and the patriarchal narratives.[31]

Early phases of research routinely placed the patriarchs within the context of the general migrations of people such as the Amorites. Scholars often spoke of the four great (and many small) migrations that allegedly occurred in the eastern Mediterranean region: first, the Canaanite transmigration (probably before 3000 B.C.E.); second, the Amorite (ca. 2000 B.C.E.); third, the Aramean (at the end of the second millennium B.C.E.); and fourth, the Arabic (in the mid-first millennium C.E.). These migrations were superimposed onto the history of the ancient Near East and believed to provide an intelligible paradigm for major sociopolitical changes. The idea of large-scale migrations is based on the well-documented Arabian migrations, which were fueled by a warlike spirit and religious fanaticism. Other migrations include the Hurrian (at the beginning of the second millennium B.C.E.) and the Aegean (ca. thirteenth–twelfth centuries B.C.E.).

The historians who developed these theoretical models about migrations of whole nations did so on the basis of a paradigm they found in sources from the classical world. Greek historians such as Herodotus and later Roman historical writers often used this model to shape their historical works. Furthermore, these attempted explanations of changing sociopolitical circumstances in the ancient Near East are conceived through illegitimate comparisons with later European and Asian migrations: first, all the Germanic migrations that contributed to the destruction of the Roman Empire; second, the Mongolians who in the Middle Ages sacked vast sections of Europe.

Today, these theories have lost a great deal of their appeal. New knowledge has arisen from historical research, the social sciences, and from literary studies. Most importantly, it has become clear that when historians of the classical world chose to employ the scheme of popular migrations, they did so from literary and ideological reconsiderations. Thus the Roman intellectual elite would hardly have entertained the idea

---

Benjaminites. The normal way to write their name in Mari is DUMU-*Yaminu*, that is with a nonphonetic Sumerian logogram, DUMU, meaning "son." This logogram was believed not to render a word of Amorite origin. The nomads were therefore called only *Yamina*. Now, the complete name of *Binu-Yamina* has been found at Mari, however, so far only as a personal name. Even if the *Binu-Yamina* share their name with the Benjaminites of the Old Testament, it is probably only a coincidence and does not prove any historical connection between the two.

[31]The best-known advocate of this theory is the American archaeologist E. A. Speiser, who spent many years investigating Nuzi. A basic version of his interpretation is contained in his commentary, *Genesis* (Anchor Bible 1; 3d ed.; Garden City: Doubleday, 1964).

that they were descendants of Troy if they had not been acquainted with the Homeric poetry and its Greek heritage.

Furthermore, a real, historical large-scale migration almost never resembles the image of transmigration created by classical authors. When historians speak about a mass migration, they think of a unique event: a people or nation decides because of hunger or lack of space to leave its country and move elsewhere, almost as if such a thing were decided by a referendum. This people, then, quickly migrates to another region, butchering or displacing the local population in the process. Although this description agrees with the Roman accounts of the wanderings of the Cimbrians and Teutonians to Italy and southern France about 100 B.C.E.,[32] a number of logistical problems remain unsolved. For example, how did the migrating people survive? Modern parallels suggest that such massive migrations are liable to end catastrophically; that is, most people die along the way from hunger or exhaustion. A twentieth-century example will suffice: in 1916, 90 percent of the Armenians died after their expulsion from Asia Minor.

This is not to say that migrations never happened, only that they had little in common with the picture created by ancient writers. A migration is not a relatively brief episode; it develops over a long period of time. First, individuals break from the main group in search of new locales. Only later do larger groups follow in their footsteps and achieve their own relocation goals. Thus, the first wave of settlers paves the way for subsequent immigrants. While the new area's population may hardly notice the initial phase of the migration, which establishes a new settlement, later mass migrations may lead to substantial demographic change and reaction, including extensive assimilation between the newcomers and the previous population. The assimilation process can follow either of two paths: a blending of both the new and old populations, or a total absorption of the new into the old or the old into the new. In either case, either the immigrants or the previous population lose all or part of their ethnic identity. As a matter of fact, even when one population appears to absorb the other, *both* tend to lose their unique identities. Subtle changes begin to take shape with the reciprocal influence of one group upon the other. Thus the Mongols, who in the Middle Ages conquered China, ended up as Chinese. On the other hand, as a result of the Arab conquests, the Middle East became "Arabic."

Neither the literary structure of the patriarchal narratives nor the socioeconomic problems that relate to the notion of large-scale migra-

---

[32]Of course, modern literature also recounts these travels. Thus, the Cimbrian migrations are covered by the Danish novelist, Johannes V. Jensen, in *The Long Journey* (trans. A. G. Chater; Nobel Prize ed.; New York: A. A. Knopf, 1945). Inspired by Darwinism, Jensen views human history as a series of migrations dating from the Stone Age to Christopher Columbus.

tions of nations preclude the possibility that an actual transmigration did occur around 2000 B.C.E. If one did, ancient Near Eastern sources should provide clues to such a migration. Did the Amorites migrate to Syria, Palestine, or Mesopotamia sometime between the end of the third or beginning of the second millennium B.C.E.? Is there circumstantial evidence to support such a migration? The answer is no. No extant recollections point to Amorite migrations into Syria or Palestine around 2000 B.C.E. Previous research suggested that the Amorites and other Semitic groups originated in the Arabian wilderness. According to this opinion, after the last ice age the Arabian Peninsula gradually became a dry place to live, a climatic change that compelled them to seek refuge in more fertile sections of the Middle East. While it is true that a continuous drought starting probably more than seven thousand years ago created the desert landscape of modern Arabia, this process was complete before 3000 B.C.E. From that time the Syrian-Arabian climate and ecology have remained practically unchanged to the present day. On the other hand, periodic and regional droughts have sometimes forced residents—nomads as well as farmers and urban dwellers—to leave their homes. The most unfavorable areas of the Middle East included the outlying areas around the desert's perimeter. More favorable conditions existed in Mesopotamia, western Syria, and the Mediterranean coastal regions. Undoubtedly, around 2000 B.C.E., demographic changes occurred in Palestine and Syria. Thus, a period of drought from the Early to Middle Bronze Ages probably caused the relocation of several smaller communities, but archaeological evidence suggests that the larger populations remained relatively intact, which would not be the case if there had been any major infiltration of foreigners into those areas. Most migrations seem to have involved displacements of people within a region, rather than movements across regional borders. Furthermore, five thousand years of relentless, though nondescript, population shifts in Syria and Palestine suggest the habitual nature of the early migrations under discussion here.

The biblical chronology places the patriarchs at the end of the third millennium B.C.E. At this time no major migration developed that also included the families of the patriarchs. There is no reason to see them as newcomers to the Near Eastern stage. A close reading of the biblical text comes to the same conclusion. Nowhere are the patriarchs described as newcomers who arrived in Syria and Palestine from a country far away. According to the narrative, Mesopotamia was the original home of the patriarchs, and Abraham traveled from Haran to Canaan. Their home was not in the southern desert, nor in the mountains to the north or east of Syria and Mesopotamia. Finally, their background was urban rather than nomadic.

If we eliminate any need for massive migrations, the Genesis accounts of the patriarchal journeys fit nicely into the lifestyle in Syria and Palestine around 2000 B.C.E. However, they would just as nicely fit the circumstances of, for example, 2500 B.C.E. or 1500 B.C.E. Among their many problems, the patriarchal narratives provide only general geographic information regarding the period within which the journeys allegedly occurred. Ultimately, we cannot eliminate any period within the history of the ancient Near East as a possible setting for those wanderings.

Similar problems develop with a second suggested date for the nomadic activity of the patriarchs: the Middle Bronze Age. The situation is very much the same as the Amorite "migration" and infested by the same kinds of misunderstandings. One theory suggests that Near Eastern nomads represented a unique and independent culture, constantly seeking fertile pastures as they moved from one camp to another. In time, exhausted by their wanderings, the nomads sought a permanent home. A second theory proposes the pre-agricultural milieu of the nomadic peoples—part of a cycle of human evolution from original hunter-gatherers to fully developed urbanites.

Indeed, the most important information about nomadic activity in the ancient Near East comes from the Middle Bronze Age—specifically from Mari on the eastern border of Syria. Because nomads appear in the Mari archives, many scholars place the patriarchs during the Mari dynasty of the eighteenth century B.C.E. These sources will be discussed later. At this point, we must recall briefly only that it has been assumed that the transition from full nomads to sedentary agriculturists and citizens developed through the intricate interrelationships between the nomadic tribes and Mari's government authorities. Scholars who follow this line of thinking isolate two main tribal groups: the Khaneans and Benjaminites. The Khaneans supposedly earned virtual citizenship through their positive relationship with the monarchy, while the Benjaminites successfully resisted the attempts of the central government to pacify them and force them to settle down. The latter example contradicts the idea that nomads settle voluntarily.

This false picture of the patriarchal nomads is based on a fundamental misunderstanding of the structure of Near Eastern society that is still common in the popular Western conceptions of the Orient. The theory suggests that this society embraces three different types of occupations or ways of life: nomads, villagers and agriculturists, and urbanites. But what are the boundaries? What distinguishes nomad from agriculturist, or agriculturist from urbanite? This misguided discussion among scholars is based on several misunderstandings of the Near East. Among groups in that part of the world, no clear dividing lines segregate one way of life from another. Furthermore, no clear enmities highlight the relationships among the region's native peoples: neither between the nomads and agriculturists, nor between the urbanites and agriculturists. Historically, certainly the tenuous relationship and natural discord between nomads and villagers can easily erupt into hostilities. Normal inter- and extra-societal friction can develop at any time between antagonists of all sorts, but we cannot simply reduce such hostilities to the level of occupational rivalry: nomads versus agriculturists, agriculturists versus urbanites, etc. Certainly, ethnic disputes can ignite bitter rivalries: two competing tribes bickering over well rights, or two villages arguing over borders. Even within certain towns or ethnic groups, discord can erupt without warning. For example, during droughts, nomads will often pay a "visit" to the village. Similarly, nomads and agriculturists will clash over the duties to be paid by the nomads for grazing rights. However, it would be inaccurate to construe such contrasts between these categories as basic and unbridgeable.

Skirmishes erupt throughout Genesis between the patriarchs and the people with whom they periodically come in contact. After they scuffle over well rights with the people of Gerar, the shepherds for Abraham and Isaac have to withdraw to other territories (Gen 21:22–32; 26:12–33). These are not conflicts between the nomadic and sedentary lifestyles; rather, they are *ethnic* battles between the patriarchs and the Philistines. Here the patriarchs act on behalf of their descendants, the later Israelites, who themselves were in a state of competition with the Philistines over land rights.

Upon closer inspection, the classic European theory regarding nomadic life in the Near East described above obscures the diversity of that life in favor of an artificial and erroneous tripartite division. Thus there are many forms of nomadism. Some cattle breeders may travel perpetually from place to place, while their colleagues are almost stationary. Similarly, since nomads cannot depend on a regular income, they must find other occupations to guarantee their livelihoods. Thus, it is virtually impossible to draw clear professional distinctions between the nomads and agriculturists, or the agriculturists and urbanites. Even walled cities produced only superficial divisions between urbanites and outsiders, both of whom share many occupational similarities. Before the end of World War II and the belated industrialization of the Near East, many urbanites still made their living tilling the fields outside their cities. They left their city home at dawn to manage their fields and returned that evening. Along with these "urban agriculturists" who produced food for the city, a residual urban workforce developed to process the harvested goods—a production flow that began outside the city limits and ended inside with the efforts of the city's own workforce.

Ultimately, we must use extreme caution with any theory that describes Near Eastern society as "dimorphic," that pits nomad against agriculturist and agriculturist against urbanite. Such heavy-handed theories of societal dichotomy cannot withstand the crucible of sound sociological and economic analyses. After all, scholars create analytical archetypes like "nomad," "agriculturist," or "urbanites" to clarify the nature and scope of the hypothetical groups they represent. Yet these archetypes overlook the complicated trade and social relations that develop over time—changes that produce sometimes unpredictable ethnic and professional hybrids. Undoubtedly, the complex blend of occupations and societies proves that Near Eastern life is polymorphic. Since "national" or ethnic group members engage in many different occupations, any legitimate Near Eastern social theory must understand that occupations themselves remain ethnically neutral.

It is fairly easy to reconcile the socioeconomic information in the patriarchal narratives and in other parts of the Old Testament with this description of Near Eastern society. Although 95 percent of the population bred livestock or grew agricultural produce, the Hebrew Bible has no words for "nomad" or "agriculturist."[33] One notable attempt at a more methodical representation of ancient society appears in Gen 4:17–22. The genealogy of Cain describes how he built the first city and how his descendants became the progenitors of various occupations: those who live in tents and raise livestock; artisans; and musicians. Although he is the father of urban dwellers, Cain also serves as progenitor of the Kenites: a pre-Israelite population whose nomadic wanderings covered southern Palestine and the entire Sinai Peninsula. Among nomads they represent a unique category: traveling tinkers or artisans (a kind of Gypsy tribe).

Of course, the Old Testament brims with information about people who live in encampments and breed livestock. Thus, Abraham lived in a tent at Mamre where an angel visited him. Similarly, during the Israelite monarchy, tent dwellers such as the Rechabites led a nomadic existence because they rejected urban living in favor of a desert haven (Jer 35). Even the Old Testament writers knew that desert dwellers lived in tents. After all, God lived in a tent-shrine as well. These authors knew of their contemporary, and now historically verifiable, desert dwellers like the Ishmaelites, Midianites, and Amalekites, as well as the Arabic tribes like those of Kedar. They never situated the patriarchs in a nomadic milieu. Thus, despite uncertainty and vague allusions, the Genesis narratives clearly indicate the patriarch's urban roots in Palestine's smaller cities—a lifestyle that remains relatively unchanged almost to modern times. Here and there we receive glimpses of the patriarch's livestock: mostly goats and sheep, with occasional references to camels and cows. In typical fashion, upon their arrival in Palestine, the patriarchs hire professional shepherds or family members (normally their sons) to maintain their livestock. Among all the patriarchs, Jacob worked longest as a shep-

---

[33]Of course, this is an approximate figure, the basis for which is information gathered from modern preindustrial Near Eastern society. Those circumstances remained largely unchanged until the present century.

herd; however, he never worked independently. Rather, he toiled for his father-in-law Laban, and like Laban's other employees, Jacob lived an urban rather than a nomadic life.

The third main question regarding an alleged patriarchal period concerns social conventions about which the narratives speak. Some contend that these situations only arise within certain time periods and environments within the history of the ancient Near East. Of the various narrative motifs, the "substitute child" scenario demands close inspection. In it, a slave like Hagar (Gen 16) replaces a previously sterile wife (Sarah). This raises several questions regarding inheritance and birthrights. Besides, can Sarah truly act as Abraham's half-sister and wife simultaneously? Also important in this connection are Isaac's and Jacob's choice of wives—always women from their own family—as well as questions concerning the inheritance rights of women, the transfer of inheritance rights to foreigners (Gen 15:2–3), and the relevance of the right of primogeniture.

Based on this information, some would say that the patriarchal narratives reflect customs of the second millennium B.C.E. Specifically, the Late Bronze Age (ca. 1550–1150 B.C.E.) commands much interest because of the alleged parallels between the patriarchal narratives and the fifteenth-century documents unearthed in the northeastern Mesopotamian site at Nuzi (Yorghun Tepe). Those documents provide the backdrop for the aforementioned "substitute son" motif, including written wills that furnish allowances for surrogate mothers. E. A. Speiser's work on the Nuzi documents passionately supports the sister-wife scenario. Other scholars suggest that the patriarchs' social conventions reflect different times and places during the second millennium B.C.E.

Initially, this argument based on sociological peculiarities seems convincing. Yet are these customs and social conventions really that unique? How do they diverge from "normal" Near Eastern customs and manners not limited to exactly this period? To verify the historicity of the patriarchal narratives, one must carefully scrutinize the veracity of the relevant quoted documents themselves. Have they been properly understood? Are they truly unique? The parallels between the Nuzi documents and the patriarchal narratives seem solid and unique. Yet realistically, they might simply reflect normative Near Eastern customs and social conventions of that time, or any time for that matter—situations and circumstances bound by neither time nor space.

The Nuzi materials command great interest even though they originate from Hurrian sources and thus refer to a non-Semitic environment in the Tigris Valley in northeastern Mesopotamia, a considerable distance from the geographical and ethnic milieu of the patriarchs. Some suggest that these documents echo socioeconomic circumstances that were widespread in the middle of the second millennium B.C.E. If correct, this suggestion undermines any thought of a unique relationship between the Genesis narratives and the Nuzi documents. A final verdict will depend on a more precise assessment of the character of the Nuzi documents. They belong to private archives and are not official state documents. They provide us with an excellent impression of the ordinary life of the inhabitants of Nuzi. Still, the question remains whether the customs reflected in these texts were common to Near Eastern society.

The many legal documents from Mesopotamia that have been unearthed during more than a century's excavations in Syria and Iraq may help clarify this problem. Also relevant are the Mesopotamian law codes, such as the best known example, the Code of Hammurabi (eighteenth century B.C.E.). Still, these juridical documents do not provide solid evidence for the historicity of the Genesis accounts. This is especially true of the law codes, which may have been of little relevance to daily life in Mesopotamia: court documents practically never refer to them. Moreover, the codes are not law books in the ordinary modern sense of the word; for example, several crimes, such as plain murder, are not mentioned. Instead, the law codes were probably a kind of wisdom literature or "academic" speculation removed from the practical application of law in the courtroom. Second, although most of these law codes come from the second millennium B.C.E., similar collections have survived from earlier and later periods. The most recent examples of such materials come from the Neo-Babylonian period (ca. mid-first millennium B.C.E.). Third, although law codes abound from Mesopotamia and the Hittite capital of Hattusas (Boghazkoy), virtually none originate in the patriarch's homeland in or around Syria and Palestine. Similarly, rich legal documents flow from both Ugarit (Ras Shamra) and Alalakh (Tell Atchana) in northern Syria; however, no law codes are among them. In practice, the law codes are exclusively a Mesopotamian phenomenon (with Hattusas as a notable exception). They were of no importance to the daily life in courts. In the courtroom, the judges referred to a tradition of oral law. An easy comparison is traditional Islamic law, which has until this century preferred oral law (*hadith*).

Problems always arise when our scholarly argumentation develops from obvious misunderstandings of the written material,[34] as in the case of certain scholars who misread both the biblical material and Nuzi documents. Three biblical stories tell of a husband who lies to prevent

[34] One such problem concerns those scholars who ignore redaction issues because they insist on the rock-solid connections between the customs of the patriarchs and their ancient Near Eastern counterparts. This problem can be avoided if one willingly discards the assumption of a centuries-long redaction process that reached from Solomon to the postexilic period. However, if one accepts the notion that the Pentateuch developed over a 500-year span, then one should ask how the patriarchal narratives could possibly reflect the customs of any one period.

his wife from falling into the harem of a foreign king (Gen 12, 20, and 26). In each narrative, the husband says that his wife is his sister. The husband tells the lie to guarantee his own freedom, unfortunately but inevitably at his wife's expense. In Genesis 12, as *Deus ex machina*, Yahweh spares Sarah through personal intervention. This totally amoral vignette ends when, through deception, Abraham secures a personal fortune and regains his wife. Again, in Genesis 20, when the infuriated king accuses him of fraud, Abraham persists in maintaining that Sarah is really his sister (Gen 20:12). In Genesis 26, where the wife is saved just before she is brought to the harem, the initial lie has no serious consequences. John Van Seters notes correctly that these narratives represent three interrelated versions of a single literary complex; however, Genesis 20 and 26 serve as commentaries on and paraphrases of the original version in Genesis 12, placed in their contexts to mitigate the impression of the patriarch's dishonesty in Genesis 12.[35] Thus, Genesis 12 and 20 include no historical information regarding Abraham's marriage; rather, it is a patent cover-up to excuse Abraham's scandalous behavior. The author of Genesis 20 wantonly tried to save Abraham from being a liar by insisting that Sarah was really the sister of Abraham. However, the third version (Genesis 26) plays down this theme of sisterhood, probably because its author tried to save Abraham from having transgressed the Old Testament marriage rules in Leviticus 18 (especially vv. 9–11), which forbids marriage between brother and sister.

Our analysis of the "embattled matriarch" narratives leads to a fuller understanding of the "wife-as-sister-of-the-husband" motif. These are morality plays: stories that do not parallel any ancient Near Eastern customs whatsoever. In this regard, both John Van Seters and Thomas L. Thompson note correctly that the primary editor of the Nuzi texts misunderstands the plot of these stories.[36] The Nuzi documents never deal with marriages between brothers and sisters; rather, they speak of a man's legal right to sell his sister in marriage to another man, who now becomes the first man's adopted brother.

The preceding discussion proves that, from both sides of the evidence, the irresistible urge to draw concrete, *historical* analogies between the biblical patriarchs and the ancient Near Eastern world produces faulty interpretations. Although sometimes these analogies seem plausible, they never confirm the distinctive and unique circumstances they

---

[35] See Van Seters, *Abraham in History and Tradition*, 167–91.

[36] See Speiser, "The Wife-Sister Motif in the Patriarchal Narratives," in *Oriental and Biblical Studies* (ed. Jacob J. Finkelstein and Moshe Greenberg; Philadelphia: Westminster, 1967), 62–82. The document consists of a contract located in a private archive in Nuzi (museum number JEN 78). Critical analyses of Speiser's arguments are located in Van Seters, *Abraham in History and Tradition*, 71–75, and Thompson, *The Historicity of the Patriarchal Narratives*, 239–45.

claim to depict. Those stories deal with generic events from many different times and places. Similarly, the background of the patriarchal narratives could reflect the general Near Eastern lifestyle, rather than that of a specific society within it (i.e., the small city and village milieus). For instance, the Genesis account of the father-daughter-brother marriage contract reflects a custom that persisted in those venues into this century. The sole purpose of the patriarchs is to act as the progenitors of later Israel. They are not nomads, nor are they tribesmen. How could they be? They were progenitors of a people, not themselves members of this very people. When the authors of the patriarchal narratives produced this literature, they simply placed the patriarchs in an environment and in social conditions known to the authors themselves. This, however, does not mean that the patriarchs should be considered self-portraits of the authors. They are described as kinds of "ideal" figures, rich and benevolent members of a society that also included the authors and their audience. The patriarchs do not act much differently than other people. Only their role as patriarchs distinguishes them and their activities. Thus, they represent paradigms that span the vast Israelite experience.

Along these lines, we must consider another critical issue for the patriarchs and their time, namely, religion. If their practice stems from a general knowledge of what once happened "in the land," then do their stories come from the mind of the author or from recollections of earlier events? Alt's analysis provides little help with the question. He believed in a patriarchal religion based on personal piety and the "God of the Fathers," one similar to that of ancient nomads. Although his arguments no longer compel us, his notion of a personal religion remains somewhat plausible.[37] Alt noted correctly that the religious ideas which permeate the patriarchal narratives are different from other ideas and practices mentioned throughout the Old Testament that are identified with a later stage of ancient Israel's religious history. He saw this as an example of how religious ideas developed through the ages. The patriarchal religion was in his eyes more primitive—pristine and related to Israel's nomadic past—than the later Israelite religion of, for example, the time of the Hebrew kings. This assessment is hardly correct. In contrast, modern theories concerning the origin of the patriarchal religion focus on the family environment. This religion of the family was private and different from the official religion of the state, which was common to all citizens and supported by the officers of the state and by the king himself. The patriarchal religion was family business and, therefore, not part of the past. It was a reflection of private religion as it existed side by side with the official religion. If so, the author of the narratives within which this reli-

[37] See Alt, "The God of the Fathers."

gion appears cannot retrace its practice to some dim beginnings deep in Israel's past. No, the authors who wrote the patriarchal narratives consciously placed them and their religion within their own world. These figures and their habits represented a well-known part of contemporary life, rather than a remote and unknown past.[38]

In conclusion, we return to our original question: Do the patriarchal narratives contribute anything to an understanding of ancient Israel? At first glance, these narratives concern the Canaan of pre-Israelite times; but in fact they provide no real information about their actual subject, as will become clearer in the course of this study. The patriarchal narratives are even less informative when it comes to Syria and Mesopotamia in the Bronze Age. All of this adds to the impression that the world of the patriarchs is a fiction, not reality. That world does not represent a real world. It stands outside the usual representation of time and space. As a matter of fact, all of this indicates that neither the narratives nor their world can be dated to any precise period.

Several so-called anachronisms provide additional and compelling proof of this argument. First, Genesis says that the patriarchs originally came from Ur of the Chaldeans and bred camels. This information indicates that the narratives cannot be dated to a period that precedes the first millennium B.C.E. Most importantly, Chaldea did not exist before the eighth or seventh century B.C.E., and the domestication of camels came many years after the alleged patriarchal period. It remains possible that the anachronistic elements were added later to preexisting narratives, but that hypothesis has to be demonstrated on the basis of another set of arguments. Sometimes scholars refer to archaeology as providing an analogy to this situation. During excavations it often happens that a certain stratum must be dated not according to the oldest evidence present but according to the most recent artifacts. When archaeologists dig out a house from Palestine, for example, and find in it items belonging to the fifth century B.C.E., they can conclude for certain that this house was occupied during that period. Whether it was built at that time or earlier remains unknown. However, when we find items from the fifth century B.C.E. embedded in the foundation of the house, it is certain that the house was built in that century. A house cannot be older than its foundation. This analogy indicates that the anachronistic information in the patriarchal narratives does not prove the narratives were composed in the days to which this information belongs; it only says that the narratives were

---

[38] Insightful evaluations of these theories can be found in Rainer Albertz, *Persönliche Frömmigkeit und offizielle Religion: Religionsinterner Pluralismus in Israel und Babylon* (Calwer theologische Monographien A/9; Stuttgart: Calwer, 1978); also Albertz, *A History of Israelite Religion*, vol. 1, 25–39; and Matthias Köckert, *Vätergott und Väterverheissungen: Eine Auseinandersetzung mit Albrecht Alt und seinen Erben* (FRLANT 142; Göttingen: Vandenhoeck & Ruprecht, 1988).

known and read at this time. It is, however, different if the anachronistic information belongs to the basic structure of the narrative—perhaps as part of the plot of the tale. If this is the case, the narrative hardly predates such essential information. It has to be said that none of the anachronistic notes found in the patriarchal narratives are that important. None of them are essential to the course of the narrative.

I.2.3. Egypt and the Joseph Saga: Was Israel in Egypt?

Coats, George W. *From Canaan to Egypt: A Structural and Theological Context for the Joseph Story* (CBQMS 4; Washington: The Catholic Biblical Association of America, 1976). **Dietrich,** Walter. *Die Josephserzählung als Novelle und Geschichtsschreibung: Zugleich ein Beitrag zur Pentateuchhfrage.* BibS(N) 14. Neukirchen-Vluyn: Neukirchener Verlag, 1989. **Redford,** Donald B. *A Study of the Biblical Story of Joseph (Genesis 37–50).* VTSup 20. Leiden: E. J. Brill, 1970. **Schmitt,** Hans-Christoph. *Die nichtpriesterliche Josephsgechichte: Ein Beitrag zur neuesten Pentateuchkritik.* BZAW 154. Berlin: de Gruyter, 1980. **Thompson,** Thomas L., and Dorothy **Irvin.** "The Joseph and Moses Narratives." In *Israelite and Judaean History.* Edited by John H. Hayes and J. Maxwell Miller. Pages 149–66. The Old Testament Library. Philadelphia: Westminster, 1977.

Two narratives, with two separate agendas and plots, describe Israel's stay in Egypt: the "Joseph saga" (Gen 37–50) and the Exodus narrative that some scholars refer to as the "Passover legend" (Exod 1–15).[39] The two compositions display separate narrative intentions; however, considered as a pair, two issues stand out: they display more literary coherence and a broader scope than the patriarchal narratives. The patriarchal narratives use common and recognizable themes to string together a series of episodic, anecdotal short stories that cohere only loosely with the overall context of the patriarch's history. In contrast, the Joseph saga represents an advancement in narrative technique. Of course, it does not necessarily follow that the patriarchal narratives predate the Joseph saga. Perhaps the differences between the Joseph narrative and the patriarchal history arise either from their divergent literary milieus or the greater competency of the author of the Joseph saga.

Most scholars view the Joseph saga as either a novella or a novel; however, its length and complexity do not suggest that the Joseph saga as we have it represents its original form. In this regard, scholars note the revisions and layers of redaction that were necessary to create links be-

[39] According to Johannes Pedersen. See his *Israel: Its Life and Culture III–IV* (London: Oxford University Press, 1953), Additional Note I, 728–37; also his article, "Passahfest und Passahlegende," *ZAW* NS 11 (1934): 160–75. Scholars such as Noth and von Rad partly built on Pedersen's conclusions. See esp. Martin Noth, *A History of Pentateuchal Traditions* (trans. Bernhard W. Anderson; Englewood Cliffs, N.J.: Prentice-Hall, 1972), 66–67.

tween the Joseph saga and the complex of patriarchal narratives, on the one hand, and the Exodus story, on the other. The Joseph saga serves as a literary interlude between these. Nonetheless, all these alterations and revisions neither change the narrative's intention or plot, nor introduce important new elements into it.

To some, its distinct literary character and coherent literary style verify an already popular impression about the technique of biblical authors, namely, that they used traditional narrative materials, although it does not necessarily point to an already extant epic form of the Genesis literature. Folklorists recognize the Joseph saga's numerous adventure motifs, for which a number of ancient Near Eastern parallels exist—especially Egyptian fairy tales. One such story parallels that concerning Potiphar's wife, in which a wife attempts to seduce young Joseph. When he refuses her advances, fiery vilification befalls the young man. This well-known motif also appears in the Egyptian "Story of the Two Brothers" (from the end of the second millennium B.C.E.).[40] In her husband's absence, a wife tries to seduce his brother. The brother resists, whereupon his brother's wife accuses him in front of his brother of having tried to rape her. In the end, the unhappy young man is forced to flee his home. Other well-known motifs that appear in these adventure stories include the success of the youngest brother, a startling career advancement at the king's court, and the gift of "second sight" (i.e., the interpretation of dreams).[41]

Considering the similarities between these stories and those in the Joseph saga, few have sought the historical background of this saga. Scholars have accepted its fictional character. The only historical content involved Israel's sojourn in Egypt. This element, however, is not part of the basic structure of the Joseph saga but part of the revision that established a connection between the saga and the surrounding narrative complexes.

The incorporation of the Joseph saga into the narrative thread of the Pentateuch caused a number of elements to be included, although they are really extraneous to the saga, such as Joseph's many brothers. They have no individual roles to play. The plot needs only a few of them, such as the good and the evil brothers and the innocent-victim brother. The Joseph saga conveys no information about the past of the Israelite people; it is a story about a youngster—a hero in a fairy tale who rises to eminence in a foreign country. Three important scenes outline that career: first, Joseph's stay in Potiphar's house; second, the prison scene; and finally, his release from prison, after which Joseph accepts a lofty position in

---

[40] For translations, see John A. Wilson in *ANET*, 23–25, and Miriam Lichtheim in *COS* 1.40, 85–89.

[41] A summary of such motifs can be found in Donald B. Redford, *A Study of the Biblical Story of Joseph (Genesis 37–50)*, 87–93.

Pharaoh's court. These scenes indicate that the story is not necessarily unique among Old Testament writings. In fact, one cannot deny the parallels between this story and that of Daniel at Nebuchadnezzar's court. Clearly, the Joseph saga represents an intriguing literary motif—that of the young hero who experiences great personal success on foreign soil. This topic arises again in the books of Daniel and Esther. In the latter, the heroine, like Joseph, repulses her assailants and rescues her nation.

Even many scholars who agree that these stories are fictional nevertheless persist in searching for their specific, historical backdrop. These attempted reconstructions focus on two episodes in Egypt's past: first, the "Hyksos invasion" in the seventeenth century B.C.E.; and, second, the late part of the New Kingdom when, according to Egyptian sources, some people believed to be of West Asiatic origin assumed high positions in the service of the pharaohs.

We will address the so-called Hyksos immigration into Egypt in detail later; here, however, we must mention one important fact: only a Hellenistic history of Egypt dating from the third century B.C.E. mentions such invasions. This history, written by the Egyptian priest Manetho, commands serious attention among Egyptologists, many of whom contend that his historical reflections did not simply fall from the sky. Yet the term "invasion" does not accurately characterize this immigration. The Hyksos did not overwhelm and colonize Egypt overnight; rather, small groups of Asians trickled into northern Egypt over many years. It cannot be excluded in advance—indeed, it is rather likely—that at a later date some people in Palestine had ancestors who had been part of this Hyksos movement. Perhaps, as with Jacob and his sons, these people fled a famine-ravaged land for a more hospitable environment. Yet scholars cannot positively link the Jacob and Joseph complexes to Hyksos migrations in the first half of the second millennium B.C.E.

Besides the Hyksos migrations, occasionally other people migrated from Palestine to Egypt to seek refuge or livelihood. Egyptian documents and art[42] often mention these Asian refugees both before and after the Hyksos era. Mary and Joseph, with their infant Jesus, were neither the first nor the last people from Asia to seek refuge in Egypt. In ancient times, relations between Egypt and Palestine were strong, continuing without a break from at least the beginning of historical times (from ca. 3000 B.C.E.). Thus, although the Joseph saga mentions people from Palestine moving to Egypt, that circumstance provides no concrete historical background for these stories.

---

[42] A well-known reference is a nineteenth-century B.C.E. depiction of Asian nomads which appears in the tomb of the high Egyptian official Khnumhotep in Beni Hasan. See *ANEP*, 1, plate 2.

A similar problem involves the question whether the Joseph saga was set in the Amarna Age (the middle of the fourteenth century B.C.E.) or sometime more generally during the New Kingdom. The New Kingdom has always intrigued scholars because Egyptian documents from this period reveal the presence of Hebrews. Yet these Hebrews (or better *ᶜabiru/ᶜapiru*, as they were known at that time) were not necessarily Israel's ancestors. In the Joseph saga as well as in the Exodus narrative, Egyptians sometimes refer to the Israelites as Hebrews. This is important—although in no way decisive—evidence. In the second millennium B.C.E., "Hebrews" represented neither an ethnic nor national entity; rather, they were a sociological assembly.[43]

Some Egyptologists take references to Egyptian geography and customs as arguments for the historicity of the Joseph saga. They believe this information may help them "reconstruct" a historical background of this novel.[44] Specifically, Jozef Vergote looks to the second millennium for the historical background of the patriarchal narratives. Like the quest for the historicity of the patriarchs, Vergote's case rests on feeble material. Certain elements of the saga may, indeed, belong to an Egyptian context in the second millennium B.C.E. Such elements, however, are more often than not found in combination with other elements that belong to quite a different—and, in general, later—period. In fact, the Egyptologist Donald B. Redford contends that most of the Egyptian elements in the Joseph saga originate no sooner than the end of the first millennium B.C.E. Other elements belong to the Ptolemaic period, the period after the Macedonian conquest of Egypt around the end of the fourth century B.C.E. Other scholars contend that late elements in this saga are secondary additions to the narrative, while still others think they are, in fact, older than suggested by the Egyptian evidence—something which is, of course, difficult to prove. We cannot rashly dismiss such theories if we do not possess arguments that decisively refute them. Yet the only safe conclusion is that the contested late elements appear exclusively in the Saite period (26th Dynasty, 664–525 B.C.E.) or later. Therefore, while we can speculate that they are older, we cannot let such theories detain or direct us. At this point, all that can be said for sure is that certain elements in the Joseph saga cannot be proven to be older than the Persian period.[45]

Finally, we turn to a discussion about individuals. Who are the potential models for the tradition of Joseph (or Moses) in Egypt? Even if we

---

[43] See below section II.5.6.

[44] See Jozef Vergote's summary in *Joseph en Egypte: Génèse ch. 37–50, à la lumière des études égyptologiques récentes* (Orientalia et biblica lovaniensia 3; Louvain: Publications Universitaires, 1959). See also the "revision" of this theory in Redford, *Joseph*, 187–243.

[45] Persia conquered Egypt during the reign of Cambyses, around 525 B.C.E.

accept that certain Asians in high positions in, for example, Ramesside Egypt are related in some way to either Joseph or Moses, we can still only conclude that the author of the Joseph saga composed a novel that was not totally removed from reality, although the success of the hero of this novel is, of course, exaggerated. Some Asians did rise to high positions in Egypt. For example, a Syrian official named Baye, who has sometimes been compared to Moses, served as vizier for the entire nation and lived during the time of Pharaoh Siptah at the end of the 19th Dynasty in the last years of the twelfth century B.C.E. Almost contemporary with Baye, Irsu, another Asian, is reported to have usurped the throne of Egypt, although we know of this only from a less-than-reliable Egyptian document. We could add many other names to the list. All these Asians apparently rose effortlessly to high positions when internal strife and political disintegration tore Egypt apart—common and recognizable situations at the end of the Early, Middle, and Late Kingdoms.

In conclusion, one cannot discount the *possibility* of some historical kernel underlying the Joseph saga; however, the so-called historical elements of the narrative cannot be placed within any specific historical period, neither do they refer to any specific historical person known from Egyptian history. If we consider the obvious literary character of this saga, it is clear that Joseph cannot be solidly identified with any known historical context. It hardly comes as a surprise, then, that no Egyptian document mentions Joseph. The author of this narrative was influenced by the common knowledge that it was possible for a foreigner to reach high positions in Egypt. For this reason, Joseph may be compared to other fictitious heroes who similarly rose to eminence in a foreign country. While reality, as it appears in the novel, has become "glorified," the novel does not exaggerate to the point of total unrealism.

I.2.4. Moses, Exodus, and Sinai

MOSES: **Aurelius,** Erik. *Der Fürbitter Israels: Eine Studie zum Mosebild im Alten Testament.* Coniectanea biblica: Old Testament Series 27. Stockholm: Almqvist and Wiksell, 1988. **Coats,** George W. *Moses: Heroic Man, Man of God.* JSOTSup 57. Sheffield: JSOT Press, 1988. **Koch,** Klaus. *Der Tod des Religionsstifters: Studien zur alttestamentlichen und altorientalischen Religionsgeschichte.* Göttingen: Vandenhoeck & Ruprecht, 1988. **Osswald,** Eva. *Das Bild des Mose in der kritischen alttestamentlichen Wissenschaft seit Julius Wellhausen.* Theologische Arbeiten 18. Berlin: Evangelische Verlagsanstalt, 1962. **Schmid,** Herbert. *Mose: Überlieferung und Geschichte.* BZAW 110. Berlin: Töpelmann, 1968. **Schmidt,** Werner H. *Exodus, Sinai und Mose.* Erträge der Forschung 191. Darmstadt: Wissenschaftliche Buchgesellschaft 1983. **Smend,** Rudolf. *Das Mosebild von Heinrich Ewald bis Martin Noth.* 1959. Reprint, "Die Methoden der Moseforschung." In *Zur ältesten Geschichte Israels.* Pages 45–115. Gesammelte Studien 2. BEvT 100. Munich: Chr. Kaiser, 1987. **Van Seters,** John. *The Life of Moses: The Yahwist as Historian in Exodus–Numbers.* Louisville: Westminster John Knox, 1994.

EXODUS: **Albertz,** Rainer. *A History of Israelite Religion in the Old Testament Period.* Vol. 1, *From the Beginnings to the End of the Monarchy.* Translated by J. Bowden. London: SCM, 1994. Esp. pages 40–66. **Davies,** Graham I. *The Way of the Wilderness: A Geographical Study of the Wilderness Itineraries in the Old Testament.* SOTSMS 5. Cambridge: Cambridge University Press, 1979. **Engel,** Helmut. *Die Vorfahren Israels in Ägypten: Forschungsgeschichtlicher Überblick über die Darstellungen seit R. Lepsius (1849).* Frankfurter theologische Studien 27. Frankfurt am Main: Knecht, 1979. **Fritz,** Volkmar. *Israel in der Wüste: Traditionsgeschichtliche Untersuchungen der Wüstenüberlieferung des Jahwisten.* Marburger theologische Studien. Marburg: N.G. Elwert, 1970. **Herrmann,** Siegfried. *Israel in Egypt.* SBT Second Series 27. London: SCM, 1973.

SINAI: **Moberly,** Walter L. *At the Mountain of God: Story and Theology in Exodus 32–34.* JSOTSup 22. Sheffield: JSOT Press, 1983. **Nicholson,** Ernest W. *Exodus and Sinai in History and Tradition.* Growing Points in Theology. Richmond, Virginia: John Knox, 1973. **Perlitt,** Lothar. "Sinai und Horeb." In *Beiträge zur alttestamentlichen Theologie.* FS Walter Zimmerli. Edited by H. Donner, R. Hanhart, and R. Smend. Pages 302–22. Göttingen: Vandenhoeck & Ruprecht, 1977. **Zuber,** Beat. *Vier Studien zu den Ursprüngen Israels.* OBO 9. Freiburg, Switzerland: Universitätsverlag, 1976. Esp. pages 15–72.

In the book of Exodus, we find many of the same problems that we met in both the patriarchal narratives and the Joseph saga. Now, however, the problems intensify. Again we must ask the pivotal question: Is the Exodus narrative historical reflection or literary fiction? If we insist that the Exodus narrative is not referring to a historical event, then we must be prepared to withstand opposition of a far more serious kind than was the case when we deconstructed the historicity of the patriarchal narratives.

Solid reasoning underlies this critical opposition. The social setting of the Exodus story is vastly different from that of the patriarchal narratives and the Joseph saga, which deal with the fate of a particular family. It is perhaps rather easy for us to believe that little in the way of history has survived in these latter narratives. We can accept the impossibility of either verifying or discrediting the historical details while nevertheless maintaining their religious importance as expressions of faith, which cannot and should not be part of a critical historian's agenda.

Unlike the patriarchal narratives and the Joseph saga, Exodus does not describe the fate of a single family. Now the narratives turn to a larger question: the liberation of a *nation.* The string of narratives that began with Joseph's family migrating to Egypt ends with several hundred thousand people leaving it. The patriarchs (including Joseph) are now no more than the distant ancestors of this nation. They are seen as individuals for whose acts their descendants, namely, the later Israelites, cannot assume any responsibility; they are, so to speak, "before the birth of the nation." The case is otherwise with the generation that left Egypt. Later Israelites must accept the acts of that liberated generation as their own for the sake of national solidarity and continuity. They are part of the national heritage. A saying from the exile underscores the relationship between past and present: "The fathers ate sour grapes, and their children's teeth feel blunt!" (Jer 31:29). It reflects the idea that the liberation of their ancestors ("fathers") from Egypt provided freedom for generations yet unborn, that is, the "children." These children and those ancestors are one people. The Israelites perceive themselves as heirs, identifying with their deceased ancestors, *their* people. This also means that the ancestors have determined the fate of their descendants because every successive generation relives for itself the experience of its ancestors.

The liberation from Egypt is a critical moment in the history of Israel. A nation and its religion depend upon it. Without it, Israel's nationhood would have been a historical footnote, and its faith in Yahweh as the God of Israel would have remained insignificant. The Exodus represents more than a national liberation; rather, it marks the birth of a nation and justifies that nation's very existence.

Two other events become important "foundation legends" for the Israelites: the revelation at Sinai, and the occupation of Canaan. The Exodus marks the beginning of the people and the source of its identity, but the people also need a religion and a land. Without both, the people cannot survive but will face annihilation. A national identity requires a concrete, physical space within which to develop. Without its religion, the people would wander aimlessly through the wilderness like ghostly figures. At Sinai, Yahweh presents himself as the God who liberated Israel from Egyptian bondage—the very same God who at the beginning of history entered into an exclusive relationship with the patriarchs and promised them a beautiful land. Finally, at Sinai, Yahweh becomes Israel's God *in concreto.* A contract or "covenant" seals this bond between a people and its God. Thus, the law of Yahweh becomes the legal basis for the nation and for the Israelites' everlasting obligation to their God. Two principles of this covenant inexorably solidify their religious identity. First, the collective religious consciousness of the Israelites confirms that Yahweh is and always will be their God. Second, all Israelites must now and forever conform to the law of Yahweh, in effect, Israel's "constitution." Thus, the law simplifies what it means to be an Israelite, under God's protection. And anyone who fails to obey is no longer a member of that people.

As for the land, the fulfillment of that promise lies in the future. Yet God makes a pledge at Sinai: if they adhere to the stipulations of the law, the people will inhabit the land and own it. This is not merely a story about a divine revelation; rather, it represents a program for the future of the Israelite nation. Until the people finally live in the "land," one cannot truly call the people "Israel."

In this way, the denial of the historicity of these bedrock elements of the Israelite historical narratives comes close to a denial of the very existence of the Israelite people. Thus, dismissing the Exodus narrative as a historical source is far more serious than taking a critical view of the historical content of the patriarchal tradition. The patriarchal narratives contain individual vignettes—for instance, the patriarchs' journeys to and from Egypt—or disconnected divine revelations. Of course, the patriarchs, in their role as Israel's ancestors, also hold paradigmatic significance. Still, these stories recall solitary characters, not an entire people.

Predictably, many conservative Christians and Jews become troubled by skeptical voices that question the historicity of the Exodus narratives. Both Christians and Jews consider themselves Israel's true descendants; therefore, to them, these criticisms represent "negative" or even heretical opinions. They do not view these theories as objective analyses of the Exodus or the revelation at Sinai; they see them as attacks on their own religious identities.

If, however, we disregard such concerns—it is after all not the purpose of a critical investigation to protect the presumed identity between the living and dead members of a certain religious community—it is quite obvious that the Exodus narrative is largely made up of literary elements that closely resemble the ones already found in the book of Genesis. Of course, Exodus contains other literary models that demand further investigation. Like the patriarchal narratives, the book of Exodus represents a literary quilt, pieced together from the fragments of universal and timeless adventure stories and legends. These are examples of narrative art rather than specifically Israelite folk literature. Appreciating the utility of their plots and characters, the biblical authors appropriated these universal tales and reconstituted them with their own Israelite template. Consequently, the extrabiblical literature does not provide the context for determining a specific period or locale for the biblical narratives. For this reason, the biblical narratives remain relatively immune to historical analysis. To be sure, a *literary* analysis produces intriguing results: we can see in the biblical stories images of a familiar narrative style, and perhaps that type of mimicry contributed some measure of credibility to an ancient historian's message. But the modern historian can confidently confirm or deny the historicity of the narratives only after a careful analysis of every possible historical detail.

Exodus 1–19 represents a coherent narrative unit that describes the Israelite wanderings from Egypt to Mount Sinai. Yet many literary substrata appear within those chapters—individual vignettes strung together to create "scenes" within the larger Egypt-Sinai complex. The unit begins with Moses' birth and miraculous rescue and ends with his escape to Midian, where God outlines his future mission. The next contains the long section about the plagues that lead ultimately to Israel's liberation. Finally, a third pericope describes how the Israelites left Egypt and headed toward Sinai.

Initially, this Exodus-Sinai complex seems like a coherent narrative unit. Yet upon further examination, the events and legislation at Mount Sinai represent the narrative's literal and figurative high points. The importance of the Sinai event is so profound that it disturbs the narrative balance of the Exodus-Sinai complex. Sinai simply disrupts the narrative that takes the reader from Egypt to Canaan. Without regard for narrative consistency, Mount Sinai bursts into the Israelites' otherwise uninterrupted march from the Sea of Reeds to the Jordan River.

For years, Old Testament scholars have recognized the narrative discontinuity between the Sinai complex and the Pentateuch's overall narrative scheme. They have based this observation not on the narrative itself (in the books of Exodus and Numbers) but on such texts as the brief credo in Deut 26:5–9, quoted at the beginning of this chapter. These brief recollections of Israel's early history, its liberation from Egypt, and its conquest of the promised land completely ignore the Sinai events. While Israel's life in and migration from Egypt remain pivotal topics, Sinai is never mentioned. Thus, almost sixty years ago, Gerhard von Rad suggested that the Sinai complex is not one of the original narrative components of the Pentateuch. For him, these are two originally independent narrative units, on the one side the Exodus and wilderness stories, and on the other the Sinai revelation. They were written independently and only later joined together.[46]

For von Rad, the borderline between the Exodus narrative and the Sinai revelation is in Exodus 14 (Exod 15, the renowned "Song of the Sea," is an independent unit and not part of either complex). Exodus 16 begins the wilderness wanderings. From an editorial perspective, this view is both comprehensible and logical since each complex stems from its own religious background or occasion within the Israelite-Jewish community: clearly, the Exodus narrative is related to the Passover, and Sinai to the Feast of Weeks (Pentecost). The two traditions merge much later. The inclusion of the Sinai revelation into the narrative string of the Exodus and wilderness stories must perforce be later than the composition of a credo text such as Deut 26:5–9.

Of course, the late combination of two originally independent narrative units does not exclude further elaborations and additions, especially those which create smooth literary transitions between the Exodus and Sinai material. Each narrative complex carries its own religious

---

[46] See von Rad, "The Form-Critical Problem of the Hexateuch," in *The Problem of the Hexateuch and Other Essays* (trans. E. W. Trueman Dicken; New York: McGraw-Hill, 1966), 1–78. Von Rad views these credo texts as the beginning of a traditional curriculum; however, see the counterargument of Leonhard Rost, *Das kleine Credo und andere Studien zum Alten Testament* (Heidelberg: Quelle & Meyer, 1965), 11–25. Rost and others contend that these credos developed at the end of the tradition's history.

meaning and background. They arose independently and came together at a late date. Consequently, we must consider their historicity separately. If we confirm the historicity of one complex, we cannot *assume* the historicity of the other.

Moses, the towering figure of the narrative, guarantees the fundamental unity of the Exodus-Sinai-wilderness complex. Moses himself functions as the glue that holds together the Exodus–Numbers tradition, each episode of which is inexorably linked to and defined by its hero. There is, however, reason to doubt that Moses is also the historical link between the Sinai revelation and its surrounding narrative complex. From a historian's vantage point, it might be questionable to see one and the same person as the center of two originally separate narrative units. This observation is important because it is almost impossible to separate Moses from either unit and consider him primary to one of them while secondary to the other. What *is* the Exodus narrative without Moses? Could Israel accept the tablets of the law from anyone other than Moses himself? Everything points to the narrative units' having been composed from the beginning with Moses in mind.

When they wrote their stories about Israel's past, the authors and the collectors of tradition saw Moses as more important than any of the narrative elements that they combined into the Exodus-Sinai-wilderness complex. Thus, from the moment of its composition, Moses dominates the Exodus–Numbers complex. As a consequence of Moses' being an integral part of all the narrative units in Exodus–Numbers, it must be concluded that he did not participate in any of the events recorded, which is a paradox since the narratives would not live without his presence. Clearly, Moses held a unique position in the popular and corporate memory. However, it is exactly the primacy of the role he plays in the compositions that makes it difficult to uncover anything historical about his life. Martin Noth understood correctly that we can retrieve very little historically verifiable information about Moses. All we know is that he lived somewhere, at some time, and was buried in a grave east of the Jordan.[47]

This uncertainty about Moses' identity surfaces again when we consider his many different roles. In some narratives he is portrayed with a multitude of characteristics, while other narratives characterize him more uniformly. The infant Moses' rescue from the river foreshadows his role as Israel's liberator, the figure of a prototypical ancient Near Eastern adventurer-hero. Egyptians, Babylonians, and Assyrians all knew of tales about such child prodigies, a noteworthy example being the Akkadian

---

[47] See Noth, *History of Pentateuchal Traditions*, 172–91; concerning the burial ground, see 186–91. See also Noth's succinct arguments for Moses' historicity in his *History of Israel* (trans. P. R. Ackroyd; 2d ed.; New York: Harper & Row, 1960), 136 n. 2.

hero-king Sargon. His mother abandons him, placing him in a rush basket and setting him adrift; however, unlike Moses, who is rescued by the king's daughter, Sargon is plucked from the river by the water-boy Akki.[48] Except for Sargon's modest upbringing, many parallels remain between both narratives. Sargon rises above his roots through the intervention of the goddess Ishtar.

Sargon is not some vague traditional figure but a well-known Mesopotamian king and empire-builder who reigned during the latter half of the twenty-fourth century B.C.E. His personal record describes his accomplishments as a great adventurer and warrior; the subsequent literature made him a legend. Yet his miraculous rescue does not preclude Sargon's historicity. The legendary tales of Moses and Sargon foretell the future greatness of two marvelous heroes. Their authors used the rescue theme to distance their heroes from ordinary people. In this way, the hero is allowed to transgress the social conventions that normal people must follow. Without this freedom, no hero would ever succeed in radically changing the fortunes of his nation.

The subsequent story concerning Moses' escape to and return from Midian contributes to a singular narrative goal: the liberation of his people from Egyptian bondage. This story contains marvelous recollections of other folk literature. First, a hero has to prove that he is in fact the chosen one, whereupon a benefactor saves him from deadly danger. Thereafter, he has to submit to a series of trials and tribulations before he can win the princess and half of the kingdom. Of course, in Exod 2:16–24, Moses must settle for Zipporah, the daughter of Reuel, the "priest of Midian."[49] Ultimately, the hero settles every score with his enemies and rescues his family—at least the part favorable to him.

Moses is both national liberator and national prophet. In this role he is called to become a prophet at the burning bush in very much the same way as other Old Testament prophets, and like Jeremiah in particular he is most reluctant to assume the mantle of his new vocation. The role of a prophet is not secondary to the character of Moses, that is, something that has only loosely been attributed to him. On the contrary, much of the Exodus narrative's logic and flow depend on this prophetic motif. It allows Moses to negotiate with Egypt and his people as God's exclusive agent. Understandably, this snapshot of Moses-as-prophet con-

---

[48] E. A. Speiser's translation of this text appears in *ANET*, 119; see also Benjamin R. Foster's translation in *COS* 1.133, 461. The story is preserved in both a Neo-Assyrian and a Neo-Babylonian version from the first millennium B.C.E.

[49] The Old Testament employs several names for Moses' father-in-law. In Exod 2:18 he is called Reuel; however, in Exod 3:1 he is known as Jethro (cf. also Exod 18). In Judg 4:11 he is neither Reuel nor Jethro but Hobab, and by now he has changed from being a Midianite to being a Kenite. Amazingly, in Num 10:29, Hobab is described as "the son of Reuel the Midianite"!

forms to similar motifs in the prophetic and historical books of the Old Testament. In every case, the prophet in those narratives functions as a politician and national leader as well. Of course, the people are often reluctant followers of these politician-prophets (including Moses) and their decrees. Ultimately, the story of Moses combines two traditions: the ancient Near Eastern hero adventures discussed above; and the literary motifs from the Old Testament prophetic tradition. Because the Israelites continuously sin against God's will, we often see Moses speaking on behalf of his people when negotiating with God. Perhaps this is a traditional relationship between Moses as prophet and as spokesperson. While we will not develop this relationship here, other interesting characteristics of this complex figure emerge, such as the occasions where Moses acts like a magician or wizard. He must, among other things, draw water from a rock in order to satisfy the needs of the Israelites (Exod 17:1–7; see also Num 20:2–13). He also acts like a magician in the story about the plagues (Exod 7–11). This picture of Moses as a magician cannot be dismissed as secondary; it might instead be an old element of his characterization.

When we consider the several components of the image of Moses in the Pentateuch, his role as the creator and legislator of the Israelite religion is clearly central. At Sinai, Moses mediates the covenant between Yahweh and Israel and conveys the content of God's law to the Israelites. That Moses should also function as Israel's supreme judge and ruler with the same power as the later Israelite kings will, in light of his other functions, hardly come as a surprise.

Moses is simply the unifying literary component in the Egypt-Sinai-wilderness complex. Through him the authors spin a red thread that connects all the different episodes belonging to this complex of narratives. Yet one question persists: does any of this relate to a historical person called Moses? As we already noted, the Exodus-wilderness complex on the one hand and the Sinai pericope on the other were originally two independent literary units. Unity between them was only reached by introducing the figure of Moses to both narrative complexes. Before that happened, these narratives developed independently; without Moses, their authors would hardly have succeeded in bringing them together.

It is frequently said that the history of Israel's origin and religion presupposes one central and historical individual and is totally unfathomable without that person. Thus, it is quipped that if there had been no Moses, somebody would have to invent one! They say that Israel's early history is inconceivable without a genuine architect. The answer is easy: yes, they did in fact invent him! On the literary level, Moses' role as catalyst decides Israel's peculiar self-identity. Without him, there is no Pentateuch that bears his name, and no substance to the narrative about the emergence of early Israel; however, this role need not necessarily conform to any historical reality, although neither does it by itself say that

Moses never existed. Perhaps this Egyptian name entered into the Hebrew tradition very early. If so, we may have evidence for a historical Moses.[50] Much speaks in favor of Moses having never set foot in Palestine; rather, one should look for his home in a region east of the Jordan.

Again, we return to the daunting question: Do the Exodus, Sinai, and desert experiences recall historical events? This question persists in spite of the fact that the narratives manifest obvious literary and stylistic reshaping. The narratives still consist of sequences that might have existed before they were joined together in the Exodus-wilderness complex or in the Sinai pericope. If we try to retranslate these narratives as history, many problems arise. Did a massive Asian migration from Egypt occur during the second millennium B.C.E.? Did the Israelites really accomplish what the narrative suggests? If so, how large was this migration? Did it involve a major displacement of people, or was it only a minor incident involving no more than a small segment of the Israelite ancestors who lived in Palestine in the first millennium B.C.E.? Did the Old Testament writers retouch the details of the Exodus? For example, did they superimpose onto the biblical narrative their own, contemporary experiences with Egypt? If so, this would validate the story line by way of a prototypical Egyptian-Israelite relationship.

Again, Sinai presents another dilemma. Where exactly did God appear to the Israelites? The ecclesiastical tradition that connects the present-day Jebel Musa[51] with the biblical Mount Sinai only partially conforms to the biblical tradition. In the late narrative that begins in Exodus 19, a mountain appears. However, the description of the journey—as well as other hints preserved by the narrative—does not point in the direction of Jebel Musa. Such information rather leads toward the northern part of the Sinai Peninsula and, more precisely, to the oasis Kadesh-barnea. Nonetheless, another problem persists. The divine revelation at Sinai described in the Old Testament cannot be reduced to a part of the history of early Israel. Such a revelation simply goes beyond what is from a historian's point of view acceptable, because God cannot be the subject of historical reflection. Unlike their counterparts in antiquity, modern historians cannot misapply the concept of God as *Deus ex machina* to explain things that happened in the past; rather, they must rely on empiri-

---

[50]The name Moses (Heb. *mōšeh*) comes from an Egyptian word signifying "son," but the Hebrew etymology in Exod 2:10 follows the lead of Moses' birth narrative, playing on the verb *māšāh*, which means "to pull out" (from water). Obviously, this represents a "folk etymology" taken from the narrative structure but without any linguistic support. In Egyptian, the name occurs in compounds referring to certain pharaohs, including Kamose, Tuthmosis, and Ramesses (Ramose). Some scholars feel that the Hebrew form comes from the second millennium B.C.E. because later on the word is transcribed differently.

[51]The Arab name means the "mountain of Moses."

cal facts. By nature, the Sinai revelation is not a historical subject. This does not mean we should ignore the exploration of Israel's religious roots—even its possible extra-Palestinian or desert origins in the south of Palestine. This subject belongs to the history of religions school, which has developed scientific methods to handle such phenomena.

What we said about Sinai applies as well to the desert wanderings. They must also conform to the criteria and scrutiny of scientific research. Are they generic stories or genuine reflections of Israel's experiences? Already, problems arise. The census in Numbers describes a massive migration composed of several hundred thousand people, who wandered the desert for forty years. And yet the general description in the Old Testament of the Israelites' desert sojourn has little in common with living conditions in such a place; it rather looks like a snapshot of a religious procession within a settled culture. The number of participants is astonishing. How could so many people survive in the desert? Already the biblical authors were met with such questions and they knew very well how to answer them clearly and absolutely: God provides for his people! Literature can handle miracles, history cannot.

The biblical authors interject an intriguing answer to Israel's desert dilemmas, namely, God. Repeatedly, God solves the wanderers' problems with a series of mighty deeds; for example, God provides manna and quails to nourish the Israelites during their sojourn. Both miracles reflect well-known phenomena from the Sinai Peninsula—at least according to travelers and explorers who have visited that place. Thus, the biblical narratives could reflect actual events. Yet those who know the desert understand the real miracle: that so many people could benefit so much from so little. Again we come across an authorial paradigm already noted above. From a narrative perspective, Israel's survival in the desert does not hinge on the unfamiliar or the absurd; rather, it depends on the believable, real-life experiences of people living in those days. Only the size and scope of those experiences elicit wide-eyed amazement. In the author's mind, God has taken the impossible and made it possible—the implausible is now plausible. God uses what already exists. He need not act like a wizard.[52]

So the depiction of the desert wanderings found in Exodus through Numbers is a tradition that does not relate historical circumstances of immigration or life in the desert. This narrative is no more and no less than a literary fiction that has only one goal, namely, to move the Israelites from

---

[52]It is very much the same technique the gospel writers apply when they have Jesus feed the multitude with a diet of fish and bread (e.g., Matt 14:13–21). Nothing unusual here. Jesus did not feed them with extraordinary food but with an extraordinary amount of ordinary food. It is the magnitude of the event that is miraculous.

Egypt to Canaan. Only the most dedicated believer clings desperately to the notion that hundreds of thousands of humans survived forty years in the desert: clearly a barren and inhospitable environment. To justify the historicity of the desert wanderings, we must modify the number of refugees leaving Egypt and tone down God's miraculous deeds so that we can analyze the historicity of the events they describe. Ultimately, the results will do violence to the biblical descriptions. Why? Because they run counter to the biblical version that not a few persons but a whole nation took part in those events.

The conclusion that Exodus and Numbers do not rely on historical facts accords with the testimony of extrabiblical sources from the second millennium B.C.E. Scholars have repeatedly argued that no Egyptian document from this period mentions a massive migration of Israelites from Egypt to Western Asia. Rather, such sources regularly refer to small-scale migrations of people from Western Asia in and out of Egypt. On the other hand, another source may be important, namely, Manetho's description of the Hyksos (from the third century B.C.E.). According to this Hellenistic writer, the Hyksos came from Asia and conquered Egypt, but as Egyptian resistance grew they were forced to evacuate Egypt again. We will return to the subject of the Hyksos later. At this stage, the interesting point is the feasibility of a connection between the Hyksos and the Israelites.

The Egyptian and biblical portraits differ regarding the particulars of Asiatic migration. In the former, the Egyptians forcibly evict the Asians; in the latter, Egyptian actions compel the Asians to leave. According to Manetho, at the end of the Hyksos reign, the pharaohs expelled the Hyksos population from Egypt; however, unlike the Egyptians in the book of Exodus, Manetho's Egyptians never tried to hinder the departure of their deportees. If the eviction of the Hyksos was the historical background of the Israelite exodus, then we must conclude that either the Old Testament historians or Manetho have confused matters. At the conclusion of the Egyptian-Hyksos war, the Egyptians overran much of the neighboring territory, including the Sinai Peninsula, Palestine, and Syria. Ultimately, pharaoh's armies advanced as far as the Euphrates. The biblical narrative never mentions these consequences of the Hyksos expulsion; rather, it explains the *Israelites'* intention to conquer Palestine upon its departure from Egypt. Furthermore, the chronology of the biblical events does not mesh with the Egyptian source material. The Egyptian-Hyksos war took place during the sixteenth century B.C.E. Again, the biblical and scientifically deduced periods do not agree. The biblical account places the Exodus about four hundred years before the construction of Solomon's temple in Jerusalem (ca. 1350 B.C.E.). Yet the scientific chronology suggests that the Israelites hardly arrived in Palestine before 1200 B.C.E. Ultimately, the most compelling evidence comes from a mid-fourteenth-century Palestinian source: the Amarna letters.

They do not mention any Israelite presence in Palestine. It would be difficult to maintain that the Israelites had already been in the country for more than two hundred years.

If we accept some sort of correlation between the sixteenth-century Hyksos eviction and the Israelite migration from Egypt, we must conclude that the biblical record in Exodus represents vague and imprecise recollections of ancient events and times. We cannot, however, totally ignore the fact that later Egyptian tradition up to the time of Manetho preserved the remembrance of the Hyksos expulsion. It is, therefore, not completely unlikely that such a tradition may have also inspired the biblical historians, although it is impossible to prove that it did.

Scholars note another part of Egyptian history that could serve as the backdrop for Israel's slavery in and migration from Egypt. Exodus 1:11 refers to a pharaoh, "who did not know Joseph," who hires the Israelites to build his supply cities Pithom and Rameses. This sounds similar to the old Egyptian information about *ᶜabiru/ᶜapiru* who helped construct the massive pylon gates called Ramesses Miamon of Ramesses II (ca. 1279–1213) at Memphis.[53] Yet we must employ great caution when drawing concrete parallels between this information and what the Bible says about the Israelites in Egypt.

Egyptian history refers to the cities of Pithom and Rameses. Apparently, Rameses once stood on the site of present-day Khatana-Qantir in northeastern Egypt. During the new empire, this city became known as Piramesse—a reference to that city's great builder, Ramesses II. For a brief period during the 20th and 21st Dynasties, it served as Egypt's capital. Soon the state authorities moved the residence to the neighboring city of Tanis. The Old Testament refers to this city as Zoan. During the next phase of Egypt's history, Tanis became Egypt's new political center. Exod 1:11 can hardly refer to anything postdating the move from Piramesse to Tanis, although it should be said—in the light of the reference to Pithom in the same context—that even this conclusion may be contested.

According to Exod 1:11, the cities of Pithom and Rameses are equally important. This is difficult to establish because the reference to a city called Pithom seems completely inconsistent with information from Egypt during the last part of the second millennium B.C.E. Pithom first appears as a city name around the Saite period (not before the seventh century B.C.E.). The name means, "house of (the god) Atum," which originally could have been the name of a temple or a sacred precinct.

---

[53]For the text, see Jean Bottéro's translation and annotations in *Le problème des Ḫabiru à la 4ᵉ rencontre assyriologique internationale* (Cahiers de la Société asiatique 12; Paris: Imprimerie nationale, 1954), 169–70 (text, 187–88), and Moshe Greenberg, *The Ḫab/piru* (American Oriental Series 39; New Haven: American Oriental Society, 1955), 56–57 (texts 162 and 163).

Consequently, Atum owned the temple, and his priests managed it on his behalf. Yet during those early years, it was never used as a city name. Furthermore, the excavations at the Tell el-Maskhuta yield no data regarding Pithom's existence during the reign of Ramesses II or any other pharaoh from the 19th or 20th Dynasties. The earliest evidence comes from the reign of Pharaoh Neco during the 26th Dynasty (ca. 609–607 B.C.E.).[54] Again, we find ourselves at the inevitable crossroads—the unhistorical report in Exod 1:11 of the Israelites in Pithom. Consequently, we must conclude that the information contained in that verse is anachronistic. Pithom (and the biblical report) arises no sooner than the Saite period. Perhaps during that time, Neco incarcerated and employed Israelites (or Judeans) as prisoners of war during the campaign of 609 B.C.E. (during which Judah's king, Josiah, died in battle). Of course, if this theory is not totally compelling, it is nevertheless possible that Judeans already lived in Egypt during this time. If so, perhaps Egypt employed them, along with others, to toil on its building projects.

Ultimately, a rock-solid historical milieu for Exod 1:11 remains tantalizingly elusive. The records discussed above support several conflicting dates for an Israelite presence in Egypt from as early as the thirteenth century B.C.E. to as late as the seventh century B.C.E. In either case, these details were added to the existing story line to validate and add credibility to the literary description of Israel's sojourn in Egypt.

The noted Egyptologist Edward F. Wente offers yet another view of this issue. He does not consider the relationship between Pithom and Rameses in Exod 1:11 to be a problem. In his opinion, neither Pithom nor Rameses had anything to do with the time of the Ramessides. In Exod 1:11, the remark about Rameses may refer to the new city of Tanis, which the Egyptians constructed from the stones of the older community. Workers even transported to Tanis the colossal statues of Ramesses II. Tanis then took on a religious significance involving the worship of Ramesses II, who was in Egyptian tradition never forgotten, not even in Hellenistic times. Thus, Tanis could serve as a good match for the Rameses mentioned in Exod 1:11. If so, then any reference to both Pithom and Rameses must derive from a later stage in Egyptian history.[55]

---

[54] See John S. Holladay, *Cities of the Delta*, part 3, *Tell el-Maskhuta: Preliminary Report on the Wadi Tumilat Project* (American Research Center in Egypt Reports 6; Malibu: Undena, 1982), and Donald B. Redford's discussion in *Egypt, Canaan, and Israel in Ancient Times* (Princeton: Princeton University Press, 1992), 451. For the Egyptian evidence, see also now Ernest S. Frerichs and Leonard H. Lesko, eds., *Exodus: The Egyptian Evidence* (Winona Lake, Ind.: Eisenbrauns, 1997). These, especially Frank J. Yurco's article (pp. 44–47), express an opinion of the historicity of Exod 1:11 that is vastly different from the one proposed here.

[55] See Edward F. Wente's article "Rameses," in *ABD* 5:617–18.

If Wente's theory is correct—which is not yet proven—then the puzzle of Israel's relationship with the city of Rameses is partially solved. Again, Exod 1:11 represents a classic Old Testament literary device to project the circumstances and events of a later period into Israel's ancient history and to persuade the reader of the narrative's historical veracity. Thus Exod 1:11 is no more historical than Gen 47:11, in which Joseph "settled his father and his brothers and gave them a possession in the land of Egypt, in the best land, in the land of Rameses." This is, at any rate according to the biblical chronology, a clear anachronism.

Consequently, the narrative in Exodus about the events in Egypt leaves the reader with two alternatives: either to disregard the historical references in the story or to reduce its contents dramatically. If there were no Israelites in Egypt in the thirteenth century B.C.E., then there was no wonderful rescue from the sea, no Egyptian army and its pharaoh engulfed by the sea. Egyptian sources from that time are unanimously silent about these events, and the mummies of all the kings of Egypt from this period can be found in the Cairo Museum—not at the bottom of the sea.

If we reduce these stories in the usual, but unlikely, way—taking them to be the memory of only a very small and unimportant group of Asians who escaped from Egypt sometime in the late second millennium B.C.E.—then we must conclude that the Old Testament narratives are unhistorical. The Israelite people never lived in ancient Egypt. The authors of the biblical narrative may have borrowed from the remembrance of a small group of persons who once had been in Egypt. This group eventually might have become part of the Israelite nation and their tradition a part of the national heritage.

When scholars accept a "small group" hypothesis, they do so to bypass the many historical problems raised by this narrative. Consequently, it is impossible to prove that such a group of emigrants from Egypt ever existed. By drastically reducing the number of people involved in the escape from Egypt, scholars have made them invisible to the historian. Therefore, no historian is in a position to decide whether such a hypothesis has a historical foundation or should be dismissed as a modern fiction. The crucial problem still remains: Does the Exodus narrative have a historical background or did the biblical historians invent this story, its roots originating from circumstances in their own time (or at least to a period predating their time by only a few years)? The last option conforms best with the information in Exod 1:11: while in Egypt, the Israelites built the supply city Pithom, founded in the first millennium B.C.E., and maybe also the supply city Rameses.

We now arrive at a crucial point in the discussion. Two stories help us either confirm or deny the historicity of the Exodus narratives: Moses' miraculous rescue from the Nile, and the ten plagues. Traditionally, the plagues lack no attention from biblical scholars, many of whom try to provide scientific explanations for them. In each instance, scholars point to natural, recurring phenomena in Egypt: plagues and locusts; firstborn children killed by chronic pest infestation; a "red" Nile besieged by algae. Nevertheless, such "scientific" explanations are not supposed to undermine the miraculous character of the text. As with the author of the manna story, the person who put together the plague story probably used natural phenomena and turned them into miracles by expanding and combining these elements. Each plague by itself may represent only a natural phenomenon, but this circumstance is hardly important or interesting; the important thing is the combination and scope of the plagues. A reader easily understood that a plague could kill children. Undoubtedly, disaster struck when locusts devoured entire grain fields, a persistent problem for ancient farmers. Only in our own time have we seen locusts controlled in the Third World. In their unique way, the narrators describe the reality of plague; however, as in the case of the "manna from heaven," they transform the ordinary into the extraordinary. The authors of the Pentateuch did not sketch some wizard-god for Israel; rather, they depicted a creator who treated his creation "according to the rules." However, who or what would hinder that god from transforming the normal and natural of his creation into something unheard of, into true miracles?

Perhaps the narrators of Exodus used an extant literary tradition that described the migration from Egypt of the Israelite nation, or at least of those people whom the authors considered to be Israelites according to their own criteria. Due to the lack of evidence, we cannot leave out this possibility; indeed, a number of references and hints at these events in the prophetic literature support it.[56] Ultimately, the authors of the book of Exodus created the narratives as we know them. These writers—just like the authors of the patriarchal narratives in Genesis—created their own narrative universe. They wrote about places and events that never existed. Perhaps at one time Israel lived in Egypt. Perhaps not. Yet one thing is clear from our study of the Exodus narratives: they describe a literary world, not historical facts. Thus, it is fruitless to contemplate the exact form of an Israelite migration from Egypt or to calculate exactly when it may have happened. Similarly, what do we gain by knowing the particular sea through which they passed? Is it the Gulf of Suez or the Crocodile Sea (through which the present-day Suez Canal cuts) or an area near Pelusium (at the northern end of the Suez Canal)? Furthermore, did the biblical writers understand the geographical loca-

---

[56] See, for example, Hos 9:3, "Ephraim shall return to Egypt," or the famous verse in Hos 11:1: "When Israel was a child, I loved him, and out of Egypt I called my son." Although one might question the authenticity of these passages, they may represent relatively early attestations of the enslavement of Israel in Egypt.

tion and history of the sites referred to in their narratives? Even Mt. Sinai's exact location causes problems for the biblical writers. Do they place it at Jebel Musa in the south or Kadesh-barnea in the north? Perhaps they, like many scholars,[57] looked toward a location in southwest Arabia, where the Midianites also lived.[58]

We seek neither to exacerbate nor to solve these problems. We do not intend to reconstruct Israel's religious history from its dim beginnings through the Hellenistic period; however, we will make the following observations. First, the Exodus and Sinai narratives were combined in a religious environment where the Law—the Torah—was already dominant, in other words, in an Israelite, or preferably Jewish, context. Sinai witnessed not only the conclusion of a covenant between God and Israel but also the divine installment of the Ten Commandments and the law of Moses among the Israelites. The lofty elevation and expansion of the Law reflect the transition from Israelite to Jewish religion—clearly a later phase in the religious tradition of Israel. Previously, the Sinai narrative recalled the Feast of Weeks, that is, Pentecost. Here we may seek the original setting of the idea of the divine covenant. Nevertheless, this covenant was not deemed important enough to be included in the short historical credo texts in the Pentateuch.

In spite of the preceding observations, we cannot dispute every last historical connection for the Sinai narratives. Both the Old Testament and ancient Near Eastern sources provide circumstantial evidence of Yahwistic practice at Sinai, although the god Yahweh only later came into possession of a major temple in Palestine. The book of Exodus tells us how Yahweh reveals himself initially to Moses (Exod 3) and then later to all of Israel (Exod 19ff.). These revelations take place south of the border of ancient Palestine, where we should probably look for Yahweh's original home. Most of the Old Testament evidence appears in material dating from a relatively late literary period; however, other Old Testament passages refer to the mountain of God. As we noted previously, in 1 Kings 19 Elijah ventures into the desert and encounters God at Mount Horeb, evidently a second name for Mount Sinai. In Judg 5:5, Yahweh is

---

[57] See, e.g., Martin Noth, "Der Wallfahrtsweg zum Sinai (Nu 33)," in Martin Noth's *Aufsätze zur biblischen Landes- und Altertumskunde* (ed. H. W. Wolff; Neukirchen-Vluyn: Neukirchener Verlag, 1971), 1:55–74.

[58] Despite the literary imagery contained in it, Exod 19ff. does not recall volcanic activity. Historical-critical scholarship sometimes went overboard on this issue, forcing into the discussion the *a priori* assumption of natural phenomena to explain every inexplicable biblical text. We should think of the way Greek drama sometimes introduces a deity—with thunder and storm. Perhaps in 1 Kgs 19 (God's revelation to Elijah at Mount Horeb), we find a veiled criticism of the revelation at Mount Sinai as it appears in Exod 19ff.; however, this does not deny the literary staging of God's revelation at Sinai created by the Old Testament authors.

"the one from Sinai." In such texts, Yahweh is also seen as an immigrant from the south, ultimately from Edom or Seir.

Furthermore, Yahweh is mentioned outside the Old Testament narratives. Egyptian sources relate stories about an area known as "Shasu Yahweh" (*š3s.w yhw3*), inhabited by Shasu people.[59] According to the Egyptian sources from the second millennium B.C.E., the nomadic Shasu lived in Syria-Palestine, east of the Jordan, and on the Sinai Peninsula. In this context, Shasu Yahweh is located in the Sinai Desert.

In light of the preceding discussion, new life is breathed into an old hypothesis concerning the origins of Yahwism. Long before scholars began to interpret the Egyptian clues about Yahweh, many tried to find the historical background for Moses' visit to Midian, the first place Yahweh confronted Moses. Apart from the question of the historicity of Exodus 3, one unique feature stands out in this Moses-in-Midian story: if Yahweh appeared in Midian, then Israel's God lived in a foreign land and mingled with foreigners (the Midianites). Evidently, this *was* the case. Second Kings 5 provides an example of the important connection between Yahweh and a land: the Aramean Naaman, who had converted to Yahwism, had to bring a "piece" of the land of Israel back to Damascus. On this piece of land he could continue to worship Yahweh. Thus it is only possible to worship Yahweh "in" (i.e., "on") his own land. Clearly, the Old Testament consciously connects Yahweh with southern Palestine, indicating the originality of the information contained in these narratives. These historical kernels in the Exodus narratives suggest that either the Israelites lived in southern Palestine or Midianites (according to other biblical information, the Kenites) brought the worship of Yahweh to Palestine. Consequently, Yahwism spread throughout the region until finally Yahweh became Israel's national God. In support of such a theory, scholars refer to the evidence that Moses' father-in-law was either a Midianite or a Kenite.

Ultimately, this hypothesis does not yield concrete proof. It is only a theory, one that does not completely mesh with the Exodus narratives in which the Israelites bring the worship of Yahweh to Palestine. The old tradition-historical method might be fit to solve such a problem: the Old Testament authors knew that Yahweh once "came out of Sinai" and was a Midianite or Kenite deity. In the emerging biblical narratives, Yahweh remains the same, although he chooses another people as his own. This is one more example of the intensive redactional activity carried out by the Old Testament authors, who worked with a plethora of diverse infor-

---

[59]See Raphael Giveon, "Toponymes ouest-asiatiques à Soleb," *VT* 14 (1964): 244; cf. also S. Herrmann's assessment of these materials in "Der Name *JHW3* in den Inschriften von Soleb," in *Fourth World Congress of Jewish Studies*, vol. 1 (Jerusalem: World Union of Jewish Studies, 1967), 213–16.

mation—some of which was historical—but who were interested not only in the question of historicity. Their interest was to create a dramatic and entertaining story that covered Israel's history from the election of Abraham to the conquest of the promised land.

I.3. SYNTHESIS: THE BIBLICAL SOURCES AND HISTORY

Edelman, Diana. *The Fabric of History: Text, Artifact and Israel's Past.* JSOTSup 127. Sheffield: JSOT Press, 1991. **Friedman,** Richard E., ed. *The Poet and the Historian: Essays in Literary and Historical Criticism.* HSS 26. Chico: Scholars Press, 1983. **Garbini,** Giovanni. *History and Ideology in Ancient Israel.* Translated by John Bowden. London: SCM, 1988. Esp. pages 1–20. **Lemche,** Niels Peter. *Ancient Israel: A New History of Israelite Society.* The Biblical Seminar. Sheffield: JSOT Press, 1988. Reprint, 1996. Esp. pages 29–73. **Lemche,** Niels Peter. "On Sociology and the History of Israel: A Reply to Eckart Otto—and Some Further Considerations." *BN* 21 (1983): 48–58. **Lemche,** Niels Peter. "Rachel and Lea. Or: On the Survival of Outdated Paradigmas in the Study of the Origin of Israel—I–II." *SJOT* 1 (1987): 127–53; *SJOT* 2 (1988): 39–65. **Miller,** J. Maxwell, and John H. **Hays.** *A History of Ancient Israel and Judah.* Philadelphia: Westminster, 1986. Esp. pages 54–79. **Otto,** Eckart. "Historisches Geschehen-Überlieferung- Erklärungsmodell: Sozialhistorische Grundsatz- und Einzelprobleme in der Geschichtsschreibung des frühen Israel." *BN* 23 (1984): 63–80. **Otto,** Eckart. "Sozialgeschichte Israels: Probleme und Perspektiven. Ein Diskussionspapier." *BN* 15 (1981): 87–92. **Soggin,** J. Alberto. *An Introduction to the History of Israel and Judah.* London: SCM Press, 1993. **Thompson,** Thomas L. *The Early History of the Israelite People from the Written and Archaeological Sources.* SHANE 4. Leiden: E. J. Brill, 1992. Esp. pages 1–26, 77–126.

This study demonstrates that the biblical portrayals of Israel's earliest history (or protohistory)—set in the larger contexts of Mesopotamia, Syrian Palestine, and Egypt—are literary compositions rather than historical sources. The biblical authors consulted various ancient tales and legends, but did not approach them with a critical eye. This conclusion needs no historical proof. A literary analysis of the Pentateuch proves incontrovertibly that its narratives are not reliable sources for the study of antiquity; rather, they are works of art. Without regard for exact historical data regarding the development of their people, those writers used every weapon in their literary arsenal to create powerful and dramatic narratives.

The chronological information in the Old Testament narratives presumes that the events in the Pentateuch occurred during the Bronze Age (i.e., in the third and second millennia B.C.E.). Solid historical analysis belies this assumption and confirms what literary analysis indicates, namely, the Pentateuch's purely literary makeup. One cannot reconstruct ancient Near Eastern history from these narratives; rather, we must be content with what they are: adventure stories and legends, crafted and written by late author-compilers to discuss "the old days" with their audience. Clearly, that audience did not measure the historic by *historical* standards.

It is comparatively simple to unearth certain narrative elements that "stand out from their historical context." Some of those narrative elements we categorized as anachronisms. Such anachronisms help authors conform essentially older narratives to their own world and time. These elements may often be obviously secondary and easy to detect. In other cases, such elements seem to be part of the narrative plot and are therefore not easy to isolate, possibly implying that the whole narrative is late, that is, that the "anachronism" dates the narrative in which it is present.

The reference in Gen 11:31 to "Ur of the Chaldeans" does not show any sign of being an anachronism. Yet Abraham could not have lived there before the eighth century B.C.E., since the Aramaic-speaking Chaldeans did not inhabit southern Mesopotamia before this time. It cannot, of course, be ruled out that the note "of the Chaldeans" was added to the text by a late copyist of the text, by somebody who knew that the Ur of his own time was inhabited by Chaldeans. Because of such considerations, the presence of this reference says little about the date of the main narrative—it only indicates when the note was added to the narrative.

A number of other references in the patriarchal narratives create problems if one wishes to find an early date for these compositions. For example, in Genesis 24, Abraham's servant travels to Mesopotamia in search of Isaac's future wife. The servant rides on camels, with camels as beasts of burden at his side. When he arrives in Mesopotamia (or better, Aram-Naharaim), the servant encounters Abraham's family members, whom the subsequent Jacob narratives call Arameans. Specifically, Isaac's brother-in-law is referred to as "Laban the Aramean" (Gen 28:5; 31:20, 24). In this story, two issues command our attention. First, ancient Near Eastern peoples domesticated camels around 1000 B.C.E. Individuals may have domesticated a camel or two earlier than that; however, we have no evidence to support such a theory. We only know that the author of Genesis 24 assumes the use in his own time of domesticated camels for riding. Thus, the pericope cannot predate 1000 B.C.E. A second problem concerns the servant's ultimate destination: Aram-Naharaim. Aram Naharaim means "Aram between the rivers" or "Aramaic Mesopotamia" (or "Mesopotamian Aram").[60] This could hardly have been the name of the region before it turned into Aramean territory at the end of the second millennium B.C.E.[61] The earliest Assyrian

---

[60] The Greek word "Mesopotamia" simply means "between the rivers."

[61] Several other possible sites for Abraham's relatives have been suggested, including Paddan-aram (Gen 25:20; 28:2; 31:18). The actual name is meaningless, for it only confirms what we already know, namely, that the authors of the patriarchal narratives viewed Abraham's family as Aramean.

sources do not mention the Arameans before the twelfth century B.C.E., and we possess no sources that support the existence of Arameans during the Late Bronze Age.

Earlier in ancient Near Eastern chronology, completely different peoples inhabited the Upper Mesopotamian region about which we are speaking. Amorites and some Hurrians lived there around 2000 B.C.E., neither of whom are mentioned in the Genesis narratives.

From the third millennium B.C.E. to the present day, this area of the world has seen many empires and smaller nations come and go. Yet the patriarchal narratives mention neither the small nor large entities in Syria or Mesopotamia during the so-called patriarchal period, for example, Ebla in the third millennium, or Mari, Yamkhad, and Qatna in the second millennium. Similarly, we hear nothing of the ancient Assyrian state that by the start of the second millennium had already begun dominating the area as well as trading with distant lands and peoples. Indeed, in the first half of the second millennium B.C.E., the Assyrians founded a trade emporium in Asia Minor. Documents pertaining to this trade station testify to limited trade relations between this Assyrian colony and Harran, the home of Laban the Aramean (cf. Gen 27:43).

We could offer many more examples and richer conclusions regarding the disjunction between the biblical narratives and the actual ancient Near Eastern milieu from 2300 to 1200 B.C.E. For example, we could note the discrepancy between the depiction of ancient Near Eastern civilizations in Genesis and the established and well-known Bronze Age Syrian and Mesopotamian states. Again, the Old Testament never deals with the political landscape in the alleged period of the biblical narratives. One exception is Egypt, the home of the pharaohs, which plays an important role in the Genesis and Exodus tales. Indeed, among its ancient Near Eastern neighbors, Egypt was typologically exotic, geographically isolated, and ethnically independent. First, Egypt was mainly limited to the Nile Valley; it was also protected against outsiders by natural borders, with deserts to the east and west, an ocean to the north, and rapids to the south that effectively cordoned off Egypt from the Nubians. Second, Egyptians differed from their Asian neighbors in another key respect: the Egyptian language is quite distinct from the Semitic languages, representing an altogether different branch of the Afroasiatic language family called Hamitic. If these two language groups developed from a common heritage, already in prehistoric times the Semitic and Egyptian strains were so distinctive that those who spoke them could not easily communicate with each other. Third, the Egyptian empire began around 3000 B.C.E. Several times during its history Egypt withstood insurrections and invasions; however, it never totally lost its independence or identity before or during the Israelite period. From an "Egyptian" point of view, it is not important whether the Pentateuch was composed in 2000 B.C.E.,

1000 B.C.E., or 500 B.C.E. At any point in time, Egypt could act as the backdrop for the "Egyptianizing" parts of the pentateuchal narratives.

In comparison, other ancient Near Eastern civilizations left relatively few traces of their existence or activities in the Old Testament. Sometimes the Bible provides bits and pieces about those societies; however, those recollections usually point to individual places and events removed from any historical contexts. For example, Genesis 14 mentions several huge societies from Mesopotamia and Asia Minor. The text tells of four powerful kings "from the East" who invade the patriarch's property; however, the information is a jumbled and nebulous mishmash of historical information. The narrative only knows that these large empires once existed.

When the Old Testament provides information about other ancient Near Eastern peoples, it does so without any regard for specific historical details. A good example is the narrative information about the Hittites. On the one hand, such information may sound quite concrete. Thus Genesis 23 provides an elaborate account of Abraham's purchase of a family tomb in Hebron from Ephron the Hittite. On the other hand, lists such as Gen 15:20 provide very general information about the Hittites among the pre-Israelite nations in Canaan. The Hittite empire was centered in Asia Minor during the second millennium B.C.E. and became one of the most influential nations of the ancient Near East, facts about which the Old Testament says nothing. Yet the Old Testament erroneously places the Hittites in ancient Palestine, though Palestine never functioned as part of the Hittite empire (its southern border never went beyond the Beirut-Damascus line). John Van Seters offers intriguing insights into this discussion. His study of Assyrian and Babylonian documents leads him to the conclusion that the ethnic designation "Hittite" changed after the fall of the Hittite empire. Afterwards, the Hittites in Assyrian and Babylonian documents simply represented people that lived west of the Euphrates.[62] Few scholars question Van Seters's conclusions. If he is correct, then the author of Genesis 23 may have borrowed ideas about the Hittites living in Palestine during Abraham's time from Assyrian or Babylonian sources, although this material said little about the ethnic composition of ancient Syrian and Palestinian society.

It is more difficult to analyze the social relationships described in the Old Testament. Unfortunately, extrabiblical sources do not often verify social and political relationships described in the biblical narratives. In its typical narrative style, a story portrays a private individual who gains an audience with the king. Whether this king is the monarch of a

---

[62]See John Van Seters, "The Terms 'Amorite' and 'Hittite' in the Old Testament," *VT* 22 (1972): 64–81. As the title suggests, Van Seters believes the terms "Amorite" and "Hittite" are almost indistinguishable in the Old Testament.

small Palestinian state or an Egyptian pharaoh, the narrative describes a social impossibility in ancient Egypt or Syria: a common person did not appear before royalty. The gulf between regent and subject was virtually impenetrable. Sovereigns avoided such audiences because strict social convention alone determined whether someone could come before the king or his court. Thus, this discussion about biblical adventure stories whose heroes associate with and perform important tasks for kings reminds us that the biblical relationship between narrative and history is very much like those of Hans Christian Andersen or the Brothers Grimm.

In light of the preceding arguments, we can now conclude that the Old Testament is a poor source for reconstructing the history of Palestine and Syria during the Bronze Age. The historian has virtually nothing with which to work. Thus, it is useless to mine the Old Testament narratives for material to reconstruct that period. Instead, historians should look for other sources. The narratives in the Pentateuch will not and cannot pretend to be historical documents pertaining to Israel's past. These stories resemble a genre much like those of chivalry novels or modern films. Like the Pentateuch, these novels and films develop from the same fiction-to-reality relationship. For example, period clothing is particularly significant for films about the Middle Ages; however, the actors who wear them remain modern people, with contemporary experiences and perceptions. A filmmaker may often employ experts to reproduce on the screen the speech patterns and thought-worlds of the Middle Ages. Yet, even if the actors successfully portray those lives and times, if the general audience is indifferent or unmoved by their efforts, the movie fails. To make a movie comprehensible, every film producer must produce a movie that speaks to its audiences' tastes and intelligence. Consequently, no reasonable historian studies Sir Walter Scott's *Ivanhoe* or Errol Flynn's portrayal of Robin Hood to reconstruct medieval English history. Yet many Old Testament scholars conduct their investigations in precisely that manner when they view the Pentateuch as a reasonably reliable historical source. No, the past is dead and should be left to the dead. Enlisting Isaiah, we might say the living should not seek the dead (8:19–20). The past can only be summoned up to understand the present. When we turn to the past, we transform it into a guide for the present, and in the process it is no longer about the past, but about the present and the future.

Instead of relying upon inadequate Old Testament texts, scholars are better served by other ancient Near Eastern sources, many of which provide important, scientifically valid insights into the actual periods to which the Old Testament adventure stories seemingly refer. To that end, several issues will command our attention in the following chapters. First, we will review the extant ancient Near Eastern source materials. Then we will outline Near Eastern history from about 2300 to about 1200 B.C.E., at which point Israel's actual history begins.

2

A HISTORICAL RECONSTRUCTION OF THE PERIOD

II.1. WRITTEN SOURCES FOR THE HISTORY OF SYRIA AND PALESTINE

GENERAL: **Sasson,** Jack M., ed. *Civilizations of the Ancient Near East.* 4 vols. New York: Scribners, 1995.

TRANSLATIONS: **Hallo,** William W., ed. *The Context of Scripture.* Vol. 1, *Canonical Compositions from the Biblical World.* Leiden: E. J. Brill, 1997 (= *COS*). **Pritchard,** James B., ed. *Ancient Near Eastern Texts Relating to the Old Testament.* 3d ed. with supplement. Princeton: Princeton University Press, 1969 (= *ANET*).

II.1.1. Texts from Syria and Palestine

EBLA: **Archi,** Alphonso. *Testi amministrativi: Assegnazioni di tessuti (Archivio L. 2769).* Archivi reali di Ebla 1–. Rome: Missione archeologica italiana in Siria, 1985.

AMARNA: **Knudtzon,** J. A. *Die el-Amarna Tafeln.* 2 vols. Leipzig: J. C. Hinrichs, 1915. **Moran,** William L., ed. and trans. *The Amarna Letters.* Baltimore: Johns Hopkins University Press, 1992. **Rainey,** Anson F. *El-Amarna Tablets 359–379.* 2d ed., revised. Kevelaer: Butzon & Bercker; Neukirchen-Vluyn: Neukirchener Verlag, 1979. **Smith,** Sidney. *The Statue of Idri-mi.* London: British Institute of Archaeology in Ankara, 1949. **Wiseman,** D. J. *The Alalakh Tablets.* London: British Institute of Archaeology in Ankara, 1953.

UGARIT: I. UGARITIC TEXTS: **Dietrich,** Manfried, Oswald **Loretz,** and J. **Sanmartín,** eds. *The Cuneiform Alphabetic Texts from Ugarit, Ras Ibn Hani and Other*

Places. Münster: Ugarit-Verlag, 1995 (=*KTU*: 2d, enlarged ed.). II. ADMINISTRATIVE TEXTS (IN UGARITIC AND AKKADIAN): **Schaeffer,** Claude F.-A., ed. *Le Palais royal d'Ugarit II–VI.* Mission de Ras Shamra; Paris: Imprimerie nationale, 1955–1970 (first volume never published). III. TRANSLATIONS OF EPIC TEXTS: **Gibson,** J. C. L. *Canaanite Myths and Legends.* Edinburgh: T. & T. Clark, 1978. **de Moor,** Johannes C. *An Anthology of Religious Texts from Ugarit.* Leiden: E. J. Brill, 1987. **Parker,** Simon B., ed. *Ugaritic Narrative Poetry.* SBLWAW 9. Atlanta: Scholars Press, 1997. IV. TRANSLATIONS OF RITUAL TEXTS: **Caquot,** André, Jean-Michel **de Tarragon,** and Jesús-Luis **Cunchillos,** eds. *Textes ougaritiques II. Textes religieux et rituels: Correspondance.* Littératures anciennes du Proche-Orient 7; Textes sémitiques de l'Ouest. Paris: Editions du Cerf, 1974–1989. **Pardee,** Dennis. *Les Textes para-mythologiques de la 24e campagne (1961).* Paris: Editions Recherche sur les civilisations, 1988. **Xella,** Paolo. *I testi rituali di Ugarit I.* Rome: Consiglio nazionale delle ricerche, 1981.

We possess an extensive collection of inscriptions from ancient Palestine and Syria, including present-day Lebanon. These documents come to us mainly in two forms: the occasional monumental inscription etched in stone, and the more prevalent clay tablets. Generally, the latter contain Akkadian cuneiform script and language; however, some are also written with local cuneiform alphabets and in a local Syrian dialect. Monumental inscriptions may likewise be either in Akkadian or in one of the local dialects. Sometimes foreign conquerors—not least Egyptian pharaohs—ordered that monumental inscriptions of their conquests be composed and erected at important crossroads, mountain passes, and other visible and widely traveled places. Unfortunately, erosion has to a large extent destroyed the content of inscriptions dating from the third and second millennia B.C.E.

The surviving source materials from Syria and Palestine vary in several respects. For example, whereas various Syrian sites—especially those including royal palaces—contain significant and substantial text collections, only a few inscriptions that date between 2300 and 1200 B.C.E. have survived from Palestine. This gap reflects the divergent social and economic realities of both areas during those years. Palestinian cities paled in comparison to their larger and more complex Syrian counterparts. Syria's urban centers were complex social organizations. Their comprehensive archives helped keep local affairs in order as well as recorded and maintained relations with neighbors. Most Palestinian cities, on the other hand, were small—at times more like fortified villages or simple fortresses. Consequently, they did not require extensive record-keeping or written communications to regulate or monitor interpersonal and interstate relations. It is no surprise, then, that not a single written document has survived from third-millennium B.C.E. Palestine, and only a few are extant from the first half of the second millennium. Only the extensive excavations of the Middle Bronze city of Hazor in Upper Galilee provide a few insignificant tidbits from this part of the second millennium. Predictably, Hazor was by far the largest city in the region.

In contrast to these disappointing findings stands the impressive palace archive unearthed during the past twenty years at Tell Mardikh (the site of ancient Ebla, situated forty kilometers south of Aleppo), whose findings date to the second half of the third millennium B.C.E. Before the Ebla texts came to light, scholars had to base their assumptions about Syria in this period on the imprecise information provided by Mesopotamian documents. Consequently, these texts—so far confined to only this place—provide revolutionary insights into Syrian society from 2500 to 2300 B.C.E. Most of this documentation concerns Eblaite society, supplying only scant information about areas outside its confines.

The most significant document discovery from the beginning of the second millennium B.C.E. comes from Tell Atchana, the ancient city of Alalakh. Alalakh lies on the Orontes River and once served as the capital of the kingdom of Mukish. Unfortunately, its archive contains documents that date no earlier than the eighteenth century; therefore, it contributes limited information about the Middle Bronze Age. Its importance to scholarship lies in the details it provides about Syrian society at that time.

Far more numerous are the source materials from the latter stages of the second millennium B.C.E. (i.e., the Late Bronze Age). This period also furnishes important documents from both within and outside of Palestine—documents that contain significant clues about Palestinian life and society. The important sites include the major Syrian archives at Alalakh (fourteenth century) and Ugarit (the present-day ruins of Ras Shamra; fourteenth–thirteenth centuries). Ugarit, which was at that time the capital of the kingdom of Ugarit, stood on the coast of the Mediterranean Sea near the modern Syrian city of Latakia. While the Alalakh texts are generally in Akkadian, the Ugarit archive contains texts in Akkadian as well as in Ugaritic, the local language spoken at that time in western Syria. The texts composed in the Ugaritic language are written in cuneiform signs, but in comparison to Akkadian it is an uncomplicated writing system. Many texts from Ugarit are not documents pertaining to the administration of the Ugaritic state; these include literary texts and sources that provide important clues about Syrian religious practices during the second millennium B.C.E. Finally, in addition to Alalakh and Ugarit archives, we should mention other less significant text discoveries; for example, the fifteenth-century Syrian inscription of King Idrimi of Alalakh.

Archaeologists have yet to find substantial archives in Palestine. So far they have unearthed only a limited number of texts in Akkadian and a stray document or two written in Ugaritic characters. Other Late Bronze Age texts from Palestine are Egyptian in origin and mostly monumental inscriptions—although they are not really very "monumental."

Arguably the most significant Late Bronze Age texts from Palestine are the Tell el-Amarna letters. Ironically, these letters were not found in

Palestine or Syria; rather, they came, by chance, into the hands of scholars in Egypt about one hundred years ago. Around the mid-fourteenth century B.C.E., Amarna served as Egypt's capital. Its archive has yielded close to four hundred documents, the vast majority of which contain correspondence between Syrian and Palestinian vassals and the Egyptian pharaoh regarding the difficulties of daily governance.

Clearly, even a painstaking analysis of these Bronze Age Palestinian and Syrian source materials cannot provide a gap-free historical reconstruction of the period from which they spring. They provide only momentary glimpses into isolated events that might span years or decades. Thus, while we can reconstruct larger chunks of Ebla's early history, we are left with only fragments regarding Alalakh in the eighteenth and fourteenth centuries. Any facts concerning events before the eighteenth and between the eighteenth and fourteenth centuries remain beyond our grasp. To fill in these gaps, we must look elsewhere in the ancient Near East.

II.1.2. Mesopotamian Sources

The Mesopotamian inscriptions are so numerous that it is impossible to list them here. For a bibliography that covers all published inscriptions until 1975, see **Borger**, Rykle. *Handbuch der Keilschriftliteratur I–III*. Berlin: de Gruyter, 1967–1975. A collection that is of special interest here is published in the series Les archives royales de Mari I–XXV. Paris: Editions Recherche sur les civilisations, 1950–1986.

Two main types of written documentation from the third and second millennia B.C.E. comprise the Babylonian source material about Syria and Palestine. First, some materials deal specifically with Syria or Palestine. This kind of documentation reflects the close commercial links, but also the many battles between Mesopotamia and its neighbors to the west. The second kind of evidence—as a matter of fact, quite a comprehensive collection—offers more indirect than direct relevance. This evidence does not specifically refer to Syria or Palestine; rather it reflects the shared culture and common forms of social organization.

The first category of material is of rather limited value, since few documents directly refer to events in Early Bronze Age Syria. In this period, Palestine is seemingly unknown to the Mesopotamian scribes. Furthermore, documents from Mesopotamia that mention Mesopotamian kings traveling in Syria and fighting local powers are generally late and legendary. Thus, some sources refer to the heroic King Sargon (2334–2279 B.C.E.) and his successful campaigns against Syria, while others cover the less successful exploits of his grandson Naram-Sin (2254–2218 B.C.E.). However, as time goes by this kind of documentation becomes more and more precise and concrete; indeed, in the Late Bronze

Age, Mesopotamian sources become very important for interpreting the history of the small states of Syria and Palestine.

The second category of written material includes large administrative collections as well as law collections and documents pertaining to the practice of law in Mesopotamian court rooms. These administrative and legal texts have continued to fascinate scholars, not least because of the many obvious and (even more) assumed parallels to Old Testament legal texts. Sometimes scholars conclude that these parallels confirm that such ancient Near Eastern legal documents provide an accurate historical backdrop for the Old Testament narratives. Previously, we noted such connections between the fifteenth-century Nuzi documents and the patriarchal narratives. Yet the value of Mesopotamian legal documents lies elsewhere. They offer interesting insights into daily life in the ancient Near East—details about places and events that often remain unchanged over many years. For example, some of the laws in the Code of Hammurabi (eighteenth century B.C.E.) had a prehistory in the Mesopotamian law tradition that reached far back. Furthermore, just as many or even more of the laws in this code were transmitted to posterity in some form or another. In this way, it would be correct to speak of a continuous law tradition lasting for more than a thousand years. Very few of the laws deal specifically with circumstances in the eighteenth century B.C.E. At the same time it is difficult to pinpoint the direct connection between the written law codes and the practical application of justice in the courtrooms. Perhaps we must conclude that these legislative traditions developed in academic circles, completely apart from daily life in court. Thus it seems that the juridical tradition of Mesopotamia witnessed a consistent gap between "theory" and "practice."[1]

The regulations in the Old Testament concerning the Sabbatical Year—and also the Jubilee Year (Lev 25:8–55)—provides an excellent example of how the Mesopotamian law tradition influenced the Syro-

---

[1]More than forty years ago, the noted Assyriologist F. R. Kraus demonstrated that the Code of Hammurabi was never intended as a prescription for practical jurisprudence. He contended that the Code of Hammurabi should be regarded as a collection of verdicts and court decisions rather than a law code in the modern sense of the word. The aim and scope of this "code" was to prove that Hammurabi was a just king. See Kraus, "Ein zentrales Problem des altmesopotamischen Rechtes: Was ist der Codex Hammurabi?" *Geneva* NS 8 (1960): 283–96. Kraus's conclusions are supported by thousands of extant documents from Hammurabi's time that never refer to anything in the Code. Furthermore, the Code seems incomplete; that is, it fails to mention several important legal questions. For example, homicides required no concrete legislation because murderers were routinely condemned by judges who needed no written law to tell them how to handle such cases. For more discussion of the role and scope of Mesopotamian law codes, see Martha T. Roth, *Law Collections from Mesopotamia and Asia Minor* (2d ed.; SBLWAW 6; Atlanta: Scholars Press, 1997), 4–7.

Palestinian world. Thus, the Old Testament demands a regular cycle of Sabbath Year celebrations. Every seven years, by law, slaves who had previously sold themselves because of debt were released and their debts remitted (Deut 15:1–18). In other parts of the Torah, we find as isolated prescriptions (Exod 21:2–11; 23:10–13) the elements that were combined in the law of the Sabbatical Year. These prescriptions seem similar to the royal decrees in circulation in Mesopotamia during the time of the kings of the Hammurabi dynasty. Approximately every ten years (the actual number varied), Babylonian kings issued a decree that remitted the sentence of debt slaves and released their mortgaged properties, returning the land to their original owners. Along with this practice came very specific legal presuppositions and language, most of which are not original to Hammurabi's time. Similar language appears in ancient Near Eastern documents dating as early as the mid-third millennium and as late as the fourth or third century B.C.E.

This terminology about discharging debts in Babylonian texts can also be found in Syrian sources and, of course, in the Old Testament, although it is impossible to say that decrees of remission were also issued by the kings of Syria and Palestine. In the Old Testament, the language does not occur directly in the context of the Sabbath regulations. However, it appears in the form of the Akkadian "loan-word" *d^erôr*, "release" (Lev 25:10; Jer 34:8, 15, 17), in the Jubilee ordinance in the book of Leviticus (Lev 25), and as part of a royal decree of remission issued by King Zedekiah on the eve of the Babylonian conquest of Jerusalem in 587 B.C.E. (Jer 34). This language may also be echoed in the Psalms and in Isaiah in the form of *mêšārîm/mîšôr*, "equity" (Ps 96:10; 99:4; Isa 11:4).[2] Although we here encounter a link between the Mesopotamian and Old Testament principles of debt discharge, this does not provide concrete evidence to isolate the starting point or specific ocurrences of the Sabbatical Year celebration. At best, such similarities only affirm sporadic and indirect connections between Mesopotamia and Palestine.[3]

Among the many extant Mesopotamian documents from the Middle Bronze Age, those from the royal archive at Mari-on-the-Euphrates (nineteenth–eighteenth century B.C.E.) are particularly noteworthy. Mari (modern Tell Hariri) was an important kingdom situated at the border between Mesopotamia and Syria and was in those days governed by kings of Syrian (Amorite) origin. Consequently, Mari's extensive archive provides invaluable insights into Syrian society and some reflections on Mesopotamian social practice.

---

[2] The Hebrew *d^erôr* comes from Akkadian *andurārum*, and *mêšārîm/mîšôr* is obviously a reflection of the Akkadian *mīšarum*, the technical term for the decree of debt remission in the time of Hammurabi.

[3] We will cover this issue in more detail later in III.2.2 and III.3.2.

A significant portion of the Mari archive consists of reports from governors to the royal authorities concerning their provinces. Interestingly, some of those documents mention groups of nomads who drift in and out of the kingdom of Mari. One such group is the aforementioned Binu-Yamina, or Benjaminites. Still another interesting bit of news from this collection refers to alleged prophetic activity similar to that mentioned in the Old Testament.

Finally, the Mari archive contains important examples of royal correspondence between the great monarchs of that era. Among the Syrian royalty mentioned within those documents are Yarim-Lim, the king of Yamkhad (Aleppo) and father-in-law of Mari's king Zimri-Lim, and the king of Qatna, who gave his daughter to the king of Mari. These documents not only provide a multifaceted impression of international political relations, but they especially illuminate the interdynastic associations of that time.

II.1.3. Egyptian Sources

GENERAL TEXTS: **Breasted,** James H., ed. and trans. *Ancient Records of Egypt: Historical Documents from Earliest Times to the Persian Conquest, I–IV.* Chicago: University of Chicago Press, 1906. Reprint, London: Histories and Mysteries of Man, 1988. **Helck,** Wolfgang, and Kurt **Sethe,** eds. *Urkunden des ägyptischen Altertums, IV: Urkunden der 18. Dynastie, Übersetzung zu den Heften 17–22.* Berlin: Akademie Verlag, 1961. Reprint, Berlin: Akademie, 1984. **Kitchen,** Kenneth A. *Ramesside Inscriptions: Historical and Biographical, I–VIII.* Oxford: Blackwell, 1968–1990. **Kitchen,** Kenneth A. *Ramesside Inscriptions: Translated and Annotated, I–VII.* Oxford: Blackwell, 1993–.

EXECRATION TEXTS: **Posener,** George. *Princes et pays d'Asie et de Nubie: Textes hiératiques sur des figurines d'envoûtement du Moyen Empire.* Brussels: Fondation égyptologique reine Elisabeth, 1940. **Sethe,** Kurt. *Die Ächtung feindlicher Fürsten, Völker und Dinge auf altägyptischen Tongefäßscherben des Mittleren Reiches.* Berlin: Verlag der Akademie der Wissenschaften, 1926.

Documents from Egypt have more to say about Palestine in the Bronze Age than their Mesopotamian counterparts. This is a natural consequence of the fact that Palestine was the closest neighbor to Egypt in Western Asia, although separated from Egypt by a hundred-kilometer desert barrier. Furthermore, during the Late Bronze Age, both southern Syria and Palestine came under the New Kingdom's jurisdiction. Naturally, Egypt's relationship with its Asian neighbors intensified at that time. This situation contrasts markedly with that in the third millennium, the time of the Old Kingdom—during which Egypt's narcissistic self-occupation (it was, after all, the time of the great pyramid constructions) resulted in a complacent attitude toward its neighbors. By the end of that period, a series of revolts and civil war in Egypt changed Egypt's attitude to the foreign world and forced it out of its isolationism. During the ensuing period (i.e., the Middle Bronze Age, the time of the Egyptian

Middle Kingdom), Egypt began to interfere in the affairs of Palestine; however, Egyptians seemed reluctant to commit political and military resources to subdue Palestine and Syria completely.

Apart from isolated references, third-millennium Egyptian documents provide scant information about Asia. Most of that material focuses on Egypt's trading posts in the Levant and its various trade relations with Lebanon and throughout the Near East. As the Middle Bronze Age approaches, Egyptian references to Palestine and the wider Near East become more frequent and detailed. Two types of documents stand out.

First, the so-called Execration texts emerge from a period between 1850 and 1750 B.C.E. These texts are inscribed on figurines that represent renegade monarchs. Smashing the figurines while reciting the inscribed vilifications was a way to curse the Palestinian sovereigns—much the same as "voodoo magicians" maltreat dolls. Interestingly, some of the inscriptions contain references to important cities such as Jerusalem, Shechem, Hazor, and Ashkelon.[4]

Second, a renowned tale from this era is the Story of Sinuhe, hardly a historical report but a novel that outlines the life of this Egyptian official. Sinuhe is a fugitive who is forced to live as a refugee among the Palestinian barbarians whom the narrator describes as uncivilized primitives. The historical value of this material is highly debatable; that is, it paints an extreme and caricatured portrait of Palestinian society in the days of the Middle Kingdom, during the Middle Bronze Age. The narrator is only concerned with impressing upon the reader the great cultural and domestic chasms between Egypt and its seemingly uncouth neighbors.

Excerpts from the Story of Sinuhe

Then I made my way northward. I reached the "Walls of the Ruler," which were made to repel the Asiatics and to crush the Sandfarers. I crouched in a bush for fear of being seen by the guard on duty upon the wall.

I set out at night. At dawn I reached Peten. I halted at "Isle-of-Kem-Wer." An attack of thirst overtook me; I was parched, my throat burned. I said, "This is the taste of death." I raised my heart and collected myself when I heard the lowing sound of cattle and saw Asiatics. One of their leaders, who had been in Egypt, recognized me. He gave me water and boiled milk for me. I went with him to his tribe. What they did for me was good.

. . . .

---

[4] Today, these documents are housed partly in Berlin and partly in Brussels.

There came a hero of Retenu,
To challenge me in my tent.
A champion was he without peer,
He had subdued it all.
He said he would fight with me,
He planned to plunder me,
He meant to seize my cattle
At the behest of his tribe.

The ruler conferred with me and I said: "I do not know him; I am not his ally, that I could walk about in his camp. Have I ever opened his back rooms or climbed over his fence? It is envy, because he sees me doing your commissions.

. . . .

At night I strung my bow, sorted my arrows, practiced with my dagger, polished my weapons. When it dawned Retenu came. It had assembled its tribes; it had gathered its neighboring peoples; it was intent on this combat.

He came toward me while I waited, having placed myself near him. Every heart burned for me; the women jabbered. All hearts ached for me thinking: "Is there another champion who could fight him? He [raised] his battle-axe and shield, while his armful of missiles fell toward me. When I had made his weapons attack me, I let his arrows pass me by without effect, one following the other. Then, when he charged me, I shot him, my arrow sticking in his neck. He screamed; he fell on his nose; I slew him with his axe. I raised my war cry over his back, while every Asiatic shouted. I gave praise to Mont, while his people mourned him. The ruler Ammunenshi took me in his arms.

Then I carried off his goods; I plundered his cattle. What he had meant to do to me I did to him. I took what was in his tent; I stripped his camp. Thus I became great, wealthy in goods, rich in herds.[5]

By the time of the New Kingdom-Late Bronze Age, Egyptian information on Syria and Palestine becomes abundant. We already mentioned the Amarna archive that was discovered in Egypt but originated in Syria and Palestine. Numerous monument inscriptions also describe in pompous language the exploits of pharaohs who conquered Asia and deported Asians to Egypt for slave labor. Other documents from this collection include more stories and scribal discourses. In one vignette,

---

[5] Translation of "Sinuhe" by Miriam Lichtheim, *COS* 1.38, 77–79; see also "The Story of Sinuhe," by John A. Wilson, *ANET*, 19–20.

scholar-scribes debate among themselves the subtleties of Palestinian geography and politics. The author proves his own superior intellect by calling his adversary an idiot and offering to the reader several geographical tidbits about Palestine.

To round out this discussion, we could mention several indispensable resource texts for the history of Late Bronze Age Palestine; however, we will limit our discussion to one document: the so-called victory inscription of Pharaoh Merneptah (1213–1204 B.C.E.). In his inscription, Merneptah describes how he vanquished the Libyans to the west and the peoples of Asia, including Israel, to the east. For one hundred years, this document has been considered correctly as concrete proof of an Israel in Palestine around 1200 B.C.E. Clearly, the Merneptah inscription represents the earliest extrabiblical hint of Israel's dim beginnings.

II.1.4. Other Written Sources

HITTITE SOURCES: **Beckman**, Gary M. *Hittite Diplomatic Texts*. SBLWAW 7. Atlanta: Scholars Press, 1996.

CLASSICAL SOURCES: **Attridge**, Harold W., and Robert A. **Oden** Jr. *Philo of Byblos: The Phoenician History*. Washington, D.C.: The Catholic Biblical Association of America, 1981.

The Hittite Sources

With the information from Egyptian documents, our discussion about extrabiblical sources for the Syrian history and culture during pre-Israelite times is almost complete. A few other documents require our further attention, the first of which come from the various Hittite archives unearthed during the last hundred years, especially in the ancient city of Hattusas. Hattusas once served as the Hittite capital and lies near the present-day Turkish city of Boghazkale, meaning "the fortress in the mountain pass"—perhaps better known as Boghazkoy, meaning "the village in the mountain pass" (it changed names as a consequence of the discoveries)—in central Anatolia. Already during the Middle Bronze Age, the Hittites for a short time communicated with Syrian and Mesopotamian states. Most of the information regarding those relations come from a single source: the late seventeenth-century campaign of King Mursilis I against Aleppo and Babylon.

During the Late Bronze Age, Hittites battled the Egyptians for control of Syria. Several types of documents from Hattusas describe events during the fourteenth century B.C.E. that involve situations in Syria and Palestine. First, the historical materials describe kings and their fates in war. Other documents contain extensive correspondence between the Hittites and the other major powers or between the Hittite "great king" and his subordinates—materials we have come to expect from the archives of powerful nations. The Hattusas materials contain treaties concluded between the Hittites and their Syrian minions, or between Hittite kings and their Mesopotamian and Egyptian associates. Among these documents, one type has particular significance for students of the Old Testament: the treaties between the great kings of Hatti and their vassals in Syria and Asia Minor were formerly seen as paralleling some important covenant texts in the Bible. Some scholars believe that these documents verify the historicity of the Sinai regulations. Of course, those same investigators overlook a crucial point, that is, the tradition of concluding covenants between overlords and their vassals did not stop with the Hittite examples. Even in the seventh century B.C.E., treaties were concluded with a similar form and content, for example, among the Neo-Assyrian overlords and the petty kings of Syria and Phoenicia.[6] In fact, such treaties seem more appropriate for comparisons with the biblical evidence. Finally, another category of the Hittite state archives consists of law collections, at times very different from the Mesopotamian ones, although in general part of the same academic law tradition.

This discussion about the relationship between Hittite texts from the Late Bronze Age and the Old Testament shows how important even Near Eastern documents originating in the periphery of the ancient world could be for biblical studies. Such texts are certainly to be considered important additional evidence. The Hittites wrote in their own language, a sort of Indo-European one. For their script, they mostly used Akkadian cuneiform, and they communicated in Akkadian with the nations of Syria, Mesopotamia, and Egypt. Because Akkadian was in those days used as an international koine, it is hardly surprising that literary and religious texts of Mesopotamian origin have shown up in the Hattusas archive.

The Classical Sources

Although especially the Late Bronze Age was rich in communication between the various parts of the ancient world, the Greek sources add nothing to our discussion. Mainland Greece and the Greek archipelago, including Crete and Cyprus, had regular commercial relations with Syria and Egypt, but none of the written texts so far found in these quarters has added to our knowledge about Syria and Palestine. The later Greek literary tradition (including Homeric poetry) may in places focus on previous times; however, those texts are so colored by artistic storytelling that they are virtually useless for historical reconstruction of the times and places they describe. The same can be said of most Hellenistic

[6] For these, see Simo Parpola and Kazuko Watanabe, *Neo-Assyrian Treaties and Loyalty Oaths* (State Archives of Assyria 2; Helsinki: Helsinki University Press, 1988).

documents. Occasionally, those texts reveal information regarding religion and science—the details of which must be carefully scrutinized. Except when those stories directly support religious aspects to which other ancient Near Eastern sources already attest, it is safer to exclude those Greco-Roman documents from the mix. Ultimately, the classical recollections regarding the ancient Near East are those that merchants and explorers brought back from their journeys. Predictably, they recalled mysterious adventures in wondrous lands—engaging for the reader, but useless for our investigative purposes.

In this section, the collections of sources to which we have referred provide modern historians with useful information regarding the history and culture of Bronze Age Syria and Palestine. Clearly, the information gathered from those sources is sketchy and fragmented; however, from them, we can draw a composite sketch of the culture and history of Syria and Palestine during that time. To fill in those gaps, we must look elsewhere. To that end, in the next section, we will explore archaeology as yet another important source of information.

II.2. ARCHAEOLOGY

GENERAL: **Binford,** Lewis R. *An Archaeological Perspective.* New York: Seminar Press, 1972. **Fritz,** Volkmar. *An Introduction to Biblical Archaeology.* JSOTSup 172. Sheffield: Sheffield Academic Press, 1994. **Meyers,** Eric M., ed. *The Oxford Encyclopedia of Archaeology in the Near East.* 5 vols. Oxford: Oxford University Press, 1997. **Redman,** Charles L. *Social Archaeology: Beyond Subsistence and Dating.* Studies in Archaeology. New York: Academic Press, 1978.

PALESTINE: **Ben-Tor,** Amnon. *The Archaeology of Ancient Israel.* New Haven: Yale University Press, 1992. **Mazar,** Amihai. *Archaeology of the Land of the Bible, 10,000–586 BCE.* New York: Doubleday, 1990. **Stern,** Ephraim, ed. *The New Encyclopedia of Archaeological Excavations in the Holy Land.* 4 vols. Jerusalem: Israel Exploration Society and Carta, 1993. **Weippert,** Helga. *Palästina in vorhellenistischer Zeit: Handbuch der Archäologie, Vorderasien II/1.* Munich: C. H. Beck, 1988.

SYRIA: **Kempinski,** Aharon, and Michael **Avi-Yonah.** *Syria-Palestine II: From the Middle Bronze Age to the End of the Classical World (2200 B.C.–324 A.D.).* Geneva: Nagel, 1979. **Perrot,** Jean. *Syrie-Palestine.* 2 vols. Geneva: Nagel, 1978–1980. **Weiss,** Harvey, ed. *Ebla to Damascus: Art and Archaeology of Ancient Syria.* Washington, D.C.: Smithsonian Institution, 1985.

The ancient Near Eastern civilizations declined steadily over many centuries, from Greco-Roman intrusions to the Islamic-Arabian conquests. Yet through the years, Europeans never entirely forgot their Near Eastern neighbors. From late antiquity to the early Middle Ages, Palestine was the *Holy Land,* a chief destination for Christian pilgrims. During that time, Europeans also developed an interest in neighboring areas such as the Sinai Peninsula, Syria (particularly Damascus), and so on.

This curiosity culminated in the Late Middle Ages when the crusaders—mostly inspired by ecclesiastical and religious motives—conquered and colonized these lands. For several centuries after the Muslims recaptured Palestine, Italian merchants were among the few Europeans to have direct contact with the Near East. As time passed, and with continued isolation from the West, the Near East became a dim memory in the European mind.

Eventually, Western European expansion was thwarted by other concerns. Instead of being the offensive force, the Europeans had to defend themselves against the expanding Ottoman empire, which brought the Turks to the gates of Vienna. Only a Herculean effort by the great Central European powers repelled the invasion. Nevertheless, the Turks maintained control of the Balkans; the formerly Christian city of Constantinople was renamed Istanbul after its overthrow in 1453 C.E. Finally, with the dissolution of the Turkish empire in the late nineteenth and early twentieth century, some Near Eastern states again reclaimed their independence. Furthermore, many Europeans began to visit the Near East, not only to establish lucrative trade relations but also to become acquainted with the mysterious and enticing world of the Orient. During the eighteenth century C.E., enlightened Europeans desired a new, scientific understanding of their Near Eastern neighbors. Those yearnings inspired a number of voyages of discovery and scientific expeditions. The results were not overwhelming; however, they did help to renew interest in the region and became the foundation of nineteenth- and twentieth-century Oriental research.

Denmark's Frederick V was the first to summon a large scientific expedition to the Near East. In 1761, his German secretary of state, J. H. E. Bernstorff, arranged a scientific exploration that consisted of not only Danish scholars, but also German, Danish, and Swedish scientists. One member of that team was a student of the renowned Swedish natural scientist Carl von Linné (Carolus Linnaeus). The only member to survive the expedition and return safely to Copenhagen in 1767 was the surveyor, Carsten Niebuhr, who came from the Danish possessions in North Germany (Holstein-Friesland). This expedition deserves special mention because it was the first state-funded, Western European scientific expedition to the Near East with clearly defined research goals. Thankfully, Carsten Niebuhr's diligence and accuracy provided invaluable information for subsequent international Oriental research. Amazingly, considering his inability to decipher the signs, Niebuhr accurately transcribed some important cuneiform inscriptions that he discovered. Those transcriptions became the basis for the decoding of cuneiform script by the German Orientalist Georg Friedrich Grotefend. Shortly after 1800, Grotefend published his initial results: a pioneering work that inspired more sophisticated analyses of cuneiform. Among those who forged the new trail was the English researcher Henry Cheswicke Rawlinson. By the mid-1800s, Rawlinson's well-known work on the cuneiform alphabet and script inspired the first rudimentary translations. Soon, new and heightened interest in Mesopotamia were fed by concrete insights into that ancient milieu.

A short time after the discovery of the cuneiform texts, Egyptian hieroglyphics were deciphered; however, this breakthrough was not the result of scientific expeditions. It happened as a consequence of Napoleonic incursions into the Near East during the 1798–1799 campaigns. Napoleon overran Egypt to establish a link between Europe and the Near East. Yet the intentions of that expedition went far beyond conquest. The first consul's entourage included many scientists, and he kept a copy of Niebuhr's notes on his night table. These expeditions yielded a series of extensive publications, including surveys and drawings of ancient Egyptian monuments and hieroglyphic transcriptions. The latter became the foundation for subsequent scholarly investigations and a twenty-year effort to decode those transcriptions. Shortly after 1820, the French Egyptologist Jean-François Champollion published his interpretation of the hieroglyphs.

These initial discoveries of ancient and long-forgotten languages were followed by the first archaeologists armed with picks and shovels. Earlier archaeologists were fortune hunters rather than scientists; by the early nineteenth century, however, those former soldiers of fortune began to apply scientific methodology to their investigations of the ancient Near East. Inspired, on one hand, by the research strategies of philologists and historians and, on the other, by the embryonic European archaeological education gained especially from the experiences at Pompeii, archaeologists hoped to expand their knowledge of ancient Near Eastern monuments and improve their study of ancient remains.

Generally, excavation teams have had different agendas. Some archaeological digs have been no more than well-organized treasure hunts that concentrated on identifying and unearthing spectacular royal palaces and large temples. Predictably, such researchers have paid little attention to the homes of ordinary people. Ostensibly, these primitive archaeological research methods yielded impressive discoveries. The excavation of large palaces and temples uncovered valuable artwork and extensive libraries. Even the most questionable research criteria produced valuable materials for future scholars. By the end of the nineteenth century, those scholars could and did publish previously unknown details about Mesopotamian culture and history. Most scholars could not identify the precise date of the stratum around which they worked; however, the evidence provided by their text discoveries more than compensated for most archaeologists' imprecise methods.

The early Egyptologists worked from a position vastly different from those working on ancient Mesopotamian sites. After all, no one could ignore the stark reminders of Egypt's past, such as the pyramids. Therefore the first excavations in Egypt were more cleaning expeditions than proper archaeological digs. Their job was simply to clear the monuments from the sand dunes. During this process, however, several monumental inscriptions were discovered. Other significant texts were discovered at various Egyptian grave sites, some of which yielded spectacular archaeological finds. For example, in 1881, the mummies of pharaohs dating from the sixteenth to thirteenth centuries B.C.E. were discovered in a burial cave near Thebes in southern Egypt. The mummies had been concealed in the cave to prevent looting. Perhaps the most incredible discovery of all occurred in 1922 when the English archaeologist Howard Carter discovered the pristine grave of the fourteenth-century pharaoh Tutᶜankhamun at Thebes's so-called Valley of the Kings.

From a methodological point of view, archaeological exploration progressed much the same in Palestine as in Egypt and Mesopotamia. In Palestine the excavators brought with them the same methodological deficiencies; here, however, no significant discoveries offset the effects of those shortcomings. Ambitious explorations were nevertheless undertaken before the turn of the century. The pioneering archaeologists who started excavations on Palestine's small *tells* (the technical term for archaeological mounds in the Near East), such as the British William Flinders Petrie, had almost without exception been active in other parts of the Near East. Now they turned their attention to Palestine and carried on in the same manner as before. Although they arrived in great numbers, they found little in the way of texts and archives. Even so, these first excavations provided a rich harvest of material. The explorers were inspired by biblical considerations and chose sites carefully, such as the well-known biblical sites of Shechem, Megiddo, and Jericho. Excavations in Jerusalem, however, were limited until the Israeli occupation of that city in 1967.

Eventually, the dearth of text discoveries in Palestine, Jordan, and Syria inspired the evolution of new and more sophisticated technologies. Massive discoveries of various earthen bowls, pots, and other items in Palestinian excavation fields drew the attention of many researchers. The question was (and is): To what period or periods do these items belong? Every bowl or pot has its own history of production, one that reveals technological and artistic changes from one period to the next. Thus, given the proper scientific tools, it was at least theoretically possible to place ceramic items in their respective time frames. In reality these procedures entail so many problems that additional and better technology is required to produce more reliable results.

For Palestinian archaeologists, the first priority is to stratify individual sites correctly. Ancient Near Eastern tells resemble layer cakes; that is, each field contains several strata, each of which represents a successive settlement phase. Many sites are so ancient and the strata so numerous that they show building and rebuilding on the same spot across several millennia. Over time, with systematic building demolition, each stratum is squeezed between the ruins of the previous and subsequent periods; therefore, strata are often no thicker than a meter. As a result, archaeologists will sometimes overlook the smallest historical layers. In our century, Palestinian researchers developed sensitive new technologies to prevent such disastrous omissions. These new methods made it possible not only to furnish museums in the Near East, America, and Europe with spectacular art objects, they also provided reliable insights into the history of those sites. Of course, because inscriptions rarely provide specific information regarding the history of strata, the people and places in the resulting histories are often nameless. Yet modern research strategies have been able to yield important clues to the history of each tell. Were its residents rich or poor? Was it a large or small city? Did it have extensive trade relations with the surrounding communities? If so, how widespread were its commercial networks? Ultimately, modern science provides the means to explore the nuances hidden beneath the surface of these basic findings. In recent times archaeologists have applied methods borrowed from the natural sciences, such as neutron activation analysis (NAA),[7] carbon-14 analysis,[8] dendrology, and paleobotany.[9]

In recent decades, the stratigraphical investigation of tells has undergone important changes. Today, archaeological digs and investigations in Palestine are much as they have always been; that is, most archaeologists throw their efforts into extracting and analyzing historical data from specific sites. Yet there is also a powerful urge to go beyond the excavation of individual towns and cities in order to unmask the history of the entire region. Doing so entails the scientific exploration of much smaller sites. One fact above all others precipitated this methodological shift: no ancient Near Eastern city could survive in isolation. Consequently, even the largest city was part of a complex network that linked it with other smaller towns and villages. The fate of every municipality was intimately connected to another. However, the history of a city might not in all cases be identical with that of the surrounding

---

[7] See Patrick E. McGovern, "Science in Archaeology: A Review," *American Journal of Archaeology* 99 (1995): 19–142.

[8] Every living organism absorbs carbon 14. Theoretically, the time period within which an organism lived can be determined by the percentage of carbon-14 degeneration in its remains. For almost thirty-five years, this method has yielded important and reliable results; however, the toxicity of carbon 14 has created some insecurity concerning its use. Thus, other methods have developed to circumvent those perceived shortcomings.

[9] Paleobotany concentrates on the botanical remains of ancient and extinct cultures. Dendrology explores trunk rings to verify the age of trees and shrubs. Since the annual growth of a tree produces a ring, it is possible to determine the tree's age. The oldest dendrological results come from the California Redwoods (ca. 3000 B.C.E.).

towns and villages. Every small town or village might have developed its own unique tradition and history. Thus, any scientifically valid analysis of the region must hold in delicate balance the micro- and macro-information gathered from sites within its borders. Ultimately, the cultural and historical data gleaned from individual sites will become small pieces in a successfully completed jigsaw puzzle: the history of the ancient Near East.

This philosophy has in recent times yielded exciting archaeological results. Especially fruitful has been the combining of classical excavation of single sites with "surveys."[10] Traditional excavation has proven to be of only limited value in reconstructing Palestine's ancient history; over the past few years, however, rejuvenated archaeological methods have produced amazing insights. For example, by comparing surface data with results from traditional one-site excavations, the Israeli archaeologist Israel Finkelstein has provided impressive insights into Palestine's history during the Early Iron Age (the alleged period of a historical Israel).[11]

Another important project, this one led by Americans, has sought to explore the old city of Heshbon in an area east of the Jordan River—an undertaking that involves combining a traditional stratigraphic excavation of the major archaeological site of Tell Hesban, the location of the ancient city of Heshbon, and surface data from the surrounding area. Furthermore, the investigation also includes ethnological, cultural-geographical, technological, and socioeconomic analyses of the region in which Heshbon was evidently the most important site.[12] This modern development in archaeology promises to yield fresh archaeological data that undoubtedly will aid the reconstruction of Palestine's ancient history.

Syrian and Jordanian archaeological sites are similar to those in Palestine; however, most major Syrian excavations occurred prior to World War I or in the decades that preceded World War II. Particularly significant sites excavated between the two world wars include Ras Shamra (Ugarit), and Tell Atchana (Alalakh)—both of which provide important clues about Syrian society during the second millennium B.C.E. During the last thirty years, the political and economic conditions in Syria and Jordan have severely hampered archaeological investigations in those regions. In

---

[10] A survey is an investigation of an archaeological site that is limited to an analysis of the ceramic material found on its surface. In the case of small and shallow sites, this might produce an overview of a site's settlement history.

[11] See Israel Finkelstein, *The Archaeology of the Israelite Settlement* (Jerusalem: Israel Exploration Society, 1988).

[12] See the excavation reports published by Roger S. Boraas, Siegfried H. Horn, and Lawrence T. Geraty, *Heshbon* (5 vols.; Berrien Springs, Mich.: Institute of Archaeology and Andrews University Press, 1969–1979); and the list of studies by Øystein S. LaBianca and others, published in the series Hesban (Berrien Springs, Mich.: Institute of Archaeology and Andrews University Press, 1986–).

addition, private funding for expeditions to these places is very scarce. Archaeological data from Syria and Jordan are consequently sparse in comparison to the material unearthed in Palestine. In spite of these problems, for more than twenty-five years Italian archaeologists have excavated at Tell Mardikh near Aleppo—one of the most significant archaeological discoveries ever in the Near East—a site that has yielded the extensive archive from Early Bronze Age Ebla. Ebla is a perfect example of how archaeology yields knowledge from one day to the next, so to speak, even about centuries formerly almost unknown to us.

II.3. THE STAGE: GEOGRAPHY AND ECOLOGY OF THE NEAR EAST

Edzard, Dietz Otto. *Gesellschaften im Alten Zweistromland und in den angrenzenden Gebieten.* Munich: C. H. Beck, 1972. **Moscati,** Sabatino. *Alba della civiltà: Società, economia e pensiero nel Vicino Oriente antico I (La società) and II (L'economia).* Turin: UTET, 1976. **Roaf,** Michael. *Cultural Atlas of Mesopotamia and the Ancient Near East.* New York: Facts on File, 1990.

II.3.1. The Names of Syria and Palestine

The Near East

Designations for the Near East are diverse and bewildering. For example, today one speaks of the Middle East, West Asia, the Near East, the Levant, or the Orient—names that refer to the same general area and its component parts. Generally, the "Middle East" includes those modern Islamic states from Morocco to Pakistan; however Morocco, Algeria, Tunisia, Libya, and Egypt are all situated in northern Africa. The "Near East" refers to the classical Middle East that stretches from Iran and Iraq to Egypt, including part of the Arabian Peninsula.

Palestine

Generally, Palestine is seen as the countryside in which ancient Israel allegedly existed. The name "Palestine"—meaning "the (land of) the Philistines"—goes at least as far back as the first millennium B.C.E. At this time Assyrian documents sometimes refer to the land of the Philistines, although the Philistines (by the end of the second millennium B.C.E.) only populated part of the area known as Palestine. In later European parlance, Palestine referred the entire area from the Jordan River to the Mediterranean Sea. This reflects classical usage, when Greek and Roman authors called this region "Palestine." For example, in the fifth century B.C.E., Herodotus called it "Palestinian Syria." For the modern Israeli state, "Israel"—or better "Eretz Israel" (literally, the "Land of Israel" or "Israel's Land")—is the name of the whole region. For their Arab counterparts, Palestine is both a geographical region and political concept. Another complication comes with the future Palestinian state. This state—if it ever becomes a reality—will have as its main territory the part of the country that was in ancient times definitely "Israelite," while the modern Israeli state certainly includes areas once possessed by the Philistines.

Syria

Similar problems arise with the term "Syria." During the classical period, Greek historians and geographers imported the name Syria—a heretofore unknown expression in the West. Modern Syria includes several different areas, all of which had their own names, which in turn often changed along with their identities. For example, during the third millennium B.C.E., Ebla was the name of both a state *and* its capital city. The same happened to other Syrian places in the second and first millennia B.C.E. Damascus identifies both the city and the region. The same phenomenon holds for Qadesh, Emar, and Ugarit. On the other hand, Aleppo—or Halab as its ancient name was (and once again is)—was the capital of a major kingdom called Yamkhad. Likewise, the city of Alalakh was the capital of the west Syrian state of Mukish.

The actual term "Syria" was initially probably a Greek rendering of the name "Assyria." Assyria—originally a city name, Ashur—was in the Iron Age a major north Mesopotamian state that collapsed at the end of the seventh century B.C.E. Although Assyria was never to emerge again as a state, the tradition about Assyria obviously survived, and its name shifted to cover a different territory to the west of old Assyria. Perhaps the confusion is actually traceable to ancient Syrian kings who appropriated the name of Assyria in order to legitimate their claim over former Assyrian territory. The beginning of this tradition may go back to the time after the fall of Nineveh, the Assyrian capital, in 612 B.C.E. After the destruction of Nineveh, the last pocket of Assyrian resistance moved to northern Syria, until the battle of Carchemish (605 B.C.E.) forever ended any Assyrian aspirations of revival.

Today, several relatively new states have sprung up in the territory of ancient Syria. Contemporary Jordan and Lebanon were formed after World War I when the Western powers divided and conquered provinces of the Turkish empire.[13] Prior to the twentieth century, "Lebanon" re-

---

[13] Actually, in the aftermath of World War I, the Near East was artificially carved into several states without regard to local priorities or ethnic relationships. Thus, centuries-long dreams of sovereignty among the indigenous Arab populations were summarily shattered by the dictates of the "great" Western powers. In every case, tactical economics inspired the new Near Eastern political landscape. France annexed Lebanon from Syria to deny the Syrians access to the important trade centers along the Levantine coast, while Great Britain seized Kuwait from Iraq to exploit that region's immense oil reserves.

ferred to a major mountain range, never to a state. In antiquity, the territory of present-day Lebanon was divided into a number of minute city-states, all part of greater Syria. The same political conditions prevailed in the territory owned by the modern state of Jordan. Insofar as the region was not part of foreign empires, local potentates, city kings, and chieftains continued in office.

Thus antiquity did not recognize a collective term for the area known as the Near East or West Asia. Consequently, we find confusing and often changing collections of names for smaller locales within this region. As we will see, the political situations in ancient Syria and Palestine were equally bewildering; however, we must first explore the geographical, economic, and demographic peculiarities of this region's history.

II.3.2. The Geography of Syria and Palestine

GENERAL: *Tübinger Atlas des Vorderen Orients*. Wiesbaden: Reichert, 1974–. **Aharoni,** Yohanan, and Michael **Avi-Yonah.** *The Macmillan Bible Atlas*. 3d ed. revised by Anson F. Rainey and Zeev Safrai. New York: Macmillan, 1993.

SYRIA: **Wirth,** Eugen. *Syrien: Eine geographische Landeskunde*. Wissenschaftliche Länderkunden 4–5. Darmstadt: Wissenschaft Buchgesellschaft, 1971.

PALESTINE: **Aharoni,** Yohanan. *The Land of the Bible: A Historical Geography*. Translated by Anson F. Rainey. London: Burns & Oates, 1967. **Baly,** Denis. *The Geography of the Bible*. Rev. ed. New York: Harper & Row, 1974. **Karmon,** Yehuda. *Israel: A Regional Geography*. New York: John Wiley and Sons, 1971.

The stage for the narratives in the Bible is confined to a territory about 350,000 square kilometers in size. Today, several states occupy this space: modern Israel, Lebanon, Jordan, Syria, northwest Iraq, and southern Turkey. Although it is roughly the size of Germany, this region's population hovers around only 15 million—a figure that was probably much lower in antiquity. Unfortunately, with few exceptions, there is no way to verify concretely the actual population density during that time. It is safe to say that during the Late Bronze Age, the Kingdom of Mukish (Alalakh) covered 5,000 square kilometers with a population of around 35,000–40,000 people, which equals an average of seven to eight persons per square kilometer.[14] At the same time, Ugarit occupied a slightly larger area, with a population of perhaps 50,000. Both states lay within the most fertile area in the region. Frequent rains and numerous rivers and tributaries provided plentiful

[14] In comparison, Germany has 230 people per square kilometer, and the Commonwealth of Massachusetts has 280.

water. The areas to the east were not so fortunate, since the fertile ground gradually degenerated into patches of uninhabitable desert. In Lebanon and Palestine, the annual precipitation is sufficient, but the mountainous terrain was not conducive to the development of large, stable human settlements. Ultimately, this explains the great disparity between the populations of Syrian states, such as Ugarit and Mukish, and that of their southern neighbors. At the beginning of the first millennium B.C.E., the population in the mountainous landscape of Judah ranged between 10,000 and 15,000 people. At the end of the nineteenth century C.E., the Baedeker Guide estimated the population in Palestine at around 500,000. Today, that number has increased at least tenfold! This indicates that as late as in the nineteenth century C.E., the total population of Palestine and Syria, including Lebanon, did not exceed 1.5 million. In antiquity, that figure was far lower.

Although the entire Syro-Palestinian region was quite large, its population was relatively small and its distribution very uneven, the population density being higher in the western part of the region and gradually decreasing as one moved eastward. Two key factors contributed to these situations. First, few subregions provided the necessary topographical space to support large population centers. Second, like today, inadequate agricultural techniques, inconsistent water supplies, and poor soil also made many regions unprofitable for farming.[15]

Palestine

Palestine itself is only about the size of Vermont (about 25,000 square kilometers). The Old Testament writers sometimes describe this region as "the land between Dan (at the Jordan's source) and Beer-sheba (in the Negev)"—a distance of approximately 250 kilometers. Its width varied from 50 kilometers in the north to around 120 kilometers in the south. Yet, over the years, Palestine's political boundaries often stretched into smaller and larger portions of neighboring areas: in the southern region to the Gulf of Aqaba; and in the east, the western regions of modern Jordan. Nevertheless, despite its very small area, Palestine's landscape remains very diverse. The country is dominated by a number of mountain ranges, although they only occasionally reach a height of 1,000 meters. Many mostly small valleys are tucked among those mountains. Larger, more extensive valleys line the western coast of the Mediterranean and southern Galilee. Finally, the deepest valley of all is the Jordan River basin; a rift valley which at its lowest point is more than 500 meters below sea level.

---

[15] The transparent and plausible explanation for the tenfold population in this area since the turn of the century is the tenfold increase in the fertility of the soil.

The Mediterranean Sea forms Palestine's natural western border. In the south, the Negev Desert and the Sinai Peninsula mark a natural borderline: a geological gauntlet between Palestine and Egypt 100 kilometers wide. The eastern borderlands include the Jordan River and three larger bodies of water: Lake Huleh in the north (drained by modern Israel); the Sea of Chinnereth (Gennesaret); and the Dead Sea in the south. The narrow Jordan River provides a rich water table; historically, however, its functional utility as a natural border has been subverted at points where it is easily crossed. Ultimately, the Jordan is more an ideological than geographical eastern border.

Palestine's northern border will only in places be a natural one. One example is the Ras en-Naqura (Hebrew *Rosh Hanniqra*) palisade on the Mediterranean coast near the border of present-day Lebanon. A better choice might be Mount Carmel, which once formed the border between Palestine and Phoenicia. Less than 100 kilometers northeast of Mount Carmel lies Mount Hermon, a truly impenetrable barrier 3,000 meters high. At the western foot of Mount Hermon, the Baqᶜah Valley (an extension of the Jordan rift valley) splits Lebanon in half. East of Hermon the Palestinian countryside gradually develops into the tableland known today as the Golan Heights (Arabic *Al-Jawlan*). To the east, this plateau continues almost without interruption as far as the outskirts of Damascus.

Jordan

To the east, in the modern state of Jordan, a mountain range appears. Originally an extension of the highlands to the west of the Jordan River, it became separated from those highlands at one point in the region's geological history by the appearance of the Jordan rift valley. Farther east, the land flattens gradually and ultimately forms the fertile tableland of Moab. In the south we encounter mountain ranges, which form the Arabian Peninsula's western fringe. Toward the east, the flatlands gradually flow into the Syro-Arabian desert.

Lebanon

Lebanon, to the north of Palestine, can be subdivided into four zones, all running from the south to the north. In the far west, the narrow coastal plain yields to the steep Lebanese Mountains that form its eastern rim. These mountains are divided into two ranges—the Lebanon and the Anti-Lebanon ranges—by the aforementioned Baqᶜah Valley.

Syria

From Damascus to the Euphrates River, a series of desert regions dominate Syria's landscape. Damascus lies within a large oasis that is irrigated by water supplies that flow from Hermon and Anti-Lebanon west of the city. The journey northward from Damascus along the main road to Aleppo crosses a series of plains increasingly adaptable for agriculture. The region stretching to the north of Lebanon as far as the Tarsus mountain range (in present-day Turkey) greatly resembles the Palestinian countryside; that is, the coastal lowlands on the Mediterranean shore are confined to the east by a mountain range. The Euphrates River forms an expansive northwest-to-southeast diagonal boundary for Syria's eastern frontier. The Euphrates Valley is rich, fertile, and heavily populated.

II.3.3. The Environment of Syria and Palestine

Brice, William C., ed. *The Environmental History of the Near East Since the Last Ice Age.* London and New York: Academic Press, 1978. **Frey,** Wolfgang, and Hans Peter **Ürpmann,** eds. *Beiträge zur Umweltgeschichte des Vorderen Orients.* Wiesbaden: In Kommission bei Reichert, 1981. **Rowton,** Michael B. "The Woodlands of Ancient Western Asia." *JNES* 26 (1967): 261–77. **Zohary,** Michael. *Geobotanical Foundations of the Middle East 1–2.* Geobotanica Selecta 3. Stuttgart and Amsterdam: G. Fischer, 1973. **Zohary,** Michael. *Vegetation of Israel and Adjacent Areas.* Wiesbaden: In Kommission bei Reichert, 1982.

The subtropical and Mediterranean climate of the Near East produces long, dry summers and short winters. Rainfall varies from one region to another, normally remaining consistent and plentiful in the west and diminishing as one moves eastward. Interior Syria and eastern Jordan remain relatively parched. The areas bordering the Mediterranean between Tarsus in the north and Sinai in the south receive ample rain. Generally, the north receives more rainfall, averaging never less than 500 millimeters per year. In Lebanon and Palestine, this zone is limited to the east by the north-south mountain range, beyond which the land becomes very dry. The Baqᶜah Valley is an exception, as the presence of another mountain range, the Anti-Lebanon, secures sufficient precipitation for agriculture; but the eastern slopes of the Anti-Lebanon receive mostly inadequate rainfall, so that inhospitable, arid conditions persist from the base of the Anti-Lebanon foothills. To the north of the two ranges of Lebanon, no other mountain range is present. Consequently, the regions east of the coastal mountains receive only sporadic rain; Aleppo—situated in a major plateau—is that area's only agriculturally productive city. East of Aleppo rain is too sporadic for agriculture. Agriculture in almost every region east of those mountains depends on other irrigating sources. First we should mention a series of rivers and rivulets that crisscross the landscape of western Syria, Lebanon, Palestine, and Jordan. One such perennial stream is the Jordan River between Palestine and Jordan, another the Orontes River that flows from the Anti-Lebanon range through western Syria and finally to the Mediterranean Sea near the city of Antakya (ancient Antioch) in southern Turkey.

Cisterns also supplement inadequate water supplies, but during the Bronze Age cisterns were impractical because they were not adequately waterproof. Only later did people begin to seal them by plastering their sides with a burnt-limestone finish. Aqueducts, which are so characteristic of the Hellenistic-Roman landscapes of the Mediterranean, and which supplied ample water to the great cities of these periods, were previously unknown. Another resource consisted of the many mountain springs. Finally, the familiar Near Eastern oases—local, natural water depots—offered plentiful supplies. Two important oases in the Syrian wilderness were occupied by the well-known city of Damascus and the almost as famous city of Palmyra (Tadmor), which lies halfway between Damascus and the Euphrates. During the Hellenistic period, when it became common to cross the desert with camel caravans, Palmyra enjoyed great prominence. Similarly, in the Jordan Valley, Jericho was founded more than 10,000 years ago—probably the oldest settlement in the region—in a fruitful oasis.

Today, the Near Eastern climate remains relatively constant; from year to year, however, rainfall and drought can vary dramatically. Fortunately, modern dams, barrages, and water lines alleviate the effects of such fluctuations. In antiquity, without such defenses, entire populations faced extinction in times of severe weather. Periods of drought recurred and often lasted more than a year. Modern experience suggests at least two or three years of drought in every decade. While ancient people adapted to survive droughts, a prolonged period of insufficient rainfall spelled death for a great many people.

Most climatologists who study the historical evolution of the Near Eastern climate believe that conditions have remained relatively stable for the last 5,000 years. Possibly, around 3,000 years ago, in the dim beginnings of recorded history, the Syro-Palestinian climate was more favorable than today. After 3000 B.C.E., periods of relatively favorable conditions have alternated with drier periods. Some suggest that the social upheavals of the Early Bronze Age, which led to a series of primary state formations, reflect the deteriorating Near Eastern climate. Such changes have significantly affected livelihood throughout the region. Scholars still generally believe that such changes caused the decline of Bronze Age civilizations.

Most of the animal species—both wild and domestic—that currently roam the Near East also lived in ancient Syria and Palestine between 3000 and 1000 B.C.E. By that time, domesticated sheep, goats, and cattle were integral parts of the household. The domestication of the camel followed later, shortly before 1000 B.C.E. Ultimately, it became the most significant and economically viable domesticated animal in the Near East. Many other animals that once roamed this region are now extinct, the victims of years of systematic hunting and human neglect (especially elephants, lions, ostriches, and bears). At the conclusion of the last Ice Age, almost tropical conditions blanketed the African savannas and the steppes surrounding the Near East, making the whole territory a single ecological zone. Elephants, lions, and ostriches all thrived in this environment and soon became prime targets for human hunting expeditions. Kings could not resist the temptation to seize personal bragging rights over a lion's dead carcass—a situation that eventually doomed all such animals to annihilation. These animals survive today only in their skeletal remains and in cave drawings and written accounts of "the hunt." Further confirmation of the existence of these wild animals in the ancient Near East comes from surviving panthers in a remote region of the Judean desert, a location that has protected them from the hunt since antiquity.

The flora has experienced the same vicissitudes as the fauna. In antiquity, the ecology provided conditions favorable to certain types of growth, particularly large forests. To the west of the watershed the mountain ranges were covered not only with bushy woodlands (the maquis) but also with lush forests. One particularly dense forest between Damascus and Hama (ancient Hamath) in Syria was virtually impenetrable. Mesopotamian documents recall these Syrian forests, in which the Mesopotamians searched for wood to replenish their own limited supplies. Years of pillaging for building and agricultural purposes has left the area barren. Centuries of rapacious human behavior reduced the vegetation of the mountainous countryside to unproductive bushlands, causing deadly and widespread soil erosion and making agriculture impossible. Thankfully, several Near Eastern states (especially Israel) are currently trying to reforest these lands.

II.4. LIFESTYLE AND ECONOMY

II.4.1. The Continuity of the Traditional Social System: The So-Called Ideal Types (Nomad, Farmer, and Urbanite)

Bar-Josef, Ofer, and Anatoly **Khazanov.** *Pastoralism in the Levant: Archaeological Materials in Anthropological Perspectives.* Monographs in World Archaeology 10. Madison, Wisconsin: Prehistory Press, 1992. **Klengel**, Horst. *Zwischen Zelt und Palast.* Leipzig: Koehler & Amelang, 1972. **Lemche**, Niels Peter. *Early Israel: Anthropological and Historical Studies on the Israelite Society before the Monarchy.* VTSup 37. Leiden: Brill, 1985. **Rowton**, Michael B. "Enclosed Nomadism." *JESHO* 17 (1974): 1–30.

Now that we have described the "stage" upon which ancient Syria and Palestine's history occurred, we turn our attention to the actors of the drama. Previously, we covered some aspects of ancient Near Eastern society while discussing the historicity of the patriarchs. Among these themes belonged the classic perception that Near Eastern society is divided into three sectors—the nomadic, the agricultural, and the urban lifestyles—and also the belief that nomadism is a necessary precursor to fully developed agriculture and sedentary farming communities. Now we must refine this discussion in order to arrive at a methodologically sound depiction of the full range of ancient Near Eastern experience.

Near eastern society does not consist of three "ideal types": nomads, farmers, and urbanites. Clearly, these categorizations are artificial and misleading simplifications based upon a distinctly European bias.[16] Ultimately, it is far better to rely on a polymorphic societal model that accepts varied and sometimes unpredictable socioeconomic deviations from the so-called ideal types. Of course, most Near Easterners did not participate in major lifestyle shifts, for example, one day a nomad, the next a settled peasant. They mostly adapted to a changing environment. The Near Eastern ecology produced a bleak and burdensome existence; therefore, any change in lifestyle would be predicated on the need for personal survival. We mentioned earlier that the Syro-Palestinian area is roughly the size of Germany, but only a third of it remains inhabitable. Consequently, population levels remain very low.

In the more fertile areas of Syria and Palestine, larger populations huddle around more plentiful water supplies. The general picture of traditional (i.e., preindustrial) Near Eastern society is clear: between 90 and 95 percent of the peasant population is involved in some form of agribusiness. Very few people are involved in trades or administrative work. Finally, around 4 or 5 percent of the remaining group engage in cattle breeding. Previously, many thought this last group actually represented the ubiquitous semi-nomads who since the Early Stone Age had tamed sheep and goats; however, they have never become a dominant group in ancient Near Eastern society.

---

[16] This tripartite model is typically "European." A scholar such as Georges Dumézil would argue that the European would instinctively stick to the number three, even when his evidence militates against it. The partition of oriental society into three sectors is one example of this. Other examples include the usual division of antiquity into three ages: Stone, Bronze, and Iron. The Stone Age is often divided into three chronological ages: the (older) Paleolithic, the (middle) Mesolithic, and the (later) Neolithic—not to mention the Early, Middle, and Late Bronze Ages. Although these are not totally inaccurate designations, upon further examination the subdividing process has no practical limit. Thus, history is subdivided into a number of "mixed periods" that attempt to describe more precisely the actual situations of each individual epoch (e.g., the "Copper-Stone" or Chalcolithic Age, an intermediate period between the Neolithic and Early Bronze Ages at the end of the forth millennium B.C.E.). Later we will note a similarly artificial distinction between the Middle and Late Bronze Ages.

Nomads are not the only breeders of livestock. Several subcategories of breeders also exist, some of whom are heavily engaged in agriculture.[17] Generally, they raise prime livestock like sheep and goats, sometimes also cows. In many places throughout the Mediterranean and the ancient Near East, peasants practice a very special kind of animal husbandry called mountain economy or transhumance: they seek the best grazing land by shifting their herds to the lowlands in winter and the mountains in summer. This practice involves a combination of agriculture and cattle breeding that often makes the line of division between nomads and farmers hard to discern for a casual European observer.

Earlier, we disputed the artificial divisions between urbanites and people who live beyond the city walls. First, in the Near East, many urbanites are engaged in some form of agribusiness. In any city, some will produce the crop of the fields belonging to the city, some will process it, and some will sell it. Second, cities provide the most viable markets for agriculturists as well as cattle breeders. The city is also the place where a farmer or a nomad can go and buy special tools, jewelry, and other commodities. Finally, the city is a hub for gathering and maintaining capital that rich urbanites reinvest in agricultural zones. Certainly, such transactions have created turmoil throughout history; however, rural society depends heavily on the flow of money, especially during periods of drought and crisis.

II.4.2. The Development of a Diverse Society: Trade

GENERAL: **Adams,** Robert McCormick. *The Evolution of Urban Society: Early Mesopotamia and Prehistoric Mexico.* The Lewis Henry Morgan Lectures, 1965. Chicago: Aldine, 1966. **Fritz,** Volkmar. *The City in Ancient Israel.* The Biblical Seminar 29. Sheffield: Sheffield Academic Press, 1995. **Nissen,** Hans J. *Grundzüge einer Geschichte der Frühzeit des Vorderen Orients.* Darmstadt: Wissenschaftliche Buchgesellschaft, 1983. **Redman,** Charles L. *The Rise of Civilization: From Early Farmers to Urban Society in the Ancient Near East.* San Francisco: W. H. Freeman, 1978. **Ucko,** Peter J., and Geoffrey W. **Dimbleby,** eds. *Domestication and Exploitation of Plants and Animals.* Research Seminar in Archaeology and Related Subjects, London University, 1968. London: Duckworth, 1969. **Ucko,** Peter J., R. **Tringham,** and Geoffrey W. **Dimbleby,** eds. *Man, Settlement, and Urbanism.* Research Seminar in Archaeology and Related Subjects, London University, 1970. Cambridge, Mass.: Schenkman, 1972.

TRADE: **Klengel,** Horst. *Handel und Händler im alten Orient.* Vienna: Böhlau, 1979. **Muhly,** James D. *Copper and Tin: The Distribution of Metal Resources and the Nature of the Metals Trade in the Bronze Age.* 1973. Reprint, Hamden, Conn.:

[17] One crucial factor is that human diets depend on a combination of animal protein and vegetables. Nomads cannot survive without grains, although their livestock is more important from an economic point of view.

Archon Books, 1976. **Polányi,** Karl, Conrad M. **Arensberg,** and Harry W. **Pearson,** eds. *Trade and Market in the Early Empires.* 1957. Reprint, New York: Free Press, 1965.

THE ORIGINS OF STATES AND THEIR DISSOLUTION: **Cohen,** Rudolph, and Elman R. **Service.** *Origins of the State: The Anthropology of Political Evolution.* Philadelphia: Institute for the Study of Human Issues, 1978. **Yoffee,** Norman, and George L. **Cowgill.** *The Collapse of Ancient States and Civilizations.* Tucson: University of Arizona Press, 1988.

Every contrived model of preindustrial Near Eastern society yields to many exceptions. Only rarely did the environment produce the plentiful supply that permitted tenuous alliances between the various economic sectors of the region. We noted above that the Near Eastern ecology is rather severe. Consequently, survival in that region is a struggle against both the elements and other human beings. Humans try to maximize productivity and profitability when climatic conditions become erratic and water and food supplies dwindle. In the harsh conditions of the ancient Near East, additional periods of famine exacerbated the relentless fight for survival.

Under these conditions, people worked endlessly to secure their livelihood, all with the one goal of survival in mind. Basic necessities were often in short supply but could be "collected" from neighbors who suffered under similarly deprived conditions. The second most important concern was to defend one's possessions against intruders. This struggle for the scant resources in the Near East has sometimes helped establish highly hierarchical societies with a diversity of occupations: some citizens, being more able than their compatriots, prosper at the expense of their comrades; other citizens are hardly able to provide for themselves and their families. To protect their belongings, they established regional defense systems, which would later evolve into states.

Of course, to preserve the little wealth the populace of a certain region may have collected, everyone followed the clearly defined and simple social contract to live and work together for the common good. Part of that compact was to secure new settlements, build fortifications around them, and protect them from foreigners.[18] Whenever such systems of defense were created, they soon suffered new forms of attack. Each new situation demanded sturdier and more durable fortifications. Small, lightly defended settlements had to merge to create more stable and better-fortified villages and cities. These village and town confederations produced the first walled cities capable of maintaining an adequate

---

[18] As many scholars suggest, this is the only meaningful explanation for the first village and walled city at the Jericho oasis 10,000 years ago. Thanks to the lush oasis ecology, its inhabitants sought to protect their foodstuffs from foreign hunters and opportunists.

defense against intruders. Similarly, within their organization, such communities also found space to accommodate a standing army, eventually in the form of hired mercenaries.

Within this context, Palestine's urbanization began between 3300 and 2300 B.C.E. These years produced the rudiments of a differentiated society. For the first time, not all of the population was involved in manufacturing foodstuffs; rather, a new interdependence took shape. Now personal survival often depended on new types of social organization dominated by the efforts of soldiers and administrators—new classes of citizens, segregated from the general populace. These classes were disconnected from the production of foodstuffs; ironically, however, their very existence made food production even more urgently necessary.[19]

This evolution produced two aftereffects. First, states or statelike social systems—the so-called chiefdoms—developed within which "specialists" used their power and status for society but also for personal enrichment. Second, the settlements, villages, or cities within which these specialists operated became administrative and economic centers of the entire surrounding area. Soon, those centers became the capitals of regions or states. The area close to the city became fixed to the city, while surrounding villages and towns acted as satellites under the capital's jurisdiction.

The next stage in the development of political society happened when the chieftain (soon to become "king") appropriated more power than rendered necessary by his services. In order to keep his exalted position, he must make himself indispensable, even in periods when his society did not need a dictator to direct its course, when he perhaps should have—like Cincinnatus—returned to tilling his fields after fulfilling his tour of duty. The king was accordingly obliged to create a prestigious aura surrounding the monarchy, including elaborate rituals and mighty palaces.

This development is well attested throughout Near Eastern history. Palaces and palace complexes became abundant, particularly the ostentatious structures that bespeak the great chasm between royal dwellings and a commoner's hovel, between the elite and the masses. In Syria-Palestine, this trend reached its zenith in the Late Bronze Age. By then, the palace-state was firmly entrenched. Moreover, now the king was not simply the sovereign of a clearly defined geographical area—he *owned* it.

The need for international trade grew naturally from this last trend. Long-distance trade created new markets for domestic produce. Local trade was limited to the supplies and merchandise produced

---

[19] Perhaps we should use the term "group" rather than "class" to avoid a Marxist social analysis. After all, ancient Near Eastern society had few of the class distinctions of modern European society.

within the confines of a very small area. Local peasants and cattlemen produced limited items such as produce, and agricultural implements were among the few tradable domestic commodities. Wine and olive oil were produced to be sold at foreign and sometimes quite distant markets. Commerce, however, was hamstrung by an inadequate transportation system. Inefficient shipping methods produced soaring export expenses. Perishable items such as foodstuffs could not economically be sent more than a few kilometers. Only the highly successful Roman merchants with their massive freighters could successfully conduct far-flung, cost-effective trade between Egypt and Rome. No comparable system existed in the ancient Near East. One rare exception to this restriction on long-distance trade came during the Late Bronze Age when Egypt sent food to famine-ravaged areas of Asia Minor.

Only a few goods were so precious as to justify long-distance trade, such as bronze weaponry and other luxury items. Of course, the needs and wealth of individual markets determine the marketability of luxury items and other durable goods. Egypt and Phoenicia at an early date established a mutually beneficial trade agreement between willing parties: Byblos sent Lebanese wood to Egypt in exchange for Egyptian gold that was distributed throughout the Near East. Yet the range and depth of international trade through the Bronze Age never compared favorably with the intense commerce of the Greco-Roman period—not to mention modern times. Extensive trade demands willing and able buyers. Ancient Near Eastern merchants conducted business within an incredibly restrictive market comprised of buyers from equally constricted strata, namely, sovereigns and the aforementioned specialized classes. Also, with poor resources, potential Syrian and Palestinian buyers lacked viable forms of payment.

Yet the people of Syria and Palestine were not totally impecunious. Their land stood between two great commercial centers: Mesopotamia and Egypt. The highly energetic Babylonian merchants yearned to barter with potential buyers from the Iranian highlands and the interior sections of Asia. They also fancied Egyptian gold, but to get it their trade caravans had to cross through Palestinian and Syrian soil—a formidable, even precarious, journey. Syrian and Palestinian sovereigns supplemented their meager resources by soliciting protection money from these itinerant salespeople. In exchange for duties on all items transported between Mesopotamia and Egypt, sovereigns guaranteed that merchandise would reach its intended recipient.

Traditionally, trade through Syria and Palestine was vital to the sustained affluence of individual sovereigns. Consequently, many important cities in that region lay along the major Egyptian-Babylonian trade routes. For example, the Palestinian city of Megiddo lay close to a strategic Carmel Mountain pass on the Jezreel Valley's southern fringe and provided a safe haven for traders. By the third millennium B.C.E., Megiddo already possessed a significant urban social system with strong fortifications. The large city of Hazor lies north of Megiddo in Upper Galilee and is situated on a plateau between Syria and the Lebanon range. During the Bronze Age, Hazor was Palestine's largest city. Syrian cities that grew around major trade routes include Damascus, Qadesh (on the Orontes River), Ebla (by the third millennium), Aleppo (by the second millennium), and Haran. Haran was an important trading post in Upper Mesopotamia whose name ("road" in Akkadian) refers to its status as a caravan station and rest area for merchants traveling to and from the large Mesopotamian cities.

Other important trade centers sprouted along the shores of the Mediterranean, and many of them played similar roles to their counterparts in the Syro-Palestinian interior. These international trade centers included Byblos, which by the third millennium had become an important center for wood trade with Egypt. By the second millennium, Ugarit was the preeminent metal import station in the eastern Mediterranean. Tin was traded through Ugarit from as far away as Cornwall. Because of their role in trade, these cities experienced significant and steady growth. For instance, at its height, Ugarit's population topped 10,000 inhabitants.

International trade held little meaning among the general population. Generally, trade was conducted solely among the privileged classes to maintain their prestige. Yet urban societies continued to blossom throughout antiquity.[20] Local sovereigns enhanced such growth by employing specialists who analyzed and refined production methods, prepared local goods for export, or handled foreign imports in transit. Ultimately, a new class of craftspeople developed whose rank and file did not produce foodstuffs but accepted them as payment for services rendered. Mostly, during the Bronze Age, these persons were employed by the sovereign; however, some of their wares were traded locally.

Of course, trade relations spread far beyond the local, more restrictive markets. Syrian and Palestinian traders particularly relished trading with neighboring communities in Egypt and Mesopotamia; however, these were highly volatile markets with which to conduct business. An uninterrupted flow of merchandise depended on the capriciousness of

---

[20] Of course, Syrian and Palestinian cities were still relatively small. Few of them ever grew beyond 1,000 people. One exception was Hazor, which in its heyday reached a population of approximately 25,000—estimates run as low as 10,000 and as high as 50,000. Generally, Syrian cities were larger, with populations running between 5,000 and 10,000 inhabitants. The populations in most Mesopotamian urban centers dwarfed those of their Syrian and Mesopotamian counterparts. Several of those cities housed more than 100,000 people, including Nippur (about 150,000), Nineveh (about 300,000), and Babylon (about 500,000). In Syria and Palestine comparable metropolises developed much later during the Greco-Roman period. The Greco-Roman concept of *oikoumenē* (the "common market") provided systems and terms of trade that made such growth possible.

political and social conditions in both Egypt and Mesopotamia. If those major powers faced internal or external strife, trade lanes withered and royal income and prestige were seriously threatened. In such circumstances, the urban upper classes that depended on these trade relations could suffer great personal hardship while the lower classes remained relatively unaffected. Of course, everyone inevitably felt the effects when the royal household was crippled. In such situations, contingency plans were enacted, the nature of which we will address in section II.4.3 below.

Trade with Egypt and Mesopotamia created another problem, namely, the balance sheet. Egyptian and Mesopotamian traders were forced to cut into their own profits by filling the coffers of Syrian and Palestinian monarchs and contributing to their wealth and prestige. The cost was too high; therefore, these merchants sought alternatives. Ultimately, Syrian and Palestinian sovereigns faced invasion from neighbors whose main purpose was to secure free and inexpensive trading lanes through the Near Eastern corridor. Local sovereigns lost everything: their income from transit trade, their prestige, and their autonomy. Furthermore, against their will, they often paid tribute to their conquerors. Theoretically, this did not preclude collecting duties from other traders. For instance, the rapid growth of Ugarit in the second millennium B.C.E. might be attributable to new trade duties imposed on traders from the Aegean world. Under such circumstances, one could say that the former Syrian and Palestinian monarchs who made their fortunes by importing "money," now were primarily exporters of "money." This reversal had disastrous consequences for Syro-Palestinian society. Now regents taxed their own people to pay the required tribute to their conquerors.

This threat to Near Eastern survival crystallized in the Late Bronze Age when the very fabric of society itself began to dissolve. Ultimately, the plight of the people reached critical mass in this dynamic societal metamorphosis. A fundamental reshaping of the texture of the society was unavoidable.

II.4.3. The Center Versus the Periphery: The Struggle between the Desert and the Sown (Two Forms of Government)

Briant, Pierre. *Etat et pasteurs au Moyen-Orient ancien.* Collection production, pastorale et societé. Cambridge and New York: Cambridge University Press, 1982. **Rowlands,** Michael, Mogens Trolle **Larsen,** and Kristian **Kristiansen,** eds. *Centre and Periphery in the Ancient World.* New Directions in Archaeology. Cambridge and New York: Cambridge University Press, 1987. **Rowton,** Michael B.. "Dimorphic Structure and Topology." *OrAnt* 15 (1976): 17–31. **Rowton,** Michael B. "Pastoralism and the Periphery in Evolutionary Perspective." In *Colloques internationaux de CNRS 580.* Pages 291–301. L'Archéologie de l'Iraq. Paris: Centre national de la recherche scientifique, 1980.

In the Near East, survival has never been a private enterprise. Historically, people always had to combine forces in order to survive and defend their territories against foreign intervention. This insecurity contributed to society's diversification and segregation. Contributing to this development was also a differentiation of interest. Some people preferred to employ people to protect them. Administrators and soldiers were in demand. States arose. However, as time went by, the costs might become too high. The state might demand too much in exchange for protection from its citizens. It might also be unable to fulfill its obligations to the general populace. In this case, people would have to find alternative protection specifically in the tribal organization. Anyone who was a relative—or was accepted as a relative—could become a member of a tribe.

Near Eastern social structure is based on family relations. Its nucleus is the family, mostly consisting of five to seven members. Exceptional and mostly found among the elite were the so-called extended families (i.e., between fifteen and twenty members). Contrary to a popular misconception about Near Eastern society, only the very rich can afford to have big families. Moreover, modern ethnographic investigators suggest that the size of a given family will normally remain stable irrespective of its social status. On the other hand, the richer part of the population shows a tendency toward smaller families. During the Late Bronze Age, the Near Eastern population remained relatively constant at about 6.5 members per family. This figure is based on information from Alalakh in Mukish and compares well with present-day family sizes. Thus, we must reject the notion that the Near Eastern family was a predominantly extended one. Actually, since antiquity, the average Near Eastern family size has remained remarkably constant.

No family was politically or economically autonomous; rather, it was connected to a larger social unit, namely, its lineage. Ethnographers suggest that these lineages were often very extensive. Historically, Near Eastern people hold their lineage in high esteem, more so than their nuclear or extended families. The lineage is believed to be strong enough to protect and support its members. Often, the lineage itself—not the nuclear family—owned the farmland on which it lived and worked. Lineages could be very different in size and function. Each lineage had to adapt more or less to the local social, economic, and political circumstances. Nonetheless, the strong bond between the nuclear family and its lineage remains a dominant feature of Near Eastern society.

The same cannot be said about the larger social organizations: the clans and tribes. Superficially, clans resemble the aforementioned lineage; however, in practice, the clan remains a looser organization, and its members are not bound by the same feeling of mutual solidarity. Traditionally, social anthropologists have searched unsuccessfully for a better and more precise definition for "clan," one that adequately differentiates between clan and lineage. Although the clan is often larger than a lineage, this may not always be the case. Thus, the common definition of a clan focuses on its unique inner group relationships and how these relationships compare with those within the lineage. In a lineage, membership and its rationale are clearly defined. Clan members "know" they belong, but cannot concretely explain this affiliation. This definition is not terribly gratifying; it does, however, crystallize important and highly complicated ethnological facts. In real life, so many subforms of both the ideal lineage and clan exist that the border between them becomes blurred.

The social makeup becomes even more convoluted when we turn to a definition of the tribe. Again, the social anthropologist is hard pressed to isolate a satisfactory definition of this latter group. Initially, the tribe looks much like a lineage; that is, all members of a tribe see themselves as descendants of the same person or progenitor. Every tribe member is a relative. Actually, tribal affiliation often depends on many other factors that can vary from one tribe to another. For example, some tribes define themselves based upon the specific territory within which they live. Others consist of people engaged in a collective occupation such as farming, cattle breeding, or trades. Tribes might be nomadic, or sedentary, or both at the same time. They can move about at will or become urban dwellers. Ultimately, with so many variations, it is difficult to determine what does or does not constitute an authentic tribal member.

From a sociological perspective, some scholars compare the tribal organization to a cul-de-sac. In their view, no development leads from a tribe to, for example, a state. The question is, however, whether this is a real problem or a problem resulting from an inadequate definition. There will always be political connections between the tribal and other social organizations. Typically, as with other areas of Near Eastern society, the essential element of the tribe is the nuclear family and the lineage. On the other hand, it can be discussed whether the clan really was part of the tribal system or had to do with the system of patrons and clients (patronage).[21] As political organizations, however, the tribe and the state seem to be mutually exclusive, with no room for both organizations in the same area. In state societies, the tribes will always be on the defensive, and their importance will diminish. Conversely, in areas where tribes roam freely, the state will often be ephemeral or struggling against the tribal influence as much as it can. Tribe and state are two competitive types of political organization vying for the loyalty of people living in their territory.

The image of an idealized tribal organization that acts as a viable alternative to the traditional, centralized Near Eastern state is compelling. Under this circumstance, the tribe is a collective, extensive, and

---

[21] See section II.4.4 below.

solid organization to which the people look for their political and temporal requirements. Similarly, it conjures an image that precludes the coexistence of tribe and state in the same territory for any appreciable time, though, in fact, the actual relationships between tribes and civil judicatories were very dynamic. In this model, the tribe becomes a surrogate government that seizes control of and responsibility for that which the state apparatus normally oversees.

From this model, we can see the similarities and differences between the two major Near Eastern social systems—tribal society and the centralized state—during the past 5,000 years. Since the beginning of recorded history, these two entities have continually exchanged roles. The ebb and flow of power favors now one system, now the other. Thus, during the third millennium B.C.E., small central states throughout Syria and Palestine underwent a predictable, cyclic metamorphosis: from central state to tribal rule and vice versa. This process is often called "retribalization." It is believed to be caused by a general shift of occupation. It is often thought that in the Near East, tribes were always nomadic and states were always sedentary. This is only partially correct. As we have already noted, since the beginning of Oriental history, tribal organizations operated in both nomadic and sedentary environments—even in cities. Yet tribal organizations in cities are exceptional and usually depend on a wider system whereby they also control the environment surrounding the cities.

We need to address one other Western stereotype, namely, the perception that antagonisms between the tribe and the state in the Near East have been a "struggle between the desert and the sown." This notion is only partially correct. First, we must refine the terminology by replacing "desert" with "periphery" and "sown" with "center." Thus it could be said that Near Eastern history is characterized by a kind of power play between the center and the periphery. In the center, city dwellers are subservient to a central state authority and its sovereign. On the periphery, people preserve their independence from the state, its authorities, and its distant capital. Occasionally, when central governments and their societies began to decay and resources dwindled, the region's economic viability also deteriorated precipitously. Economic disintegration sparked a series of concurrent centripetal actions against and centrifugal flights from the center. Consequently, the people turned to tribal rule: first, on an ideological level, to separate themselves from state authorities; and second, as refugees, to flee the center and live as peasantry or cattle breeders. In other words, they became stereotypical "nomads." During such times, the terminally weakened central authority did not possess the necessary power to maintain control of its outlying territory. Consequently, the tribes took over that land and converted it to tribal territory. This massive emigration from the center to the periphery by dislocated urbanites often caused a centripetal counter-movement of the periphery against the center. Ultimately, as the center became part of the tribe's annexed territory and state power disintegrated, the tribe became the center's new political force.

Of course, this was not the only possible scenario. At other times, strong states grew from the ashes of former tribal territories. Tribal society was thoroughly inequitable. Its imbalances stemmed from the capriciousness of a tyrannical system. Local tribal leaders often became so powerful that they began to demand tribute that was extorted from tribal members and other residents of the territory. Since they were not beholden to any state regulations, tribal leaders remained virtually invulnerable. Often, several tribes coexisted in the same territory, sometimes as offshoots of one original *Ur-tribe.* In those early tribes, when conditions became insufferable, many members sought refuge from those restless times in a centralized state system.

Finally, in some instances, another evolutionary trend took hold: some tribal leaders and their families could become so mighty that they governed like despots. By the Middle Ages, the noted Arabic historian and cultural philosopher Ibn Khaldūn had already noted these trends and suggested an evolutionary theory of Near Eastern social development that went from tribal "proto-state" to principality to statehood. Khaldūn suggests the inevitability of the centralized state's downfall rests in its inability to replicate the basic feeling of solidarity so apparent and significant to tribal members. Ultimately, the centralized state cannot provide social cohesion, a situation caused by the career goals and aspirations of its members. Accordingly, no dynasty will last long. After only few a generations in power, another dynasty with its power base in a tribal society will take over and the process will repeat itself. While not in itself absolutely wrong, Khaldūn's theory may seem oversimplified and idealistic. Realistically, the evolution from tribe to state (or vice versa) is highly complex and capricious.

In the next section we will show how the relationship between the periphery and the center formed an extraordinarily important element in the history of Bronze Age Syria and Palestine. We will also explore an amazing phenomenon that confounds Khaldūn's evolutionary hypothesis: sophisticated "high" cultures replaced by simpler "low" cultures, as when the centralized state is replaced by tribal society.

II.4.4. The Patronage System

Eisenstadt, Shmuel N. *Patrons, Clients and Friends: Interpersonal Relations and the Structure of Trust in Society.* Cambridge: Cambridge University Press, 1984. **Eisenstadt,** Shmuel N., and René **Lemarchand,** eds. *Political Clientelism, Patronage, and Development.* Beverly Hills: Sage, 1981. **Gellner,** Ernest, and John **Waterbury,** eds. *Patrons and Clients in Mediterranean Societies.* London: Duckworth, 1977.

Our discussion of ancient Near Eastern society and politics remains incomplete without proper consideration of the patronage system. In this system, a client is defined by his patron and a patron by his clients. Powerful individuals and their families recruit clients so that at critical moments the patron can call upon them for support. In the Roman Empire, patrons buttressed the state and governed public and private life.

Patronage has a long and sometimes inglorious history throughout the Mediterranean world; its manifestations include international criminal organizations such as the "Mafia" as well as other less imposing groups. Since antiquity, the specific makeup of these groups has remained hidden. Ancient documents from rediscovered state archives provide almost no concrete data about their internal mechanisms or actual existence. The stringent confidentiality among members of the "family" effectively precludes any substantive ethnological analysis of its operations. For the client, these sociopolitical groups sometimes represent a compelling and effective alternative to the natural family. The patron inspires loyalty through concrete, contractual agreements with and unconditional protection for the client, whereas the natural family coheres "only" on the basis of more or less vague feelings of solidarity. In effect, the patronage system is an insurance company that guarantees a bilateral agreement between consenting parties. The patron agrees to protect his client in any crisis. Concomitantly, the client agrees to remain loyal to the patron. This loyalty remains important both in daily life and in extraordinary circumstances that demand collective action.

In the ancient Near East, the patron-client system extended well beyond the borders of local jurisdictions. Patrons existed on all levels: from local honchos who oversaw the general populace to kings who monitored the activities of all their far-flung governing agents. Internationally, the most influential kings contracted with each other for mutual support and protection. All of these relationships were initiated and regulated through contracts. Many Late Bronze Age contract texts testify to the number and scope of these patron-client relationships, from international alliances to the kingly donations of land to loyal and successful officers. On the local level, however, we know little about such operations. We occasionally get a glimpse of how it worked. That is all. Undoubtedly, Near Eastern patronage and the Central and Northern European feudal systems are related. They shared the double-edged sword: protection of the weak, and the omnipresent potential for tyranny.[22]

---

[22] It is both strange and easily understandable that ancient sources say so little about the system. Ancient documents are never very precise about ethnic and social definitions. For instance, the ancient Near Eastern languages do not distinguish between peasants and farmers. Peasants were so omnipresent that they required no special title. Other groups, however, were clearly and specifically defined as specialists within their respective societies (i.e., "craftsmen" or "soldiers"). They *earned* their

II.5. THE HISTORY OF SYRIA AND PALESTINE

GENERAL: **Cassin,** Elena, Jean **Bottéro,** and Jean **Vercoutter.** *Die Altorientalische Reiche I–II.* Fischer Weltgeschichte 2–3. Frankfurt: Fischer, 1965–1967. **Edwards,** E. S., Cyril J. **Gadd,** and Nicolas G. L. **Hammond,** eds. *Cambridge Ancient History I, 1–II, 2.* 3d ed. London: Cambridge University Press, 1970–1975. **Garelli,** Paul. *Le Proche-Orient asiatique, des origènes aux invasions des peuples de la mer.* Nouvelle Clio 2. Paris: Presses universitaires de France, 1969. **Liverani,** Mario. *Antico Oriente: Storia, società, economia.* Rome: Laterza, 1988. **Sasson,** Jack, ed. *Civilizations of the Ancient Near East.* 4 vols. New York: Scribners, 1995.

CHRONOLOGY: **Ehrich,** Robert W., ed. *Chronologies in Old World Archaeology I–II.* 3d ed. Chicago: University of Chicago Press, 1992.

PALESTINE: **Ahlström,** Gösta W. *The History of Ancient Palestine from the Palaeolithic Period to Alexander's Conquest.* Minneapolis: Fortress, 1993.

SYRIA: **Klengel,** Horst. *Geschichte Syriens im 2. Jahrtausend I–III.* Berlin: Akademie Verlag, 1965–1969. **Klengel,** Horst. *Syria, 3000 to 300 B.C.: A Handbook of Political History.* Berlin: Akademie Verlag, 1993.

EGYPT AND THE NEAR EAST: **Helck,** Wolfgang. *Die Beziehungen Ägyptens zu Vorderasien im 3. und 2. Jahrtausend v. Chr.* Wiesbaden: O. Harrassowitz, 1962. **Redford,** Donald B. *Egypt, Canaan, and Israel in Ancient Times.* Princeton: Princeton University Press, 1992.

II.5.1. The Period of Ebla: The Early Bronze Age

EBLA: **Gordon,** Cyrus H., Gary A. **Rendsburg,** and Nathan H. **Winter,** eds. *Eblaitica 1–3: Essays on the Ebla Archives and Eblaite Language.* Publications of the Center for Ebla Research at New York University. Winona Lake, Ind.: Eisenbrauns, 1987–1992. **Matthiae,** Paolo. *Ebla: An Empire Rediscovered.* Translated by Christopher Holme. London: Hodder & Stoughton, 1980. **Pettinato,** Giovanni. *Ebla: A New Look at History.* Translated by C. Faith Richardson. Baltimore: Johns Hopkins University Press, 1991. **Waetzoldt,** Hartmut, and Harald **Hauptmann,** eds. *Wirtschaft und Gesellschaft von Ebla: Akten der internationalen Tagung, Heidelberg 4.–7. November 1986.* Heidelberger Studien zum alten Orient. Heidelberg: Heidelberger Orientverlag, 1988.

PALESTINE: **Esse,** Douglas L. *Subsistence, Trade, and Social Change in Early Bronze Palestine.* Chicago: University of Chicago Press, 1991. **Kempinski,** Aharon. *The Rise of Urban Culture: The Urbanization of Palestine in the Early Bronze Age, 3000–2150 B.C.* Jerusalem: Israel Ethnographic Society, 1978. **Miroschedji,**

right to be called soldiers or craftsmen while peasants or cattle breeders represented the gray, silent majority distinguished only by family bloodlines. Ultimately, social standing hinged on wealth and reputation, things about which a peasant could only dream.

Pierre de, ed. *L'urbanisation de la Palestine à l'age du Bronze ancien*. Oxford: B. A. R., 1989.

PHOENICIA: **Saghieh,** Muntala. *Byblos in the Third Millennium BC: A Reconstruction of the Stratigraphy and a Study of the Cultural Connections*. Warminster: Aris & Phillips, 1983.

A thousand years before Abraham's alleged arrival in Canaan (ca. 2300 B.C.E., according to the biblical portrait), highly developed and urbanized societies already existed in small and large cities throughout the Near East. Domestic and international trade flourished. "At that time, the Canaanites were in the land," the author of Gen 12:6 confidently proclaims; but since no third-millennium documents support that claim, we must employ more judicious analyses of Palestine's ethnic makeup. From the latter stages of the Early Bronze Age through the Middle Bronze Age, Palestine's ethnic picture remained relatively constant; however, that culture was Amorite, not "Canaanite." Actually, the biblical portrayal of a unique "Canaanite" population in pre-Israelite Palestine is highly questionable. We possess no third- or second-millennium documentation supporting such a society. While Egyptian and Mesopotamian documents occasionally mention in a very general way the inhabitants of a geographic locale known as "Canaan," Palestine's Bronze Age residents never referred to themselves as "Canaanites."[23] The first known population to be called "Canaanites" was a fourth-century C.E. North African peasant population during the days of Augustine of Hippo.[24]

Ultimately, the Old Testament does not convey any concrete information about Syria and Palestine in the Bronze Age, only vague and legendary material. For example, during the so-called patriarchal period,

---

[23] Here we are reminded of the Amarna letter from Abimilki of Tyre (EA 151); in which Abimilki informs Pharaoh of the situation in Canaan: "The king of Danuna is dead, and his brother has assumed the throne. The land is safe. A fire destroyed the palace at Ugarit: one half is demolished, and the other half is missing. There are no Hittite troops in this region. Etakkama is prince of Qadesh, and Aziru battles Biriawaza." Here several names and places are immediately identifiable: Danuna with Kilikien (the southernmost part of Asia Minor); Ugarit in northern Syria; and Qadesh in central Syria, along the Orontes River. Aziru was the king of Amurru (in the northern section of modern Lebanon). His enemy Biriawaza was king of Damascus. If we take Abimilki's comments at face value, Canaan refers to the entire Near East; that is, Canaan is not associated with a specific geographic location or political entity.

[24] See Augustine's *Ep. ad Romanos inchoata expositio 13* (Migne, Patrologia latina 355:2096). For this entire issue, see Niels Peter Lemche, *The Canaanites and Their Land: The Tradition of the Canaanites* (JSOTSup 110; Sheffield: Sheffield Academic Press, 1991).

Palestine was home to many diverse peoples—some historical, others contrived. Clearly, the Hittites represent a historical entity; however, other peoples seem to exist only in the minds of the biblical authors or are derivatives of legendary and heroic figures like the Titans. In Ugaritic sources, for example, the Rephaim were the spirits of the deceased ancestors, heroes never forgotten, but in Genesis they are listed among the pre-Israelite inhabitants of Canaan (Gen 15:20). Ultimately, it is almost impossible to determine whether any of the names in the Old Testament refer to peoples who actually lived in Palestine during the third or second millennium B.C.E.

Palestinian urban culture was undoubtedly highly developed by the end of the fourth millennium B.C.E. The Early Bronze Age cities did not form spontaneously; rather, they grew slowly from their dim beginnings in the rich village cultures of the early Stone Age. By the start of the third millennium, Palestine had extensive urban settlements protected by solid masonry. One example is Arad at the northern fringe of the Negev, at that time still a productive farming region.[25] By Palestinian standards, Arad was an expansive city: 90,000 square meters, with a population of roughly 3,500[26]—almost twice as many inhabitants as Jerusalem during the Davidic period.

In Palestine, domestic and international trade blossomed during the Early Bronze Age, especially within Egypt. Circumstantial evidence suggests that Egyptians were physically present in some southern Palestinian cities; however, most scholars agree that during this time, relations between Egypt and Palestine were strictly commercial. The Egyptian regimes of the Old Kingdom could not transcend their political insulation. Consequently, efforts to occupy southern Palestine would not develop for many years.

Why did the Neolithic villages mature into cities during the Chalcolithic (Copper-Stone) Age? Several interrelated explanations have been posited. First, expanded international trade necessitated the development of commercial bureaucracies. To stabilize and protect these new economic relationships, cities gradually formed around administrative centers. Second, many climatologists suggest that the Near Eastern

---

[25] Present-day travelers will easily recognize the surroundings of ancient Arad as a fertile farming center; however, that was not always the case. Twenty years ago, Arad was still an area of barren desert. Today, thanks to Israeli development, the entire countryside has changed character.

[26] Based on these calculations, Arad's population hovered around 358 people per hectare, a figure roughly equivalent to the ghettos in modern Oriental cities like Baghdad. Other scholars might prefer lower numbers and different calculations. All such figures are only rough approximations; but they remain helpful tools for determining the size of ancient Near Eastern settlements as long as the method employed is consistent. Ultimately, these population figures are not altogether unrealistic.

climate created a need for these new urban centers. At the beginning of the third millennium the lush, moist Neolithic climate started to degenerate into a period of sustained drought that produced much less prosperous conditions for Palestine's residents. Particularly in southern Palestine, agriculture was a risky enterprise. In order to survive in spite of fewer resources and an inhospitable environment, the villagers banded together in clusters, which developed a central organization under the auspices of local chieftains, or even grew into full-fledged monarchies. This centralization process began already at the end of the fourth millennium and came to fruition no later than 2500 B.C.E.

During this period, Palestine was clearly a dynamic and well-functioning urbanized culture; however, even more extensive urbanization had taken place in other sections of the Near East. Because of the extensive third-millennium trade relations with Egypt, several prosperous cities emerged along the Levantine coast. The center of this trade was Byblos. In western Syria, too, many urban centers appeared at this time, acting as centers of trade and hubs for commerce between Mesopotamia and Egypt or for trade overseas. Thanks to the efforts of Italian archaeologists, the extensive archives unearthed at Ebla (Tell Mardikh) have earned international scholarly recognition. Once they can be scrutinized more carefully, the Ebla documents will provide unprecedented and extensive insights into Syria's history and culture between 2500 and 2300 B.C.E.

So far, Ebla's extremely complex cuneiform writing system has created significant obstacles to extracting information. Cuneiform has a long history. It was probably invented in the late fourth or early third millennium by the Sumerians of southern Mesopotamia. It became the basis for the Akkadian and later the Eblaite writing systems. Although Akkadian was a Semitic language, very different from the Sumerian language, the scribes of Akkad adapted Sumerian writing for their own purpose. This had as a consequence a major restructuring of cuneiform writing. In Sumerian, the pictographic wedges of early cuneiform gradually developed into signs. Each sign expressed a specific word or image with an equally specific meaning. Akkadian transformed these signs into syllabic values. However, these values might change considerably from time to time and from place to place. Therefore, scholars remain unsure about the phonetic values of the Eblaite signs.[27] These uncertainties suggest that we remain far from a solid understanding of this language.

---

[27] The Sumerian language is primarily "agglutinative" or uninflected. Unlike Semitic or Indo-European languages, Sumerian is rather simple: one word, one definition. For example, the Sumerian words for "man" (*lú*) and "big" (*gal*) are both phonetically and structurally unalterable. Thus, a "big man" (or "king") is called *lú.gal*. In an Akkadian speaking environment *lú* and *gal* were, however, transferred as phonemes, *-lú-*, and *-gal-*, respectively, without any regard for their pictographic value.

Clearly, the Ebla texts provide very little information about third-millennium Palestine. When an important new site is being excavated, popular magazines and newspapers often sensationalize the discoveries—as happened with Ebla. When compared to the biblical chronology, Ebla blossomed in the days of the patriarchs. Wouldn't it be nice to find references to these biblical figures among the Ebla documents? It was therefore probably inescapable that some journalists and scholars should draw connections between Ebla and the patriarchs. Of particular interest is the alleged link between Ebla's king Ibrium and the biblical Abraham (or Abram). What more could you ask? Interest waned when it was discovered that Ibrium was only a member of Ebla's officialdom.[28] Such hypotheses have fallen at the hands of researchers armed with a more sophisticated understanding of the Eblaite language. Clearly, the Ebla documents provide no special arguments favoring the historicity of the patriarchs or other individuals mentioned in the patriarchal narratives. Conversely, the Old Testament never mentions Ebla.

The Ebla documents tell us the story of its domination of northern Syrian society between 2500 and 2300 B.C.E. They also provide important data regarding the population, growth, and administration of the empire, as well as useful analogies regarding Palestinian and Syrian society at large.

Although the Eblaite language belongs to the Semitic language family, linguistic evidence suggests that it is different from the other known Semitic languages from around 2000 B.C.E., namely, Amorite and Akkadian. By that time, the many subdialects of the Amorite language had already dispersed throughout Syria, while Akkadian was the dominant language of Mesopotamia (along with Sumerian). This language difference indicates a rather complex ethnic situation in Syria. Although a certain ethnic communality can be assumed between the inhabitants of a city such as Ebla and the general Syrian population—both mostly

---

The transfer of individual signs from Sumerian to Akkadian was neither simple nor smooth. Often, the original phonetic values of specific signs were supplemented or simply substituted with other values. In different times and places, one Akkadian sign could have many different meanings. Thus, in Akkadian, the sign *gal* shared a common phonetic value with four other words: *qal, kal,* and *gala*. Similarly, *lú* shared the same phonetic value with at least six other cuneiform signs. The sign *lú* could, however, also have the value *na* and (in late texts) *at*. Another example is the Sumerian sign meaning *utu* ("sun") whose other values include *ud, ut, tam, par, pir, liḫ,* and *ḫis*. The phonetic value of a cuneiform character may therefore change from place to place. It is accordingly very important to be able to pinpoint the exact values at a certain place and time. The study of the Eblaite language is still far from having established all of these values.

[28] Perhaps Ibrium is identical to the Hebrew name Abram. If so, then it only proves that Abram existed as a name in the third millennium. It does not refer to the biblical man Abraham (or Abram).

Amorite-speaking and living at the fringe of the centralized states—the ethnic composition of Ebla was not the same as that found in its surrounding territories.

The king[29] of Ebla oversaw an extensive bureaucracy and governed a city of approximately 15,000 to 20,000 inhabitants. That city was encircled by a cluster of roughly 100 villages, the total population of which did not exceed their parent center. Realistically, Ebla's overall population hovered between 40,000 and 50,000.

As archaeologists began to excavate, many of them repeatedly called Ebla an *empire*—one that supposedly stretched from central Syria into parts of Palestine. Today, the evidence is compelling: any declaration of an empire of Ebla is ill-conceived and unsubstantiated. First, its meager population precludes such an assumption. Second, the documents from its archive describe the approximate parameters of the realm. The city lies on the main thoroughfare between Aleppo and Damascus, about forty kilometers south of Aleppo. Its western border skirts the coastal mountain ranges. Ninety kilometers south of Ebla, independent kings governed Hama (the ancient Hamath). Ebla's northern extension was delimited by a series of independent centers, from Carchemish in the northwest to Mari at the Euphrates River in the southeast.

The Ebla archive, in combination with other documentary evidence from Syria that has recently become available to scholars, suggests that no large empire existed in Syria during the third millennium. On the other hand, several major cities, such as Ebla, arose in this period, some of which survived until the Greco-Roman conquest of Syria. The Ebla archive, therefore, provides valuable information about Syria's political situation. Several substantial political entities were controlled by urban regents ("kings") who oversaw populations of between 10,000 and 50,000 people. Although large, these urban centers were not empires.

Commercial activity flourished between these city-states, which also functioned as way stations along major trade routes. The peasantry (the majority of the population) remained mostly uninvolved in mainstream trade. Favorable ecological conditions contributed to the region's affluence. The population of Syria in this period enjoyed the relative prosperity and safety afforded by the centralized political system.

Around 2300 B.C.E., the Akkadian king Naram-Sin conquered and destroyed Ebla. This event began a period of decline in Syria and Palestine that continued into the next millennium, during which many large urban societies of the Early Bronze Age either were reduced considerably

---

29 The ancient Near Eastern peoples had various terms for "king." Ebla shared its term *mālikum* with other West Semitic languages (in Hebrew *melek*). In Akkadian, the word was *šarrum* (which in West Semitic dialects means "nobleman" or "prince" but not "king").

or disappeared completely. Village life, however, remained largely unaffected by this development; if anything, more villages were founded. Thanks to extensive archaeological excavations throughout the region, Palestine's evolution is more concretely identifiable than that of Syria; however, the aftereffects of these economic and political setbacks in Early Bronze Age Syria are clear.

Several other circumstances probably contributed to the downfall of the early Bronze Age urban milieu of Syria and Palestine. The intervention of Mesopotamian sovereigns into its political affairs significantly weakened Syria's ability to keep its city-state network intact. The political sequel to such an invasion is normally that either the foreign power establishes its rule or the previous sovereign is removed by local competitors. Neither of these happened this time; rather, primitive political entities began to reestablish themselves throughout the region. In this way the population of Syria and Palestine escaped the control of the authorities of the centralized state. At the same time, however, they lost the protection that it provided.

In order to understand this development, one must realize that city-states such as those found in ancient Syria and Palestine relied on commerce including trade between regions. Such trade relations buttress the power and prestige of the political leaders. As long as commerce blossomed, the city state had a fair chance of survival. However, in combination with the fall of Ebla and the resulting disturbances in Syrian trade relations, other disasters struck, such as the demise of Egypt's Old Kingdom. The Old Kingdom—the time of the great pyramid builders—was followed by an interim period that was, according to the later testimonies of Egyptian authors, marked by a total transformation of Egyptian society. It was a time "when the slave became master and the master slave." Little time and interest were left for trade enterprises.

Some Mesopotamian kings such as Sargon of Akkad and his grandson Naram-Sin evidently planned to establish major empires that would include Syria. However, the death of Naram-Sin spelled an end to this enterprise. Thus, the dramatic initial effect of the political intervention by these two kings in the internal affairs of Syria never developed into lasting, stable situations. After Sargon and Naram-Sin left the Syrian scene, no local authority remained to inherit the position of an old political and economic center such as Ebla, which was now gone.

Another factor in the Syro-Palestinian economic and political crisis might have been the deteriorating climate toward the end of the Early Bronze Age. A thousand years before, the climate might have contributed to the appearance of centralized political authority. Now environmental conditions had the opposite effect: they forced the inhabitants of Syria and Palestine to scatter throughout the region in search of arable land. Those who could not find suitable farming conditions were forced to change occupations. Some became cattle breeders, more combined agriculture with cattle breeding. As a consequence, they were forced to give up the hope of being protected by city walls or the military forces of some central authority. No doubt the Syrian and Palestinian urbanites had a difficult choice to make. They had to abandon residence in cities and seek refuge in the periphery.

Here new options were available. The periphery had always been inhabited by societies not controlled by the centralized states. These communities—most likely already in those days organized as tribal societies—now had to absorb and integrate, even dominate, the refugees from the defunct centers. In this way, Syria and Palestine experienced a "retribalization process" as the centralized states dissolved.

Two arguments support this description of the dissolution of Early Bronze Age Syrian and Palestinian societies. First, after the destruction of Ebla, no trace remained of its local Semitic dialect. Either the entire Eblaite population perished, or the survivors integrated with tribes previously living on the fringe and speaking some form of the Amorite language. Although the Ebla documents say nothing about the presence of Amorite tribespeople, other documents from the second half of the third millennium refer to a large group of Amorite-speaking Mesopotamian residents. Undoubtedly, these Amorites were considered by the local Akkadian-speaking population to be newcomers from Syria. "Amorites" is the Akkadian term for "people from the west" and later became a collective designation for all peoples of Syria and Palestine. Since no one in Mesopotamia spoke the Eblaite language, perhaps the Mesopotamian Amorites once belonged to the periphery of Syria's urban centers or areas astride the Akkadian and Sumerian cultures.

The second argument concerns the persistent expansion of the ancient Near Eastern desert. The facts are compelling: at the end of the Early Bronze Age, a general collapse of urban culture occurred. Although most of the cities were rebuilt during the following period of urbanization—the Middle Bronze Age—some were not, or they were rebuilt as poor imitations of their former greatness. The latter was the case with Ebla. By the mid-second millennium B.C.E., Ebla once again became a meaningful regional city; however, it never reestablished itself as a dominant center in Syria. Hillside ruins of other western Syrian cities at the edge of the steppe region on the desert's fringe also testify to a deteriorating environment. Indeed, without a favorable ecology it is unimaginable that either agriculture or cities could ever have flourished in these regions. Subsequently, the deteriorating ecological conditions in these areas effectively precluded the complete rebuilding of these buried cities. Other regional cities were more fortunate than their western counterparts. Several new urban centers grew beside the important cities of the Early Bronze Age: Aleppo, Hama (Hamath), and Damascus.

In Palestine, Arad is the prototypical example of the disastrous effect of these deleterious ecological circumstances. Today, Arad lies at the edge of the Negev desert. In the Early Bronze Age, it was a dynamic, densely populated urban center surrounded by highly productive farmland. Although the precise causes are unknown, Arad disappeared by the end of the Early Bronze Age, never again to be repopulated. Subsequent habitations—first as a small village, then as a Jewish fort—never rivaled Arad's previous glory. Ultimately, the inexorable advance of the desert could not support the reestablishment of another urban center.

II.5.2. "For Hazor Formerly Was the Head of All Those Kingdoms" (Josh 11:10): Palestine and Syria under the Amorites

---

AMORITES: **Buccellati,** Giorgio. *The Amorites of the Ur III Period.* Naples: Istituto orientale de Napoli, 1966. **Liverani,** Mario. "The Amorites." In *Peoples of Old Testament Times.* Edited by Dennis J. Wiseman. Pages 100–133. Oxford: Clarendon Press, 1973. **Thompson,** Thomas L. *The Historicity of the Patriarchal Narratives: The Quest for the Historical Abraham.* BZAW 133. Berlin: de Gruyter, 1974.

MARI AND THE NOMADS: **Kupper,** Jean-Robert. *Les nomades en Mésopotamie au temps des rois de Mari.* Bibliothèque de la Faculté de philosophie et lettres de l'université de Liège 142. 1957. Reprint, Paris: Les Belles Lettres, 1982. **Luke,** John T. "Pastoralism and Politics in the Mari Kingdom." Ph.D. Diss., University of Michigan, 1965. **Malamat,** Abraham. *Mari and the Bible.* Studies in the History and Culture of the Ancient Near East 12. Leiden: E. J. Brill, 1998. **Matthews,** Victor H. *Pastoral Nomadism in the Mari Kingdom (ca. 1830–1760 B.C.).* Dissertation Series 3. Cambridge, Mass.: American Schools of Oriental Research, 1978. **Young,** Gordon D. *Mari in Retrospect.* 1981. Reprint, Winona Lake, Ind.: Eisenbrauns, 1992.

SYRIA AND PALESTINE: **Gerstenblith,** Patty. *The Levant at the Beginning of the Middle Bronze Age.* Philadelphia: American Schools of Oriental Research, 1983.

THE SUTEAN NOMADS: **Heltzer,** Michael. *The Suteans.* Naples: Istituto universitario orientale, 1981.

The first half of the second millennium B.C.E. was the most dynamic period in pre-Hellenistic Palestine, witnessing a land marked by unsurpassed urbanization and unexpected prosperity—at least among the urban elite (i.e., the ruling class and its employees). In this period, most Early Bronze Age cities reorganized. Sometimes the city area expanded and was provided with updated defenses, mostly in the form of a *glaçis*, that is, an earthen and stone rampart that reinforced the old walls using ashlar blocks and bricks. Furthermore, the slopes of the city mound were smoothed and beveled to look like slopes, thereby preventing direct access to retaining walls and the use of military war machines, such as battering rams and siege towers.

Not every city shared in this boom. One striking example is et-Tell in central Palestine, the biblical city Ai, which experienced the same general collapse of urban culture in the third millennium B.C.E. Except for an insignificant settlement at the start of the Iron Age, the city was never repopulated.[30] But other Palestinian cities experienced a renaissance. For example, during the Middle Bronze Age, the Upper Galilean city of Hazor covered more than 200 hectares—including an inner city of more than 180 hectares and an acropolis of 20 to 25 hectares. The acropolis housed most of the official buildings, including the palace and administrative headquarters. According to the already mentioned system for calculating the population of ancient settlements, Hazor housed up to 25,000 residents.[31] By ancient Near Eastern standards, this figure made Hazor a major city—at least ten times larger than David's Jerusalem.

The same evolution also took place in the remaining parts of the Near East, including eastern Jordan and especially Syria. Syria became the home of many large urban centers, many of which stood on the same spot as their Early Bronze Age counterparts. In some cases, former city-state capitals (such as Ebla) became provincial capitals in the political order of Syria. Now Aleppo (Halab), situated to the north of Ebla, became the new capital of northern Syria and the center of the influential Syrian state of Yamkhad. Ultimately, Yamkhad would dominate western and northern sections of Syria.

The size of Aleppo in the Middle Bronze Age is still uncertain. Unfortunately, the modern city built above Aleppo presents numerous obstacles to detailed excavation and analysis of the ancient city. Today visitors to Aleppo see a gigantic citadel that looms high over the old city. The image can be seductive, making it look like a possible place for ancient Aleppo. Archaeological excavations at the citadel, however, prove the citadel is situated on a natural hilltop—not on an ancient city-mound—whose only purpose was to be the acropolis of the city. In the Middle Bronze Age Aleppo was undoubtedly an extensive settlement, the

---

30 The Old Testament tradition also refers to this situation. In Hebrew, "Ai" is equivalent to the Arabic "Tell" (i.e., "hillside ruins"). If Joshua actually conquered Ai (Josh 8), then he subdued a "ruin hill."

31 Other estimates of Hazor's Middle Bronze Age population include that of William G. Dever ("Qedah, Tell el-," *ABD* 5:558–81), who suggests that in its seventeenth-century heyday, Hazor's population ranged between 15,000 and 20,000 people. In *Hazor: The Head of All Those Kingdoms* ([London: Oxford University Press, 1972], p. 106), Yigael Yadin (who excavated the city) suggests a figure of about 50,000 residents. This figure is based on a hypothetical estimate of almost 500 people per hectare, which he admits is probably on the high side. His other estimate, closer to 25,000 to 30,000, is near enough to the calculation model used here of 358 people per hectare and seems realistic.

capital of the major state of Yamkhad that stretched from the Mediterranean in the west to the kingdom of Mari in the east.

Interestingly, this empire was not governed by a strong, centralized authority. One document from the Mari archive claims that Yarim-Lim (first half of the eighteenth century B.C.E.) was followed by twenty kings, that is, he ruled a state consisting of twenty satellite states that had bowed to the sovereignty of Aleppo.[32] One of these secondary states, the kingdom of Mukish (and its capital of Alalakh) situated to the west of Aleppo and bordering the Mediterranean, is well known. Another well-known city, Ebla, fell under Yamkhad's jurisdiction.

It would be incorrect to view Yamkhad as the only substantial political entity in Syria during the Middle Bronze Age. The role of Yamkhad in this period is probably roughly comparable to that of Ebla in the third millennium. Neither Ebla nor Aleppo ruled all of Syria. The aforementioned document from the Mari archive also mentions that other cities of Syria, such as Qatna and Carchemish, were not subdued by Yarim-Lim of Yamkhad, but both commanded small empires of their own. Qatna (modern Tell Mishrifeh) lay in the proximity the modern city of Hama (ancient Hamath) in central Syria. During the Early Bronze Age, Carchemish—already a well-known and sovereign city (or city-state)—stood beside the Euphrates River northeast of Aleppo. Both states remained independent and were able to participate in the competition for power in Syria in this period. The Mari documents are particularly revealing in this regard. From them, we know that persistent attempts among the states of Syria to form advantageous military and political alliances were generally short-lived.

Thus the Middle Bronze Age seems a natural and logical continuation of the Early Bronze Age, although Syrian society at the end of the Early Bronze Age suffered from a massive reduction in scale and prosperity. However, the traditions of the first period persisted when urban culture reappeared. Not only were most of the trading centers reconstructed and the trade relations with Egypt and Mesopotamia reestablished, but also the political traditions of the Early Bronze Age reappeared.

The continuity between the Early and Middle Bronze Age also finds expression in the way Aleppo succeeded Ebla in northern Syria, while Qatna at the same time took up the leading position in southern Syria, a position probably belonging to Hamath in the Early Bronze Age. (At least evidence in the Ebla documents indicates that Hamath played the leading role in a south Syrian coalition while Ebla was ruling the northern part.) Thus the Syrian society was split between two political centers, on one side Aleppo and on the other Qatna. A third party in this power

---

[32] See William L. Moran's translation of this letter in *ANET*, 628.

game was Carchemish, which continued to play its old political role in the Middle Bronze Age. It is hardly a coincidence that the political pattern from the Early Bronze Age continued in the Middle Bronze Age, although it is unknown how and why the new political centers of the Middle Bronze Age were chosen. Maybe both Aleppo and Qatna were among the satellite states of the Early Bronze Age and now assumed the role of political leaders after the fall of the formerly ruling cities. Although we are ignorant about the details, political tradition seemingly prevented Syria from uniting under the rule of only one king. Local kings became vassals of regional rulers in a system of patrons and clients, but they never united around a single master.

We have no information indicating that Palestine took part in a similar political development. It is most reasonable to think that conditions here were not totally unlike those in Syria. Thus the city of Hazor was evidently a major regional center and must have ruled a considerable territory to feed its large population. Nothing is known about the political and socioeconomic particulars of this great city, but the mention of Hazor's former greatness in the book of Joshua (11:10) may be a late reflection on the tradition of Hazor's supremacy over northern Palestine and southwestern Syria. Hazor is the only Palestinian city named in the Mari texts (in a letter that mentions trade relations with Hazor). This is one of only a few such references to Palestine in the extensive Mari archive.

Several causes contributed to the restoration of urban culture in Syria and Palestine in the Middle Bronze Age. Climatic changes were not among them, for the climate really did not improve during the second millennium. An important factor was the resuscitation of international commercial traffic. When Egypt built the Middle Kingdom from the rubble of the Old Kingdom, it reestablished trade relations with large, influential Mesopotamian city-states that were also being reconstructed at this time. Demographics was another critical factor in Syrian and Palestinian cultural expansion. During this period, Syria, Palestine, and in fact Mesopotamia as well developed a strikingly homogeneous population. The first manifestation of this trend was linguistic. The people of the Near East, including Mesopotamia, shared a common language: Amorite. Even those who did not speak Amorite descended from people who had spoken this language.

People with Amorite ancestry were common in the cities of Mesopotamia. These cities were at the beginning of the second millennium governed by a series of dynasties that boasted Amorite origins—not only in Mari at the Syrian border, but also in the most important central and southern Mesopotamian cities, including Babylon. Even Hammurabi, the most influential of all second-millennium Babylonian kings, claimed Amorite roots. Yet the common people in these cities rarely claimed pure Amorite bloodlines; in fact, many came from diverse ethnic backgrounds. Some were descendants of the earlier Akkadian population, others traced their heritage to the Sumerians of southern Mesopotamia, and still others belonged among the Amorites. Nevertheless, the ruling class was almost exclusively Amorite, although the old Mesopotamian tradition retained enough influence within this group to replace Amorite with Akkadian as the official court tongue. The scholarly language remained Sumerian.

In Syria, the Amorites dominated the overall demographic picture; therefore, the general population probably spoke Amorite. Undoubtedly, the common language and culture shared among Syria's inhabitants contributed mightily to this region's socioeconomic boon. According to the so-called Execration texts from Egypt, Palestine and Syria also shared in this common language link. In Hazor, newly discovered inscriptions include Amorite personal names.

In Syria and Palestine, the actual administrative language during the Middle Bronze Age remains unclear. The few documents from this age that have been found in Syria and Palestine suggest that the state scribes preferred Akkadian to Amorite when they composed documents for both regional administration and international correspondence. Documents from the Alalakh archive confirm that most Middle Bronze Age documents were composed in Akkadian. Here we discover an unusual fact: a population dominated by Amorite bloodlines, but whose official writings were composed in Akkadian. Clearly, Syrians and Palestinians did not need a substitute for their own native tongue. What explains this curious situation? Syrian and Palestinian scribes were trained to follow a traditional Akkadian model for official transcriptions. These scribes constituted a unique professional class whose education was long and arduous. Apprentice scribes in scribal schools were raised in the Babylonian tradition, one whose textbooks included marvelous examples of epic and scientific literature from the Mesopotamian literary heritage.[33] Thus, although most of those students spoke Amorite, they perfected their literary skills through Akkadian models. Here we see a striking parallel to Horace's classical declaration: *Graecia capta ferum victorem cepit* ("conquered Greece captured its vicious victor"). The Babylonians compelled their Amorite governors to accept and retain Mesopotamian culture. Deep into Palestinian

[33] The Epic of Gilgamesh was perhaps the most beautiful of all epic poems to rise from this marvelous literary tradition. Gilgamesh has a long and renowned history. Its earliest versions come from the dim beginnings of third-millennium Sumer. Through many subsequent revisions, it comes to full maturity during the Late Assyrian and Babylonian periods in the first millennium, by which time the Gilgamesh Epic was universally known. The scientific treatises were not "scientific" by today's standards; they did, however, try to systematize the world of experience. Unfortunately, their working assumptions remain obscure.

territory, Amorites lived in two worlds: their own physical environment and the Mesopotamian cultural thought world.

Syria, Palestine, and Mesopotamia in the Middle Bronze Age could be viewed as a laboratory for investigating the relationships between the periphery and the center. After the end of the Early Bronze Age, the periphery defeated the center. In the Early Bronze Age, both Ebla's officialdom and its general population spoke an Eblaite dialect only remotely related to the Amorite language—although both Eblaite and Amorite belong among the Semitic languages. Upper-class Mesopotamians in the third millennium spoke Akkadian or Sumerian. Yet only a few centuries later, the situation changed dramatically: the Amorite upper class dominated Syro-Mesopotamian society. Consequently, the coalescing of the periphery and the center guaranteed that Amorite names and ethnicity would continue to dominate the region. In this way, periphery and center assimilated. This, however, did not mean that from this point forward, the periphery no longer existed.

Literally thousands of extant documents from the Mari archives have provided invaluable and in-depth insight into the social circumstances of Syria and western Mesopotamia. From them we discover that social conditions were constantly changing.

At this point, we have no intention of tackling the history of the kingdom of Mari. A short overview will suffice. It seems most likely that the fate of Mari echoes that of other Syrian and Mesopotamian states. Obviously, Mari served as the capital of a major northwestern Mesopotamian outpost that, except for a brief Assyrian interlude, was governed by an Amorite dynasty. That regime occasionally entered into contractual or marital alliances with other Amorite dynasties in Yamkhad or Qatna.

By the mid-eighteenth century B.C.E., Babylon's renowned king Hammurabi conquered and destroyed Mari. Hammurabi's untimely death ended his plans to use Mari as a launching pad to expand Babylon's western frontier as far as Yamkhad. Consequently, like so many other Syrian and Mesopotamian empires, Babylon was also short-lived.

Mari's Amorite kings traced their ancestry through local tribes. Most politicos and a large portion of the general population traced their bloodline through the Khanean tribe. Thus, Mari's king could claim two titles: the king of the "land of the Khaneans" and the king of Mari. The monarch who ruled during the time of the Mari archive (ca. 1775–1760 B.C.E.) was actually the head sheikh of the Khaneans; therefore, he maintained a dual commitment to his fellow tribesmen and to the remaining inhabitants of the city. Ultimately, he maintained peace between both.

The narrow Khanean vocational endeavors centered around cattle breeding; however, their nomadic tradition sustained their interest in and need for goat and sheep herding. Others were employed as agriculturalists within the state territory. Khaneans had one foot planted in the center and one in the periphery; the center-dwellers never fully integrated into the center. After all, except for the king, Khaneans swore to maintain a strong allegiance to their own tribal leaders and upheld their tribal organization—even though all Khaneans were obliged to pay taxes to Mari's king. In contrast, the *Binu-Yamina* tribesmen (the so-called Benjaminites of Mari) were a peripheral group mentioned in the Mari documents. This group remained mainly nomadic, constantly shifting between their summer abode in central Syria at Jebel Bishri, and their winter accommodations east of the Euphrates River. Because their route of migration ran right through the territory of the kingdom of Mari, these treks created unique problems for state officials. Reports abound about failed attempts by the state to bar the Benjaminites from leaving Mari territory once they had migrated into it.

The Mari texts give no indication that these tribesmen ever submitted to or integrated with Mari culture. At this point, the periphery remained peripheral for two reasons. First, the periphery was populated by people who preferred to remain at the fringe of urban society and only occasionally visited the territory of the centralized states. Second, most state authorities attempted unsuccessfully to suppress tribal freedom. We know very little about the end of hostilities between Benjaminite tribesmen and Mari state officials because of the fall of Mari. Yet one thing is clear: the Mari kings never succeeded in reducing the Benjaminites to servants of the state. Similarly, we have no idea of the situation in the territory of the former kingdom of Mari after the destruction of its capital. Maybe it became tribal territory again. Circumstantial evidence supports this supposition, since the city of Mari was never rebuilt. Later, only tiny villages and settlements remained on the site of the former city.

II.5.3 Hurrians, Hittites, and Hyksos: The End of the Middle Bronze Age

---

HURRIANS: **Wilhelm,** Gernot. *Grundzüge der Geschichte und Kultur der Hurriter.* Darmstadt: Wissenschaftliche Buchgesellschaft, 1982. E.T. *The Hurrians.* Translated by Jennifer Barnes, with a chapter by Diana L. Stein. Warminster: Aris & Phillips, 1989.

HITTITES: **Bittel,** Kurt. *Die Hethiter.* Munich: Beck, 1976. **Cornelius,** Friedrich. *Geschichte der Hethiter.* 4th ed. Darmstadt: Wissenschaftliche Buchgesellschaft, 1990. **Götze,** Albrecht. *Kleinasien zur Hethiterzeit: Ein geographische Untersuchung.* Heidelberg: C. Winter, 1924. **Gurney,** Oliver R. *The Hittites.* Revised ed. London and New York: Penguin, 1990.

SYRIA AND PALESTINE: **Giveon,** Raphael. *Les bédouins Shosu des documents égyptiens.* Documenta et monumenta orientis antiqui 18. Leiden: E. J. Brill, 1971.

Kempinski, Aharon. *Syrien und Palästina (Kanaan) in der letzten Phase der Mittelbronze IIB-Zeit (1650–1570 v.Chr.)*. Wiesbaden: O. Harrassowitz, 1983. **Van Seters**, John. *The Hyksos: A New Investigation*. New Haven: Yale University Press, 1966.

Undoubtedly, the Near Eastern population at the start of the second millennium predominantly spoke Amorite; however, several other groups claimed their own unique origins and languages. For instance, the Alalakh documents mention the Hurrian-speaking population in Syria during the Middle Bronze Age. This group became an influential ethnic factor in Syrian society, especially in the northern part of the region.

These Hurrians are remembered by the Old Testament historians, who refer to the Hurrites as Horites, a part of the pre-Israelite Palestinian population. However, they were not just a minority group in ancient Palestine. Their language was unique among their ancient Near Eastern neighbors; that is, it does not share a common ancestor but belongs to an independent and hitherto unidentified language family. It is often assumed that the Hurrians migrated to the Near East at the beginning of the second millennium B.C.E. This was hardly the case. It is reasonable to think that they, like the Amorites, already belonged to the periphery of the urban society before that period. While the Amorites lived in the steppe region, the Hurrians clustered in the mountainous regions of northern and northeastern Mesopotamia. Consequently, they largely appropriated Syro-Mesopotamian culture and utilized Mesopotamia's writing system (Akkadian cuneiform). Rather than composing their written material in Akkadian, the Hurrians combined cuneiform with their indigenous tongue to form their own distinctive written language. Most scholars agree that these people contributed few cultural innovations to the ancient Near East. The one exception is the horse, which they introduced to the Near East. In fact, the Hurrians produced the first textbook on horse breeding, although it is preserved only in a Hittite translation.

By the end of the seventeenth century the Hurrians found their window of opportunity when the Hittites destroyed Aleppo and Yamkhad. The Hittites were to become a dominant power of the Late Bronze Age; however, after they trounced Aleppo, they retreated to their home in the Anatolian mountain region of Asia Minor. Nevertheless, in a short time, they completely reconfigured the Syrian political landscape. They were not content with their historic Aleppo adventure; rather, they sent another military expedition to Babylon and conquered it. Consequently, Hammurabi's dynasty and Amorite dominance in Mesopotamia vanished from history.

The Hittite invasions left a power vacuum in northern Syria and Mesopotamia and created a situation roughly equivalent to the aftereffects of Naram-Sin's destruction of Ebla. This time, however, local circumstances that also included the participation of the Hurrians prevented political anarchy in Syria. Thus in northern Syria the local Amorite authorities had already yielded their positions to Hurrian masters. A generation after the downfall of Yamkhad, the Hurrians ruled a substantial empire called Mitanni. The political center of this state was situated in Upper Mesopotamia. During its height, Mitanni's borders were far reaching: from the Mediterranean Sea in the west, to the Zagros Mountains in the east, a territory that included the southern part of Asia Minor and virtually all of Syria. Mitanni's southern border stood only fifty kilometers north of Damascus. For many years, scholars searched for the exact location of Washukanni, the capital of the vast Hurrian empire. Today it is normally equated with Tell al-Fakhariyeh on the Euphrates River. Besides, maybe Washukanni played the same role as the urban centers of the other short-lived Near Eastern empires: originally city-states of limited importance that rose to eminence, only to experience decline and subsequent reduction to their original status. The Hurrian empire was clearly bigger than any of its predecessors, and its importance to Syria's transition from the Middle Bronze to the Late Bronze Age is undeniable. Yet it soon proved to be no more stable than those that came before it. Like other large Syrian states, Mitanni soon waned. Ultimately, its heritage vanished without a trace.

Palestine's experience during the Middle Bronze Age differed to some degree from that of Syria, since Egypt dominated the political landscape. Perhaps it is better to describe the situation in this way: Palestine was part of a political system of small states that developed in northern Egypt at the end of the Middle Kingdom. Ironically, the Egyptians did not conquer Palestine; instead several Amorite states appeared in Egypt that were politically allied with their cousin states of Palestine.

A portrait of this period is recorded in the reflections of the third-century B.C.E. Egyptian priest Manetho, who was commissioned by the Greek Ptolemies to write a history of Egypt and list its dynasties. Among other things, he describes a cruel population of shepherds who at the end of the Middle Kingdom swept down from Asia to Egypt, destroyed the Egyptian forces and established a large empire. Manetho calls these people the Hyksos: a Greek version of the Egyptian word *ḥk3–ḫ3sw.t* (i.e., "rulers of foreign lands"). Later tradition understood the Hyksos as "the shepherd kings" because ostensibly, they were Asian nomads who invaded Egypt. Manetho's picture of the Hyksos was often repeated by modern Egyptologists who saw them as representatives of a major migration movement that hit Egypt around the middle of the seventeenth century. They considered the majority of these Asiatic people to be Hurrians who ousted Egyptian authorities and established a large empire whose capital was Avaris in the Nile Delta. Their place of origin—Palestine—became a province of this state.

Manetho's Description of the Hyksos Invasion

Tutimaeus. In his reign, for what cause I know not, a blast of God smote us; and unexpectedly, from the regions of the East, invaders of obscure race marched in confidence of victory against our land. By main force they easily seized it without striking a blow; and having overpowered the rulers of the land, they then burned our cities ruthlessly, razed to the ground the temples of the gods, and treated all the natives with a cruel hostility, massacring some and leading into slavery the wives and children of others. Finally, they appointed as king one of their number whose name was Salitis. He had his seat at Memphis, levying tribute from Upper and Lower Egypt, and always leaving garrisons behind in the most advantageous positions. Above all, he fortified the district to the east, foreseeing that the Assyrians, as they grew stronger, would one day covet and attack his kingdom.

In the Saïte [Sethroïte] nome he found a city very favourably situated on the east of the Bubastite branch of the Nile, and called Avaris after an ancient religious tradition. This place he rebuilt and fortified with massive walls, planting there a garrison of as many as 240,000 heavily-armed men to guard his frontier. Here he would come in summer-time, partly to serve out rations and pay his troops, partly to train them carefully in maneuvers and so strike terror into foreign tribes. . . .

Their race as a whole was called Hyksôs, that is 'king-shepherds': for *hyk* in the sacred language means 'king,' and *sôs* in common speech is 'shepherd' or 'shepherds': hence the compound word 'Hyksôs'. Some say that they were Arabs.[34]

This Hyksos tradition is not totally without historical foundation. From 1650–1550 B.C.E., northern Egypt was dominated by Asiatics and the actual Hyksos headquarters stood at Avaris. To that extent, Manetho's description of the Hyksos rule is based on historical events. A review of the Hyksos phenomenon will tell us that few Hurrians participated. Most Hyksos were Amorites closely related to the population that dominated Palestine and Syria in the Middle Bronze Age. The Amorites did not "invade" Egypt; rather, Asiatic incursions were protracted throughout the Middle Kingdom period. Existing economic alliances between Egypt and its Near Eastern neighbors solidified this immigration.

---

[34] Translation from Josephus's *Contra Apionem* 1.14, as found in *Manetho* (trans. W. G. Waddell; Loeb Classical Library; Cambridge, Mass.: Harvard University Press, 1940, 79–85).

Manetho's alleged invasions turn out to be a long process that changed the population landscape of northern Egypt. It culminated when these Asians assumed power as Egyptian rule dissolved in northern Egypt, bringing an end to the crumbling Middle Kingdom. The Amorites, however, did not unite into one mighty state but created a number of small city-states very similar to what was found in their homeland. Avaris also owed its position to this old tradition of political organization now transplanted to Egyptian territory. Avaris became the major center of Amorite influence while a number of satellite states appeared that were allied to Avaris but ruled by their own "kings," all of whom were clients and vassals of the ruler of a particular metropolis. The Hyksos empire was not an "empire" as the Egyptian tradition would see it; rather, it replicated the power structure of the Near East: several relatively small, quasi-independent communities that more or less closed ranks in a voluntary and cooperative confederation.

The traditional names of their kings indicate that most Hyksos could claim Amorite bloodlines; in fact, the mingling of the Egyptian and Asiatic cultural heritage highlighted the genuinely syncretistic Hyksos period. During this time, the Amorite intruders adopted Egyptian script (hieroglyphics) and worshiped their traditional gods of Asia. They imported these gods to Egypt, where they dressed them up like Egyptian deities. Rumors of Hyksos cruelty became fashionable during the pharaonic propaganda of the New Kingdom and became eternal truths in Manetho's later depictions of them. However, the evidence does not indicate that the Hyksos committed genocide or oppressed the Egyptian populace.

Ultimately, the Egyptians never accepted Asiatics as naturalized citizens. In the sixteenth century B.C.E., the early pharaohs of the 18th Dynasty boasted of how they were able to "liberate" Egypt from foreign oppression. Manetho put a real Hellenistic spin on this situation: through his hubris, the Hyksos king of Avaris defied the pharaoh—an action that had dire consequences for his people. The fate of Hyksos rule in Egypt was sealed. Soon after expelling the Hyksos, the Egyptians began to advance into Asia. The tables were turned: the Asiatics lost their grip on Egypt while Egypt established its influence on Asia. The Egyptians changed habits. No longer peaceful traders and merchants, they became conquerors ready to establish their sway over large parts of Western Asia. The aftereffects for the societies of Syria and Palestine were ominous. In the ensuing centuries, Syria and Palestine became the political footballs of the great powers whose centers stood outside the Near East.

II.5.4. SYRIA AND PALESTINE AS THE LAND OF BOOTY FOR THE GREAT POWERS

GENERAL: **Kitchen**, Kenneth. *Suppiluliuma and the Amarna Pharaohs: A Study in Relative Chronology.* Liverpool Monographs in Archaeology and Oriental Studies.

Liverpool: Liverpool University Press, 1962. **Kitchen,** Kenneth. *Pharaoh Triumphant: The Life and Times of Ramesses II, King of Egypt.* Warminster: Aris & Phillips, 1982. **Liverani,** Mario, ed. *La Siria nel tardo bronzo.* Rome: Centro per le antichità e la storia dell'arte del vicino oriente, 1969. **Liverani,** Mario. *Three Amarna Essays.* Translated by Matthew L. Jaffe. Sources and Monographs on the Ancient Near East 1.5. Malibu: Undena, 1979. **Murnane,** William J. *The Road to Kadesh.* Chicago: University of Chicago, 1985. **Redford,** Donald B. *Akhenaten: The Heretic King.* Princeton: Princeton University Press, 1984. **Redford,** Donald B. *Egypt and Canaan in the New Kingdom.* Edited by Shmuel Ahituv. Beer-Sheva Studies by the Department of Bible and Ancient Near East, Ben-Gurion University of the Negev, Faculty of Humanities and Social Sciences 4. Beer-Sheva: Ben-Gurion University of the Negev Press, 1990.

UGARIT: **Kinet,** Dirk. *Ugarit: Geschichte und Kultur einer Stadt in der Umwelt des Alten Testamentes.* Stuttgarter Bibelstudien 104. Stuttgart: Katholisches Bibelwerk, 1981. **Young,** Gordon D. *Ugarit in Retrospect.* Winona Lake, Ind.: Eisenbrauns, 1981.

Center and periphery changed their characters in the Late Bronze Age (1550–1200 B.C.E.). In Syria and Palestine, the traditional *centers* of small states became the *periphery* of the large state centers, under whose repression they fell. Although these large states had always stood at the same place, they usually played only an indirect, though significant, role in Bronze Age Syria and Palestine. Certainly, the economic influence of those large states was critical in perpetuating the urban populations of the Near East. If the major northeastern and southwestern powers sank into chaos or political decay, the consequences for the destinies of Syrian and Palestinian society would be striking and unmistakable. Geographically, Syria-Palestine stood on the fringe; therefore, it could not depend on its own resources to survive such political and economic upheaval. Conversely, if the larger states flourished and expanded, they did so at the expense of the small states of Syria and Palestine.

From the Egyptian and Mesopotamian perspectives, Syria and Palestine were always considered a peripheral and subordinate backwoods, economically and politically. In the Late Bronze Age, the great powers effected a political metamorphosis by interfering in and ultimately taking over all of the small states in Syria and Palestine. Consequently, the two regional powers confronted each other, and at least theoretically entered into reciprocal trade agreements, without regard for the theater within which they operated.

These conquests had profound effects. Now Babylonian merchants could travel to Egypt along traditional trade routes unfettered by the previously encountered difficulties and dangers. Although the routes remained, now Babylonian and Egyptian merchants could conclude their own deals without the annoying tolls and intermediaries of the former Syrian and Palestinian authorities.

Income from this trade for the small Syro-Palestinian princes was very limited, although they attempted to create a market of their own within the international trade system. The kings of the Mediterranean coastal cities were particularly fortunate in this regard, for they could garner income by charging merchants who used their harbors for dock space. Sometimes, this commercial scheme generated significant income, as in the case of Late Bronze Age Ugarit, where the great and renowned royal palace showcases the spoils of that city's commercial acumen.[35] Yet the Syrian and Palestinian kings faced other problems. For example, their masters, the great kings, obliged them to solve all kinds of problems that arose along the trade routes. Documents from the era describe the character of such obligations and also tell us how they solved them: the problems were passed on to smaller, local communities. Sometimes commercial agents of the great kings were attacked, plundered, or even killed. If the state could not catch the offender, it would develop specific plans to obtain compensation. In some cases the entire population of the offender's home village would be held liable for the debts he had incurred.

Other trade problems had to be handled by the great kings themselves. This was particularly true with the exchange of precious merchandise. Often, a recipient would propagandize the reception of goods to increase his own prestige at the expense of the sender. In an Amarna letter, the king of Babylon complains to pharaoh about his depiction of Babylonian merchandise as "offerings."[36] From an Egyptian view, these "offerings" were tributes or taxes that were required of inferior, foreign kings. The pharaoh had to mollify his Babylonian colleague by asserting that the description of the Babylonian goods as tribute was merely propaganda intended to be used only within Egypt. Thus, this type of rhetoric was intended for Egyptian ears only. Presumably, the Mesopotamians used the same ploy; that is, Egyptian merchandise (frequently gold) was perhaps described as tribute or tax.

---

[35] Visitors to Ras Shamra/Ugarit are invariably surprised by the size and workmanship of this palace. It dwarfs all other sections of the city. The conspicuous palace ruins date to the mid-fourteenth century B.C.E. In this period the palace was either built or greatly expanded. Yet the Ugarit palace was renowned even before its reconstruction, so much so that it is mentioned prominently in the previously cited letter of Abimilki of Tyre (EA 151; see the full translation by Moran in *Amarna Letters*, 238–39).

[36] In EA 1:89–92 (for a translation, see Moran, *Amarna Letters*, 2), Kadashman-Enlil II complains because his chariots—evidently gifts from one great king to another—are placed among the chariots of the "mayors," that is, as tribute (the vassals of pharaoh are generally called mayors). On this phenomenon, see Mario Liverani, *Prestige and Interest: International Relations in the Near East, ca. 1600–1100 B.C.* (Padova: Sargon, 1990), 255–66.

Apart from such "minor" problems that inevitably arose when trade agreements between the great powers were used especially to create prestige and customarily included luxury goods, the Late Bronze Age international climate particularly favored the development of commerce. The question is how this happened, why it happened, and, moreover, why it happened so abruptly and without an intermediary period between the Middle and the Late Bronze Ages. Why did we not see another change between center and periphery in Syria and Palestine? Why did the political situation change in such a profound way without serious social upheavals like the ones that followed the breakdown of the Early Bronze Age political system?

First, to prevent a renewed marginalization of the region, the neighboring great powers intervened militarily and occupied Syria and Palestine. In this way, they sought to monitor the situation in Syria and Palestine. Unlike five hundred years earlier, no power vacuum existed during the transition from the Middle to Late Bronze Ages. Close to the borders of Syria and Palestine great and resourceful states existed that were able to master whatever kinds of problems might arise during the transition. The conquest of Syria and Palestine, however, should not be seen as something that happened overnight. It was more like a process that involved a number of great powers competing for supremacy over Syria and Palestine. The great kings only agreed on one thing: regional control would not be relinquished to local princes.

The Late Bronze Age began with northern Syria under Mitanni's control. Mitanni was a large, powerful, centralized Hurrian state whose size, political clout, and economic influence more than rivaled that of the former Syrian power center of Yamkhad. In some respects, Mitanni was more of a northern Mesopotamian state, since its center was situated on the banks of the Euphrates River. In comparison to Mitanni, Syria never had more than a peripheral importance. When Mitanni conquered northern Syria, the occupation involved some bloodshed, and some cities were destroyed; however, the Syrian urban civilization mostly survived unharmed. Palestine, on the other hand, remained practically unscathed by the events in Syria because it maintained a loose affiliation with the Hyksos regime of the Nile Delta.

The end of the Middle Bronze Age culture in Palestine came when Egyptian armies pursued the retreating Hyksos forces to their bases in Palestine and Syria. This marks the beginning of the Egyptian New Kingdom (the second half of the sixteenth century B.C.E.). In the process, the Egyptians armies managed to conquer vast stretches of the region. Through these adventures, they hoped to expunge every vestige of the Asian "menace." In the following century, most of Syria would fall under Egyptian control. More than any other pharaoh, Tuthmosis III (ca. 1458–1425 B.C.E.) succeeded in this conquest. He advanced as far north as the Euphrates River, crossed it, and dealt Mitanni a vicious blow. Although he did not completely destroy it, Tuthmosis sealed Mitanni's doom. More importantly, because of his menacing presence, he successfully exacted tribute from several distant lands, including Aleppo, Alalakh, Adana (in Cilicia), and even the Hittites of Asia Minor.

From the reign of Tuthmosis III through the Late Bronze Age and into the Early Iron Age (ca. 1150 B.C.E.), Egypt retained its foothold in Western Asia. At its heyday, this vast Egyptian empire stretched from northern Nubia (present day Sudan) to the banks of the Euphrates River, a distance of more than 2,000 kilometers.

Palestine's urban centers were broken battlements by the late sixteenth century B.C.E., the result of relentless pounding by Egyptian forces. Archaeological excavations have unearthed several destruction layers. After the Egyptians consolidated their control of Palestine, the dreadful local situation soon improved. Most cities were rebuilt within a relatively short period of time on their Middle Bronze Age sites (although it is possible to establish the extent of the rebuilding only when the total area of a city is excavated, something that almost never happens).[37] Ultimately, the cultural transition from the Middle Bronze to Late Bronze Age was relatively smooth, that is, culturally the latter was primarily a continuation of the former. There was no interim period and, from an archaeological perspective, little distinguishes the Middle and Late Bronze Ages. In Palestine, the differences were political: native sovereigns ruled during the Middle Bronze Age; Egyptian officials governed during the Late Bronze Age.

Mitanni's will to survive kept international relations unsettled for many years, continuing as it did for almost eighty years after the campaign of Tuthmosis III. Between 1440 and 1360, Syria became a military staging area for battles between Egypt and Mitanni. Consequently, official boundaries remained constantly in flux until the two great powers arrived at a mutually agreeable compromise. The border between Mitanni and Egyptian territory would stretch from just north of Ugarit to south of Aleppo and Alalakh. This compromise settled the issue between Egypt and Mitanni. However, Mitanni soon faced a new threat from the revitalized Hittite state, a situation exacerbated by a series of treaties that guaranteed the Hittite conquest and control of Asia Minor. In these agreements, local princes owed allegiance to the Hittite king and in return were granted some rights of protection as well as other privileges. Once they secured Asia Minor, the Hittites stretched their tentacles into Syria.

---

[37] Not every city experienced a renaissance. For example, Jericho (Tell al-Sultan) did not recover from its destruction around 1550 B.C.E. By the pre-Israelite period, Jericho was no longer a significant settlement and a new urban foundation would not rise again until the ninth century, contrary to the Old Testament story of Joshua's defeat of Jericho. After all, the site was virtually deserted, with nothing more to conquer.

Either its belated reaction to the Hittite menace or its already weakened condition crippled Mitanni's will to retaliate. Consequently, Suppiluliumas I (ca. 1370–1342 B.C.E.)[38] seized and destroyed Mitanni's capital at Washukanni, whereupon the Hittites secured most of the Mitanni empire. The Hurrians were relegated to the backwoods of Hanigalbat in Upper Mesopotamia and after a long period of internal deterioration were absorbed into the growing Middle Assyrian state. During its heyday, Mitanni generally maintained political control of the northern Mesopotamia hinterlands. In the aftermath of Mitanni's demise, Assyria reclaimed its independence, reasserted its imperial designs, and, by the end of the Late Bronze Age, became an imposing force throughout the Near East.

The Prologue to the Treaty between Mursilis II of Hatti and Duppi-Tessub of Amurru

These are the words of the Sun Mursilis, the great king, the king of the Hatti land, the valiant, the favorite of the Storm-god, the son of Suppiluliumas, the great king, the king of the Hatti land, the valiant.

Aziras was the grandfather of you Duppi-Tessub. He rebelled against my father, but submitted again to my father. When the kings of Nuhasse land and the kings of Kinza rebelled against my father, Aziras did not rebel. As he was bound by treaty, he remained bound by treaty. As my father fought against his enemies, in the same manner fought Aziras. Aziras remained loyal toward my father [as his overlord] and did not incite my father's anger. My father was loyal towards Aziras and his country; he did not undertake any unjust action against him or incite his or his country's anger in any way. 300 (shekels of) refined and first-class gold, the tribute which my father had imposed on your father, he brought year for year; he never refused it.[39]

Suppiluliumas's defeat of his north Syrian rivals and the ensuing Hittite incursions into middle and southern Syria led to an inevitable col-

---

[38] The study of ancient chronology is a science of its own. The Hittite chronology is especially beset with problems. Thus scholars' assessments of the date of Suppiluliumas I may differ by almost forty years. Some scholars will place Suppiluliumas I as late as 1344–1322 B.C.E. This is only one example among others. Ramesses II (see below) may according to some authorities have begun his reign in 1304 B.C.E. Other scholars prefer to place his first year in 1279 B.C.E. For further discussion of ancient Near Eastern chronology, see Frederick H. Cryer, "Chronology: Issues and Problems," in *Civilizations of the Ancient Near East*, 2:651–64.

[39] Translated by Albrecht Goetze in *ANET*, 203. See also the translation by Gary Beckman in *Hittite Diplomatic Texts*, 54–59.

lision between Egyptian and Hittite forces. When Suppiluliumas set his eyes on the Egyptian possessions in Syria, Egypt was ruled by a pharaoh who would not put himself—in person—in front of his armies and fight the Hittites. That was nothing new. Since the days of Tuthmosis III, the Egyptian operations in Syria and Palestine were generally conducted by high-ranking officers, though the pharaoh claimed the glory for himself. Furthermore, by the time of Hittite incursions into Syria, Egypt was being torn apart by a cultural crisis created by its provocative pharaoh, Amenophis IV (ca. 1352–1336 B.C.E.). This pharaoh preferred to concentrate on internal affairs, such as the religious situation in his kingdom, and spent little time speculating about the political and military situations in Palestine and Syria.

Amenophis, better known as Akhenaten, is especially renowned for his reformation of Egyptian religion. "Akhenaten" was a "throne name" that expressed his religious program, namely, his devotion to the god Aten. The king assumed this name as evidence of his conflict with the mighty priesthood of the god Amun of Thebes in Upper Egypt. Amenophis's reforms threatened grave political and financial consequences for those priests and undermined their privileges and status. After all, in the eyes of the priesthood, Amun represented a supreme deity over whom no other gods could be placed or worshiped. Consequently, Amun and his priests posed a threat to the state's unity and stability. It is too early to speak about a practical monotheism (this happened only at a later date when two rival traditions coalesced: the Upper Egyptian Amun and Lower Egyptian sun-god, Re^{c}). For his part, Akhenaten served the sun as *the* god; however, it was not the image of the hybrid Amun-Re^{c}, but the sun-disc of Aten. This might have been a transparent appeal to the uneducated masses. Clearly, it was a conscious attempt to eradicate the power of the priesthood, a goal that was supported by the simultaneous construction of his new capital north of Thebes, the present-day Tell el-Amarna.[40]

It has often been assumed that Akhenaten's interest in religious affairs prevented the Egyptians from defending their interests in Asia. Nowadays, most Egyptologists have changed opinion and no longer see him exclusively as a religious reformer—and with good reason. Today, we place more scholarly emphasis on the political and economic factors

---

40 Egyptologists and Old Testament scholars alike have attempted without success to draw tidy comparisons between Akhenaten's religion and Mosaic monotheism, most notably William F. Albright. In his seductive work, *From the Stone Age to Christianity* (2d ed.; Garden City, New York: Doubleday, 1940), Albright argues that Mosaic monotheism presupposes a similar notion in Akhenaten. Albright describes the long, inexorable march toward Christian monotheism that begins in the ancient Near East and culminates in the revelation of Jesus Christ, "in the fullness of time" (see his last chapter).

that caused the pharaoh to assault the privileges of the Amun priesthood. His religious "reformation" was really a continuation of changes set in motion many years earlier. Furthermore, during Akhenaten's reign, Egypt still launched retaliatory strikes against the Hittites. As the documents clearly show, Egypt retained a significant military presence at its northern frontier throughout Akhenaten's reign. Egyptian officials did everything within their power to preserve, protect, and defend its Asian empire—without, however, much chance of success. The Hittites pushed relentlessly southward. In the end, the situation stabilized along a border between the Hittite and Egyptian zones, which followed a line somewhere between Hamath and Damascus.

As fate would have it, Egyptian prisoners of war deported to Asia Minor brought with them a plague that significantly weakened the Hittites and claimed the life of its conqueror-king Suppiluliumas I, as well as much of Anatolia's population. Hittite documents from the ensuing period eloquently testify to the pathos and dread that accompanied this calamity, especially the poem of lament composed by King Mursilis II (ca. 1340–1310 B.C.E.), a prayer to the gods for deliverance from the pestilence. As result of this terrible blight, the Hittites could not exploit the chaotic situation that raged in Egypt after Akhenaten's death. Following the death of the heretic pharaoh, the royal priesthood at Thebes reclaimed its prestige and consolidated its power under the newly crowned Tut^{c}ankhamun. Finally, the weakened Hittites and consolidated Egyptians entered into a territorial compromise that led to an uneasy peace in Syria and Palestine. That peace—it was no more than a truce—was no bargain. Lasting economic stability remained an unfulfilled dream.

The Egyptians were partly to blame for the breakdown of this brittle peace. In 1275 B.C.E., the renowned Ramesses II (ca. 1279–1213 B.C.E.) launched a massive assault to reestablish the Egyptian empire in Syria. This campaign stopped near the gates of the Syrian city of Qadesh, where Ramesses II's expedition was ambushed by a Hittite army led—in person—by the Hittite king Muwatallis. That spelled an end to the Egyptian expansion northward. After a few more years of wrangling, Ramesses II and the new Hittite king Hattusilis III (ca. 1275–1260) reached a peace accord written in the form of a treaty that delineated the imperial boundaries between the two great powers. A short period of apparent peace ensued that changed the entire political climate of Syria and Palestine. First, a new spirit of cooperation overtook the two great kings. Relations between the royal houses of Hatti and Egypt improved so dramatically that interdynastic marriages became a real option. However, problems arose almost immediately. Although Hittite princes and princesses came to Egypt, no Egyptian princesses were brought to Anatolia. Moreover, the efforts of Egyptian and Hittite officials to arrange a state visit to Egypt by Hattusilis III came to naught.

Many suggestions have been offered to explain the breakdown of the Hittite-Egyptian peace. Perhaps both empires were exasperated by ongoing disputes, but Egypt's internal problems especially contributed to this impasse. Now the pharaoh once again tried to curtail the power and influence of the priests of Amun. The shift of the imperial capital from Upper Egypt (Thebes) to Lower Egypt (Tanis) under the Ramesside pharaohs was one sign of this struggle for political and economical control. Tanis was close to the ancient worship site of Re^{c} at On (Heliopolis). If the Ramesside pharaohs were not attempting to dismantle the traditional religious framework of the empire, surely they sought to strengthen the position of the priest of On at the expense of the priesthood of Amun. Their efforts apparently failed, for Amun's priests reached the zenith of their power when their high priest became the ruler of Upper Egypt. Other problems arose on Egypt's western borders, where Libyan tribes pressed forward into Egypt. After a few generations, Libyan chieftains integrated into Egyptian territories, so much so that by the first millennium B.C.E., a dynasty of Libyan origin—the 22d Dynasty—gained control of all of Egypt.

The Hittites also faced serious problems that included threats from the Assyrians and mountain-based tribes. The destruction of Mitanni cleared a path for Assyrian expansion. Consequently, the aggressive, vigorous, and ambitious kings of the Middle Assyrian empire made formidable foes for the Hittites. Initially, Hattusas's king categorically refused to bargain with the Assyrian kings and rejected most of their proposed agreements. Fine examples of such Assyrian overtures come from a series of letters exchanged between the kings of Hatti and the Assyrian kings Shalmaneser I (1274–1245 B.C.E.) and Tukulti-Ninurta I (1244–1208 B.C.E.). The kings of Ashur tried in vain to establish good relations with their colleagues in Hattusas, but the Hittite answers were very plain and rude: they would have nothing to do with Ashur.[41] Of course, Assyria was only a shadow of what it would become; thus, this tense relationship did not damage the well-being of the Hittite state. Another more ominous menace was on the horizon. North and northeast of Hatti there lived a mountain tribe known as the Kaskas whom the Hittites could never pacify. In this dispute we find a new twist to an old problem: the tension between center and periphery becoming acute because of the weakening of the center.

[41] The correspondence opens with the Assyrian king asking for permission to visit a sanctuary in the Amanus Mountains, deep in Hittite territory. To drive home his request, the king of Ashur claims to be the "brother" of the king of Hatti, that is, his peer. His claim and request are unceremoniously denied. The Hittite king bluntly denies both friendship and brotherhood. He will not accept the king of Ashur as his equal. For an English translation of some of this correspondence, see Gary Beckman, *Hittite Diplomatic Texts* (Atlanta: Scholars Press, 1996), 141–42, and for a discussion, see Liverani, *Prestige and Interest*, 66–78 and 197–202.

The seriousness of the political problems in the Hittite heartland surfaces in the instructions to the commander of a Hittite garrison located only a few miles north of Hattusas at the border of the Kaskas territory. In daytime, the Hittite troops could move freely around their campsite, while at night they had to close and guard the gate to protect themselves against marauding tribesmen from the mountains around the camp.[42]

The exact circumstances surrounding the downfall of the Hittite nation around 1180 B.C.E. remain a mystery. One possible scenario stands out: Kaskas tribesmen attacked the capital of Hattusas because its population was decimated by a disastrous famine that precluded any sustained defense of the city. Similarly, the famine finally forced the Kaskas to try a desperate remedy for *their* plight, namely, a raid on the seemingly strongly defended capital of Hattusas. Although we cannot concretely verify these hypotheses, we do know that a long famine raged in Asia Minor only a few years before Hatti's downfall. Pharaoh Merneptah (ca. 1213–1202 B.C.E.) tried unilaterally to mollify the effects of this catastrophe by sending ships filled with grain to his Hittite comrades—in its time, an unprecedented measure.

Egypt temporarily benefited from this situation since it successfully retained its possessions in Palestine and southern Syria. Ultimately, however, the Egyptian empire was also condemned to its own demise. Below we will outline more details of this dissolution process. For now, we conclude with a significant fact: Ramesses VI (ca. 1144–1136 B.C.E.) was ostensibly the last pharaoh to rule over Palestine. After him, the population of Palestine was free to go its own way.[43]

II.5.5. The Palace State and the Organizational Structure of the Empires

Buccellati, Giorgio. *Cities and Nations of Ancient Syria: An Essay on Political Institutions with Special Reference to the Israelite Kingdoms.* Rome: Istituto di studi del vicino oriente, Università di Roma, 1967. **Heltzer,** Michael. *The Rural Community in Ancient Ugarit.* Wiesbaden: Reichert, 1976. **Heltzer,** Michael. *The Internal Organization of the Kingdom of Ugarit.* Wiesbaden: Reichert, 1982. **Liverani,** Mario. "La royauté syrienne de l'age du bronze récent." In *Le palais et la royauté, archéologie et civilisation.* Edited by Paul Garelli. Pages 329–56. Paris: P. Geuthner, 1974. **Liverani,** Mario. "Ville et campagne dans la royaume d'Ugarit: Essai d'analyse économique." *Societies and Languages of the Ancient Near East: Studies in Honour of I. M. Diakonoff.* Pages 250–58. Warminster: Aris & Phillips, 1982.

[42] For a translation of these instructions, see Gregory McMahon, "Instructions to Commanders of Border Garrisons," *COS* 1.84, 221–22.

[43] There are some hints of Egyptian strongholds in Palestine as late as the tenth century B.C.E., particularly at Beth-shan. This, however, is not the place to discuss this question in detail.

We are indeed fortunate to have at our disposal many reliable documents that describe the history and culture of Late Bronze Age Syria and Palestine. These sources allow us not only to reconstruct the political history of the Near East and its smaller component parts but also to study the social history of Syria and Palestine in more detail. It is thus possible to describe both the internal organization of the petty states of Syria and Palestine in the Late Bronze Age and the societal consequences of their incorporation into the larger empires of Egypt and Hatti. Of these source materials, Ugarit's are by far the most extensive, supplemented by the Alalakh documents. The Amarna letters are important sources for the Egyptian area of Asia. The Hittite state archives from Hattusas provide other important evidence. When compared to Egyptian sources, the Hittite documents show that the organization of the Hittite empire was very different from its Egyptian counterpart.

There is one common denominator when analyzing the organizational structure of Syria and Palestine: large or small, every state was structured along analogous sociopolitical lines. Of course, each state's power structures had its individual nuances that resulted from local environmental factors and sociopolitical traditions. Generally, Syria's organizational structures were fully developed while Palestine's remained relatively primitive.

Without exception, royal families ruled Syrian and Palestinian states. In cities as large as Ugarit and as small as the Palestinian mountain enclaves, ruling princes were called kings of their respective kingdoms. These rulers lived and built lavishly. After all, these kings needed palaces to conduct the affairs of state. The stature of these palaces corresponded to the resources and population of the states they controlled; however, one thing remained constant: they always towered above the unsightly hovels of ordinary citizens. The possession of these petty monarchies belonged to one princely line. If the prince's son could not succeed him, another legitimate blood relative would necessarily assume the mantel of power. In Syrian society, royal succession hinged on heredity—at least ideologically. Yet in practice, exceptions were common, especially when one royal family replaced another. For example, in Late Bronze Age Ugarit, one dynastic family legitimized its long reign by tracing its roots far into the "hoary primeval past." Yet some of the Ugaritic epic poetry[44] that describes the origin of the royal family are clearly legendary and cannot be considered historically accurate.

Ugarit had a social structure of four levels. The king and his family stood at the head of the society. Their retainers formed the next rung ("the king's men"), while people employed by this second level also claimed "royalty" ("the king's men's men"). The general populace simply formed the class

---

[44] For a detailed analysis of these poems, see section III.2.4.

of "the sons of Ugarit." Furthermore, the Ugarit sources clearly show that slaves stood at the base of this hierarchy. "The king's men" were the elite royalty who served the king and were paid by public means. Both high-ranking military and civil officers belonged to this stratum. Some of these officials were rewarded with grand estates. Although originally personal rewards, these estates soon turned into hereditary possessions. "The king's men's men" were second-class military and civil officials and specialists of the state "industry," namely, the craftsmen. Artisans worked for the state and manufactured exportable products. Other members of this stratum included merchants and their sales forces, all of whom worked under state auspices; however, in time, many of them became extraordinarily wealthy, semi-independent entrepreneurs. All other citizens fell into the category of "the sons of Ugarit." Although technically "free" citizens, they belonged to the low stratum of society. They lived in villages and throughout the state's incorporated region, and their freedom hinged on the ability to produce foodstuffs. For Ugarit, these "sons" provided an essential tax base from which it could draw the necessary funds to underwrite state projects and maintain infrastructure. They also served as an unskilled labor force available to the state authorities for building projects. Most citizens fell into this stratum.

In a state organized along such lines, it is a qualified guess that at least 80 percent of the overall population lived outside the capital. Thus, Ugarit's total population hovered around 50,000: 10,000 in the city and 40,000 distributed over the countryside—impressive figures for Syria in those days and impossible for Palestinian societies to reach. Eighty percent of the population were peasants who enjoyed an illusory freedom, for they lived in abject poverty. Some peasants were employed by state-operated estates; however, their plight remained equally bleak.

The history of Late Bronze Age Ugarit is that of a rather typical Syrian city-state. At the beginning of the Late Bronze Age, Ugarit was a dependency of the kings of Mitanni. Later, after the campaigns of Tuthmosis III, the Egyptians became the masters of Ugarit until Suppiluliumas I expanded the borders of the Hittite empire to include northern Syria. From the Hittite takeover to the end of the Late Bronze Age, Ugarit remained part of the Hittite empire. Only once did a Ugaritic king revolt, and he had no chance of success. By the end of the Late Bronze Age, Ugarit shared the fate of the Hittite empire, although the precise circumstances of its destruction remain obscure. By the start of the twelfth century B.C.E., the city was destroyed by either an earthquake, a foreign invasion, or both. Nonetheless, by about 1180 B.C.E., Ugarit was no longer a vibrant city; rather, it degenerated into the pile of hillside ruins known to modern visitors as Ras Shamra. Not until the Hellenistic period was a new city built in this region, modern Latakia, located a couple of miles from Ras Shamra.

The Palestinian states were configured under the same rubrics as those of Ugarit, dominated by kings and royal families who conducted state affairs from the royal palace. The palace entourage represented a small fraction of the population, the bulk of which remained peasants. Unlike their larger Syrian neighbors, Late Bronze Age Palestinian states contained few villages. The reasons for this remain obscure; however, several theoretical models may be suggested. Palestinian village life flourished during the Middle Bronze and Iron Ages; during the Late Bronze Age, however, demographic factors changed so dramatically that life outside major urban centers became virtually untenable. Palestinian villagers faced grave security issues and sought literal and figurative protection within the walls of the major cities. Relentless military incursions by Egyptian pharaohs obliterated the Hyksos and decimated the Palestinian countryside. Consequently, a battered population either fled, died from starvation, or was butchered by marauding soldiers. The survivors resettled in cities. Since most Palestinian city-states were very small, the distance between a city and its farmland generally presented no obstacles to peasants' living within the city.

Domestic resources—land and people—limited these Palestinian states. Most cities comprised only a few hectares and housed between 2,000 and 3,000 people. Territorial boundaries were also restricted, almost never exceeding 100 or 200 square kilometers. Under such conditions, most states were hard pressed to provide adequate foodstuffs for state officials and other notables within the upper echelons of society. Thus, the elite classes remained minute. Military organizations were nothing more than local, one-hundred- or two-hundred-man militias. Problems could normally be settled by a few scores of soldiers. Thus, when a local prince turns to pharaoh for help, he never asks for hundreds of Egyptian soldiers; a much more modest number was adequate.

The administrative and social organizations in Late Bronze Age Syria-Palestine were firmly centralized around an indomitable center, namely, the royal palace. In it, all important foreign and domestic affairs were conducted. Most palaces were surrounded by impressive physical plants within which craftsmen applied their trades in workshop annexes. It has become usual to describe the political system as the one of a "palace state": the palace dominated all aspects of political and economic life. Very few activities fell beyond the pale of its influence. Predictably, rigid centralization did not always produce perfect or successful administrations. For example, it never improved the harried lives of the general populace, most of whom suffered under heavy taxation and served as corvée laborers. Eventually nonexistent social welfare unleashed civil unrest that led to the decay and ultimate dissolution of the social fabric, at which time the periphery again overtook the center.

Local tribesmen were another wild card in this equation. In the Late Bronze Age, these mostly nomadic tribes were unwilling to acquiesce to any outside control—much less that of the royal palace or state confederations. Actually, most Palestinian states were too feeble to repel these outsiders or enlist their cooperation. Late Bronze Age documents refer to two main tribal entities: the Sutu (in Akkadian language documents), and the

Shasu (in Egyptian documents). We know very few details about the society and history of these groups; however, they were important enough to command the attention of the representatives of the local authorities as well as of the agents of the great powers throughout the region. State officials constantly fretted over the potential dangers these tribes presented; however, Late Bronze Age empires and tribal populations ultimately lived side by side in an uneasy relationship within which the periphery never overpowered the center.

The real powers-behind-the-powers in all the small Syrian and Palestinian states were the Egyptian pharaohs and Hittite kings (the last group succeeding the kings of Mitanni). Generally, these overlords steadfastly refused to recognize the "kingship" of local monarchs—at least in Palestine. Egyptians referred to most local princes and potentates with the title *ḫazannu* (Akkadian for "mayor"); these were low-ranking Egyptian officials employed by the pharaoh to administer his provinces. Above these officials, Egyptian emissaries or provincial governors oversaw mayoral activities from strategic locales scattered throughout the countryside. Among these "regional offices" were Hazor in Upper Galilee, Kumidu in Lebanon (the present-day Lebanese city of Kamid al-Loz), and Sumuru (Tell Kazel) in western Syria. Thus, the Egyptian empire operated in the first place as a network of garrisons that maintained its sovereignty throughout the Near East. This system was created to levy and collect taxes swiftly and efficiently; it was not concerned with the ordinary day-to-day problems of the Egyptian provinces.

Many problems developed from the Egyptian regional administration. Petty kings throughout Syria and Palestine faced great hardships in their roles as Egyptian officials, a role they did not know how to perform well. We must not forget that this Egyptian provincial administrative network was truly "bureaucratic," that is, the relationship between master and servant resembled the relationship between an employer and employee. Asiatic princes were employed by the Egyptian state and were paid accordingly—as they saw it, extremely insufficiently. As a matter of fact, Syrian and Palestinian petty kings persistently preferred to understand their relationship with the pharaoh in accordance with their own political tradition as a patron-client relationship, that is, they saw themselves as the clients of the pharaoh. Because of this, they probably expected more from their Egyptian master than he was ready to offer. They believed that they, as pharaoh's loyal servants, would enjoy the protection of the pharaoh, a protection that would also include their families. Many problems that appear in the Amarna letters reflect this misconception of the Egyptian system of administration. Still it cannot be excluded that some princes of Asia understood the situation very well and banked on the fact that pharaoh would not get involved in local affairs so long as taxes were paid and tribute delivered. This left them in a position to play their own power game without Egyptian interference.

A Letter from the King of Jerusalem to the Pharaoh

Say [t]o the king, my lord, [my Su]n: [M]essage of ᶜAbdi-Ḫeba, your servant. I fall at the feet of the king, my lord, 7 times and 7 times. Behold, the king, my lord, has placed his name at the rising of the sun and at the setting of the sun. It is, therefore, impious what they have done to me. Behold, I am not a mayor; I am a soldier of the king, my lord. Behold, I am a *friend* of the king and a tribute-bearer of the king. It was neither my father nor my mother, but the strong arm of the king that [p]laced me in the house of [my] fath[er]. [... c]ame to me... . [...] . I gave over [to *his* char]ge 10 slaves. Šuta, the commissioner of the king, ca[me t]o me; I gave over to Šuta's charge 21 girls, [8]0 prisoners, as a gift for the king, my lord. May the king give thought to his land; the land of the king is lost. *All of it has attacked* me. I am at war as far as the land of Šeru and as far as Ginti-kirmil. All the mayors are at peace, but I am at war. I am treated like an ᶜApiru, and I do not visit the king, my lord, since I am at war. I am situated like a ship in the midst of the sea. The strong hand (arm) of the king took the land of Naḫrima and the land of *Kasi*, but now the ᶜApiru have taken the very cities of the king. Not a single mayor remains to the king, my lord; all are lost. Behold, Turbazu was slain in the city gate of Silu. The king did nothing. Behold, servants who were joined to the ᶜApi[r]u *smote* Zimredda of Lakisu, and Yaptiḫ-Hadda was slain in the city gate of Silu. The king did nothing. [Wh]y has he not called them to account? May the king [pro]vide for [his land] and may he [se]e to it tha[t] archers [come ou]t to h[is] land. If there are no archers this year, all the lands of the king, my lord, are lost. If there are no archers this year, may the king send a commissioner to fetch me, me along with my brothers, and then we will die near the king, our lord. [To] the scribe of the king, my lord: [Message] of ᶜAbdi-Ḫeba, (your) servant. [I fa]ll a[t (your) feet]. Present [the words that I hav]e offered to [the king, my lord]: I am your servant [and] your [s]on.[45]

In the parts of Syria ruled by the Hittites, such problems never arose. The Hittites were themselves part of the traditional patronage system of western Asia. Even before Suppiluliumas I's invasion of Syria, the Hittites had already established an elaborate patronage system in Asia Minor. Although the patron always enjoyed substantial leverage, these connections were sealed with written contracts that benefited both parties—a system implemented by the Hittites after their takeover of Syria. When

[45] This translation of Amarna Letter 288 is from Moran's *Amarna Letters*, 331.

he agreed to oversee the welfare of his clients and their families, the king of Hatti expected services to be rendered and taxes (tributes) paid with unflagging fidelity. These contracts contained an important proviso: vassals were not allowed to meddle in international matters. They were expressly forbidden to make contact with the petty monarchs of the Egyptian zone.

Undoubtedly, even these well-conceived contracts could not prevent occasional uprisings against the Hatti regime. It would have been against the laws of nature, so to speak, for the Hittites to succeed completely in preventing their vassals from establishing relations with their colleagues across the border or even from getting involved in Egyptian affairs. The situation was particularly acute in the borderlands where every king sought to pit one neighboring empire against another for his own political or economic advantage. Among these tactics were international exchanges of contraband (smuggling!) and unilateral political alliances with competing empires. Even faithful vassals such as the king of Ugarit who engaged in such intrigue were punished for their actions—though never too harshly. However, when the king of the ancient Syrian political center at Carchemish once tried unsuccessfully to extract himself from the Hittite yoke, he and his family were removed from power. Soon Carchemish became a semi-autonomous state governed by a Hittite prince. Yet this political transformation had a residual benefit: Carchemish became the administrative regional headquarters for the Hittite provinces in Syria. Furthermore, the Hittite-born king of Carchemish became the governor or viceroy of the surrounding region, and Hittite bloodlines persisted well after the demise of the empire at the end of the Late Bronze Age. Consequently, the Hittites never vanished totally from the Syrian stage; rather, the resilience of the Hittite royal line led ultimately to its resuscitation in the so-called Neo-Hittite states of Syria in the first millennium B.C.E. This political regeneration probably explains why the Hittites never disappeared totally from the biblical or ancient Near Eastern traditions.

To show how this system worked, we will turn to the history of Amurru, a short-lived state that mirrors the fate of all small Syrian states during the Late Bronze Age. During the Amarna period, specifically, Amurru was a small state in the region between Ugarit and Byblos. Local monarchs controlled its political structure, sometimes as clients of Egypt, sometimes as clients of Hatti. Many local princes complained to pharaoh about the activity of the kings of Amurru: they were traitors who instigated rebellion against their lord (the complainant was, of course, always a loyal officer of the king!). More than one king of Amurru had to travel to Egypt to explain his intrigues—seemingly successfully as we hear of no retaliations from pharaoh. In one such case, after many excuses and apologies, King Aziru finally set off to Egypt to answer the charges leveled against him. Immediately upon his return, he went before the Hittite king to whom he swore eternal loyalty. That spelled an effective end to Amurru's independence. From then on Amurru remained a staunchly loyal vassal of Hatti, so much so that dynastic marriages between the client and patron states became a reality. Amurru was never to reappear as an independent state. Only for a short period could the princes of Amurru play the game of serving two masters without really obeying either one.

II.5.6. THE *HABIRU*, THE SEA PEOPLES, AND THE DISSOLUTION OF BRONZE AGE SOCIETY

GENERAL: **Liverani**, Mario. "The Collapse of the Near Eastern Regional System at the End of the Bronze Age." In *Center and Periphery in the Ancient World.* Edited by Michael Rowlands, Mogen Trolle Larsen, and Kristian Kristiansen. Pages 66–73. New Directions in Archaeology. Cambridge: Cambridge University Press, 1987. **Wertime**, Theodore A., and James D. **Muhly**, eds. *The Coming of the Age of Iron.* New Haven: Yale University Press, 1980.

THE *HABIRU:* **Bottéro**, Jean. *Le problème des Ḫabiru à la 4*^{e} *rencontre assyriologique internationale.* Cahiers de la Societé asiatique 13. Paris: Imprimerie Nationale, 1954. **Liverani**, Mario. "Il fuoruscitismo in Siria nella tarda età del bronzo." *Rivista storica italiana* 77 (1965): 315–36. **Loretz**, Oswald. *Habiru-Hebräer: Eine soziolinguistische Studie über die Herkunft des Gentiliziums* ʿibrî *vom Appellativum* ḫabiru. BZAW 160. Berlin: de Gruyter, 1984. **Rowton**, Michael B. "The Topological Factor in the *ḫapiru* Problem." *Assyriological Studies* 16 (1965): 375–87. **Rowton**, Michael B. "Dimorphic Structure and the Problem of the *ʿapirû-ʿibrîm.*" *JNES* 35 (1976): 13–20. **Rowton**, Michael B. "Dimorphic Structure and the Parasocial Element." *JNES* 36 (1977): 181–98.

THE SEA PEOPLE: **Crossland**, Ronald A., and Ann **Birchall**, eds. *Bronze Age Migrations in the Aegean: Archaeological and Linguistic Problems in Greek Prehistory.* Park Ridge, New Jersey: Noyes Press, 1974. **Dothan**, Trude. *The Philistines and Their Material Culture.* New Haven: Yale University Press, 1982. **Dothan**, Trude, and Moshe **Dothan**. *People of the Sea: The Search for the Philistines.* New York: Macmillan, 1992. **Helck**, Wolfgang. *Die Beziehungen Ägyptens und Vorderasiens zur Ägäis bis ins 7. Jahrhundert v.Chr.* Erträge der Forschung 120. Darmstadt: Wissenschaftliche Buchgesellschaft, 1979. **Noort**, Edward. *Die Seevölker in Palästina.* Palaestina antiqua 8. Kampen: Kok Pharos, 1994. **Sandars**, Nancy K. *The Sea Peoples: Warriors of the Ancient Mediterranean, 1250–1150 B.C.* Revised ed.; London: Thames and Hudson, 1985. **Strobel**, August. *Der spätbronzezeitliche Seevölkersturm.* BZAW 145. Berlin: de Gruyter, 1976.

PALESTINE: **Gonen**, Rivka. *Burial Patterns and Cultural Diversity in Late Bronze Age Canaan.* Dissertation Series of the American Schools of Oriental Research 7. Winona Lake, Ind.: Eisenbrauns, 1992.

Within the Amarna letter collection, six letters (EA 285–290) are from King Abdi-Heba of Jerusalem to the pharaoh. Among other things, these letters describe the destructive activity of certain people who, according to him, threaten the safety and security of the Egyptian regime in Palestine. Abdi-Heba refers to these people in Akkadian[46] as *amēlūtu*[47] *ḫa-bi-ri*.[48] When the Amarna letters first appeared in 1888, most scholars prematurely concluded that these *habiru* referred to the Old Testament Hebrews. For them, the linguistic connection between *habiru* and the Hebrew *ʿibrî* was unmistakable. Clearly, the Old Testament authors understood "Hebrew" to be another name for an "Israelite." In the Old Testament, most references to the Hebrews are found in the stories about the Israelites' Egyptian captivity, in the Joseph saga and the first part of the book of Exodus. Similarly, 1–2 Samuel interchanges Hebrews and Israelites in connection with the Israelite-Philistine wars. It was therefore no surprise to the scholars of the late nineteenth century C.E. that the Israelites should turn up in Egypt as Hebrews. Even before then, scholars knew of some Egyptian sources that included references to people who were active in Egypt and were called *ʿpr.w*. Now they also appeared in letters from central Palestine. Consequently, scholars surmised that the *habiru* to whom Abdi-Heba refers in his letters were the ancient Israelites; therefore, his letters prove that the Israelites or their ancestors lived in Palestine during the Amarna period.

Two subsequent observations upset these initial and pervasive notions. First, in the Amarna collection, the Hebrews are confined to the letters from Jerusalem and are never mentioned in any letters aside from EA 285–290. This is a bit odd as Jerusalem should be the last place to look for Hebrews; rather, according to 1–2 Samuel, Jerusalem only came into Israelite hands much later, when David conquered the city. Second, it is equally strange that the *habiru* are absent in letters posted from Shechem, although Abdi-Heba refers to the *habiru* as being active in the vicinity of Shechem. Here the local prince, the notorious Laba'yu, formed an alliance with the *habiru* to overturn Egyptian rule, at least according to Abdi-Heba's letters:

---

[46] Most of the Amarna letters were written in Akkadian and transcribed by poorly trained Syrians and Palestinians. The West Semitic roots of these scribes' mother tongue shows through the Akkadian. Presumably, the Egyptian chancellery made sure that each of its Near Eastern princes *(ḫazannu)* employed such scribes to maintain dependable lines of communication with the many Asian imperial centers.

[47] It is written in Sumerian as *lú* ("man") with *meš*, a sign expressing the plural.

[48] The etymology of this word is uncertain. Nowadays, most scholars agree on the value of the first consonant, which in Akkadian is rendered as a *ḫa*. The *ḫ* sound must here represent the West Semitic laryngeal ʿ *(ʿayin)*. The second consonant creates more problems as it is possible to transcribe it as either a *b* or a *p*. The Semitic etymology might therefore be either *ʿ-b-r*, "passing by," or *ʿ-p-r*, "dust." Evidence from the Hittite archives at Hattusas, however, seems to favor a rendering of the second syllable as *bi*. For more on this, see this author's article "Ḫabiru, Ḫapiru," *ABD* 3:6–10. For convenience, this discussion will use the spelling *ḫabiru*.

> Ginti-kirmil belongs to Tage, and men of Gintu are the garrison in Bitsanu. Are we to act like Lab'ayu when he was giving the land of Šakmu[49] to the Ḫapiru? Milkilu has written to Tagi and the sons <*of Lab'ayu*>, "*Be the both of you a protection.* Grant all their demands to the men of Qiltu, and let us isolate Jerusalem."[50]

If the Old Testament has anything to say in this context, it should also be mentioned that it places Shechem in the center of Israelite activity before the introduction of the monarchy. If the Hebrews were present in Palestine in the Amarna period, Shechem and not Jerusalem would be the first place to look for them!

The Amarna letters mention another group in terms strikingly similar to the ones Abdi-Heba used for the *habiru*. When the letters were deciphered, scholars were in doubt as to the identity of this group. This time the group did not carry a Semitic name but a Sumerian name, in several variations: SA.GAZ, SAG.GAZ, or simply GAZ. However, the German Orientalist Hugo Winckler soon unlocked the key to this mystery. He discovered that SA.GAZ was actually another name for the *habiru*.[51] This discovery had profound effects. Now it would be incorrect to say that there were too few references to the Hebrews' alias, the *habiru*; on the contrary there were far too many and from almost every part of the Near East! And more references followed as new texts were found and deciphered. *Habiru* now showed up in every possible place—even in places never frequented by the forefathers of the Israelites. In short, we possess references to *habiru* people living in such remote places as Asia Minor, Egypt, Elam (modern Persia), as well as in Syria, Palestine, and Mesopotamia. Moreover, the references are not limited to the Amarna period or the Late Bronze Age; they practically litter documents covering all of the second millennium B.C.E.

This time scholars were forced to formulate a different view of the *habiru*. These people could no longer simply be identified as the forefathers of the Israelites. While the *habiru* might have some remote connection to the Hebrews of the Old Testament, the exact link is unknown. The term *habiru* must refer to something else and much more general than the specific ethnic tag "Hebrew." Evidently the *habiru* should not be understood as an ethnic group, but as some kind of social segment.

When the idea of a social identification of the *habiru* was originally proposed, scholars had no precise idea what kind of social entity they were talking about. The Amarna letters made it clear that scribes considered the *habiru* a menace to the social and political order of their time, so

---

[49] Šakmu = Shechem.

[50] EA 289; translation from Moran, *Amarna Letters*, 332–33.

[51] Winckler's theory was later confirmed in the Hattusas documents, which use both terms to describe the same group.

scholars supposed the *habiru* to be nomads. This was in accordance with the image of nomads current among European scholars around the turn of the present century. Nomads were believed to constitute an unruly population that created as many problems for the settled population as possible because of their unrelenting pursuit of grazing land, if not land for themselves to settle on. We have already seen that this impression of nomadism is false. Nomads normally do not intend to settle. Moreover, it has so far been impossible to establish any connection between the *habiru* of the Late Bronze Age and the real nomads, the Sutu.

The tone of the ancient documents is unmistakable: the *habiru* were enemies of the established political system. Consequently, they remained social pariahs—true enemies of decent society. Scholars soon realized that these "outlaws" were ordinary folk who had been forced, because of life's hardships, to flee their society. Now they sought refuge at the fringe of Palestinian and Syrian society, where they survived as bandits. They mostly choose to stay in remote corners and inaccessible mountain regions in order to escape the interference of state societies. Here they were relatively safe because of the limited military resources of the small Palestinian and Syrian states. As they began to see the *habiru* as highwaymen, scholars found help in early Akkadian documents. Here the *habiru* are equated with bandits. Furthermore, the ideogram (pictograph) SA.GAZ is most likely not a proper Sumerian word but a Sumerian transliteration of an actual Akkadian word, *šaggāšu*, or "murderers." Such outlaws often sought refuge in the forested mountains of Palestine and Syria, thereby distinguishing themselves from nomads, who populated the steppe regions.

This interpretation of the *habiru* as outlaws and bandits, however, also needs some qualification. In fact, most Bronze Age documents paint a different picture of a thoroughly peaceful group that lived within the confines of civilized society. Sometimes, these *habiru* were employed as state-supported professional soldiers. Most were unskilled laborers employed by the state or private citizens. While they were never proper citizens in the states within which they resided but remained exiles, they were hardly outlaws in the proper sense of the word; rather, they were refugees (who, of course, might as well have been considered outlaws in their home states).

The increasingly frequent references to *habiru* in Egyptian and ancient Near Eastern documents suggest that during the Late Bronze Age a widespread phenomenon had developed. Clearly, many people left their homelands searching for better luck in foreign lands. Most states welcomed refugees with open arms because they represented a cheap labor force. The paucity of ordinary residents in most states of the ancient Near East made the influx of the *habiru* workers especially welcome. Once again, the *habiru* phenomenon concretely demonstrates the deteriorating Near Eastern social situation—one which spurred people to migrate in numbers. Many states that accepted and prospered because of the arrival of such refugees had to pay the price: their own citizens joined the *habiru* movement—a situation that threatened to destabilize existing states.

We must realize that the Amarna letters paint a distorted picture of the *habiru*. What is more, kings of Syrian and Palestinian states, who fled their towns or left them to the *habiru*, were sometimes dubbed *habiru* by colleagues who intended to defame them in the eyes of their overlord, the pharaoh. Sometimes *habiru* was simply used as an invective. This use of the term thus makes it precarious to conclude that the Amarna letters always refer to the real *habiru*, namely, outlaws at the fringe of society. Nevertheless, such a secondary use would hardly have developed without a reference in real life. People who wrote and read these letters would have some prior notion about the real meaning of this term.

Many other extant Late Bronze Age documents mention the urgent refugee problem. From the states' perspective, hard times demanded harsh measures. Thus the well-known Hittite vassal treaties were often edited to include paragraphs dealing with *habiru* migrations. Such paragraphs normally demanded the extradition of refugees—at least the vassal was obliged to follow these orders. Obviously, the Hittites welcomed the influx of refugees into their territory. Every newcomer would join the king's work force, which always needed more manpower. Furthermore, some immigrants were upper-class citizens of small Syrian states who had been ousted from power and had fled to the great king to gain his protection and to save their lives. Normally, the great king willingly accepted them as his personal clients. By doing so he would be in a better position to put pressure on the ruling family of their home states: he could always threaten to supplant the ruler of a rebellious state with one of his personal retainers. At the end of the Late Bronze Age, the refugee problem became so acute that the kings of Egypt and Hatti included a special section on how to solve it when they drafted a treaty that sealed the peace between these two major empires of the day. In effect, they entered into a contracted alliance whereby both parties extradited and accepted each other's malcontents.

One can follow the *habiru* question throughout the entire Late Bronze Age and study how the states responded to the problem. Hittite territory was apparently not so hard pressed by the refugee movement as the Egyptian-controlled parts of western Asia. The reason might have been the sociopolitical setup of their empire. Their political system depended on and demanded loyalty from vassal states; therefore, as patrons, the Hittites did concern themselves with disputes among those vassals and tried to intervene and negotiate a peace whenever two vassal kings started a quarrel. In Egypt, however, where the social system did not include a notion of solidarity between master and slave, officials were powerless to regulate or settle such discord or disputes. Egypt did not interfere when its petty kings infringed upon the rights of neighboring petty kings by bribing their citizens and trying to win their loyalty at the cost of their rightful masters. Again, the Amarna archive provides a concrete example of this situation in the extensive correspondence from Byblos's king Rib-Adda. In it, he details how the neighboring Amurru king was spreading vile propaganda hoping to lure away Rib-Adda's people. Furthermore, Rib-Adda contends that the king of Amurru tried to persuade the inhabitants of the city Ammiya to murder their king and install the Amurru monarch in his place. Rib-Adda's contentious response is a cool and laconic parody of his troublesome foes:

> So now ᶜAbdi-Aširta has written to the troops: "Assemble in the temple of NINURTA, and then let us fall upon Gubla. Look, there is no one that will save it from u[s]. Then let us drive out the mayors from the country that the entire country be joined to the ᶜApiru, . . . to the entire country. Then will (our) sons and daughters be at peace forever."[52]

And so they did—according to Rib-Adda!

The precise reason why so many citizens of Syria and Palestine chose to flee their homes in this period remains unknown. Whatever the exact reason, it became necessary to regulate this movement in the international treaties of the time. We can at least conclude that social and economic problems became so oppressive that the entire sociopolitical fabric of the Late Bronze Age collapsed. The refugee movement only forebodes this collapse. In different places different reasons may have forced people to leave, though again we know little about the details.

Deficits continually plagued Syrian and Palestinian civilization. In times of crisis, the state found no reason to subsidize the impoverished and debt-ridden peasantry. Thus periods of drought always created the risk that the peasantry would become permanently indebted to their lenders and eventually be enslaved. Such economic hardships could almost break the backbone of an ancient Oriental society that depended almost exclusively on the independent farming community to produce its food and create its basic income.[53] Of course, the unrelenting climate

---

[52] EA 74:30–38; translation from Moran, *Amarna Letters*, 143. The social factors affecting the politics of the Amurru kings were the subjects of several studies between 1960 and 1970. These studies dealt not only with the refugee problem but also with the generally poor social conditions of this age. Among the more important studies belongs Mario Liverani's "Implicazione sociali nella politica di Abdi-Ashirta di Amurru," *Rivista degli studi orientali* 40 (1965): 267–77; see also the English version in Liverani's *Three Amarna Essays*.

[53] Such problems are not limited to ancient times. As late as the nineteenth century C.E., the Turkish government established a state agricultural bank to furnish the peasantry with cheap loans in order to break the power of the moneylenders who

may have exacerbated this situation. Toward the end of the Late Bronze Age, the climate deteriorated and long periods of drought became common. Egyptian grain deliveries to Asia Minor in the days of Pharaoh Merneptah illustrate the plight of the local population during such a period of famine. This most extraordinary measure shows how serious the situation must have been, since grain was not normally an object of international commercial activity.

Other circumstances contributed to the refugee problem. For instance, ongoing hostilities between the massive Egyptian and Hittite regimes highlighted the Late Bronze Age political landscape. Naturally, clashes were most likely in border regions, but elsewhere things remained relatively peaceful. The same was true in Palestine. Peace never really "broke out" there because of the schemes of competing local princes, but the princes did not have sufficient resources to wreak real havoc, and most damage could be repaired. The life of the ordinary peasant was generally not endangered by such machinations. Most of them found refuge and lived within the protective walls of their towns and cities. Few dared to take up residence in unprotected villages.

Nevertheless, the political landscape remained restless and volatile. In such times, economic hardship relentlessly dogged the lower echelons of Near Eastern society, especially the peasantry. As we noted previously, the peasantry represented the lowest and largest stratum of the population. These people became tantalizing targets for heavy taxation by states always in need of money, especially in times of crisis.

Every Palestinian and Syrian prince sustained his power through persistent intrigue, skirmishes, and bribes, for which his subjects paid dearly. In the Late Bronze Age, those inhabitants also suffered at the expense of the Egyptian armed forces stationed and operating throughout Palestine and Syria. Apparently, the Egyptian overlords had established a fixed system for exacting taxes and duties from their provinces. Twice a year the Egyptian chancellery sent out a kind of standard message demanding that supplies be offered to Egyptian military contingents.[54]

---

were threatening the survival of the society. For three centuries, Syrian and Palestinian farmers had been without this facility. The Turkish regime viewed the extension of credit as an important step toward securing the independent peasants' existence throughout Syria and Palestine. Under the French Mandate, the Turkish banking system ceased to exist in Syria. Soon the peasantry became slaves of the moneylenders to which they were indebted. This process had almost come to an end when the French left Syia after the conclusion of World War II. Few independent peasants were left.

[54] This topic is illuminated by Mario Liverani in his article, "A Seasonal Pattern for the Amarna Letters," in *Lingering over Words: Studies in Ancient Near Eastern Literature in Honor of William L. Moran* (ed. T. Abusch, J. Huehnergard, and P. Steinkeller; Harvard Semitic Studies 37; Atlanta: Scholars Press, 1990), 337–48. Liverani speaks

Restlessness and instability dominated the entire Near East, especially in the Egyptian sphere of influence. Yet problems never escalated to the point where they could no longer be solved—if not by local powers then at least by committing imperial forces. Moreover, after the Amarna period both great empires solidified their provincial administration. In Syria, the Hittites installed their own viceroy at Carchemish. In the Egyptian zone, a number of military headquarters were established and distributed over the region, for example at Beth-shan, located twenty kilometers south of the Sea of Gennesaret. A thirteenth-century Egyptian inscription at that site describes how the Egyptian forces coped with local tribesmen and the *habiru* in the vicinity of Beth-shan—a strong indication that the *habiru* question remained unresolved even after the Amarna period. In the mountain regions around such places as Beth-shan, the *habiru* sought refuge and continually menaced local establishments such as the small towns of the region. Normally, such local disturbances constituted no real problem to the imperial regime unless they coincided with other crises in the center of the empire itself. When the great kings were no longer able to control matters through Syria and Palestine, the Near Eastern status quo was seriously jeopardized. The inability of the great centers to control the situation would also weaken the regional centers, which in turn would cause the center to give away to the periphery, and political coherence would be lost. This happened to both the Egyptian and the Hittite areas of Syria and Palestine.

As we mentioned previously, the great Hittite kings could never force the tribesmen who lived north of Hattusas to their knees. Hittite influence and power in the region slowly deteriorated because the empire could not find an effective remedy for this persistent menace. Soon after 1200 B.C.E., local tribesmen, along with underlying sociopolitical circumstances, destroyed the Hittite empire. This led to destabilization throughout Syria.

The death of Ramesses II (ca. 1213 B.C.E.) led to the inevitable dissolution of the Egyptian empire. We have already mentioned the tremendous burdens encountered by the centralized Egyptian government: the difficulties of maintaining a centralized administration—now situated at Tanis in Lower Egypt—while facing the problems created by the Amun priesthood at Thebes in Upper Egypt, a conflict that ultimately led to the establishment of two competing administrations in Upper and Lower Egypt. All of these factors militated against a cohesive sociopolitical

---

of a "spring letter" delivered yearly by the Egyptian chancellery. Subsequently, a "summer reply" from the indentured vassals arrived confirming that they would obey orders. At the end of the year, the pharaoh allowed his vassals to send in every kind of comment and complaint.

ethos. On the western frontier, serious problems developed with the inhabitants living on the Libyan Desert borderlands. In the east, the weakness of the tribes along the Sinai Peninsula guaranteed a *de facto* peace. Individual Asiatics retained high positions in the Egyptian bureaucracy, although the highest office of the country—that of the pharaoh—remained inaccessible to foreigners. By the end of the Late Bronze Age, a sustained period of political decay began, one that would last for several centuries. The Egyptian empire did not dissolve overnight. It was more of a prolonged political process that sometimes halted temporarily when energetic pharaohs took over and appeared in Asia with their armies. Often, however, such shows of force may have only precipitated events that accelerated the process of disintegration.

Ramesses III and the War against the Sea Peoples

The foreign countries made a *conspiracy* in their islands. All at once the lands were removed and scattered in the fray. No land could stand before their arms, from Hatti, Kode, Carchemish, Arzawa, and Alashiya on, being cut off *at* [*one time*]. A camp [was set up] in one place in Amor. They desolated its people, and its land was like that which has never come into being. They were coming forward toward Egypt, while the flame was prepared before them. Their confederation was the Philistines, Tjeker, Shekelesh, Denye(n), and Weshesh, lands united. They laid their hands upon the lands as far as the circuit of the earth, their hearts confident and trusting: "Our plans will succeed!" Now the heart of this god, the Lord of the Gods, was prepared and ready to ensnare them like birds.[55]

Initially, the dissolution of central administrative centers led to a similar degeneration of the provincial centers and the inevitable disintegration of Late Bronze Age society, although external factors also contributed to this situation. At the beginning of the Late Bronze Age a vast political entity in the Aegean began to exert its influence. Although we still know very little about the details of this organization, its effect on world trade during that period is unmistakable. One might call this a kind of sea empire (thalassocracy), whose administrative center was in Mycenaea and whose members hailed from the Aegean isles, western Asia Minor, Crete, and possibly Cyprus (at least in parts).

---

[55] Translation by John A. Wilson, *ANET*, 262. See also K. A. Kitchen, *Ramesside Inscriptions V* (Oxford: Blackwell, 1983), 39, for the text; and W. F. Edgerton and J. A. Wilson, *Historical Records of Ramses III* (Chicago: University of Chicago, 1936), 53–54, for another translation.

Around 1200 B.C.E., this grand civilization collapsed—a situation that carried with it grave consequences for international trade.

The production of bronze depends upon the availability of several raw materials, not all of which are found in the Near East. For many years, these commodities were shipped along major seaways from the western reaches of the Mediterranean and Britain all the way to the Levant's port cities. From there, they were shipped to the interior of West Asia. This important maritime trade was interrupted with the collapse of the Aegean empire. Subsequently, dwindling copper and bronze supplies led to rising inflation that seriously jeopardized the flow of consumer goods, not least military hardware.[56]

The breakup of Mycenaea's political hegemony throughout the Aegean region resulted in extensive unrest. Small and large seafaring bands now overtook the Mediterranean—a movement known as the "migration of the Sea Peoples." These migrations did not all happen at the same time but had been prepared by a development that lasted for some generations. They caused a major crisis, however, the effects of which led to changes in the ethnic composition of the population throughout the Mediterranean, including the Palestinian coastal zone. Egyptian sources refer to this situation as an "invasion" of the Sea Peoples who swept down from the Mediterranean and plundered vast populations in their path. Such descriptions give the impression of a sudden, massive population shift. This was hardly the case. So-called Sea Peoples were already present in the Near East before 1200 B.C.E. For example, in the thirteenth century, Ramesses II employed mercenaries from among the Sea Peoples during the battle of Qadesh.

The most famous confrontation between the Egyptians and the Sea Peoples occurred around 1180 B.C.E. According to the sources, the entire Levant shook during this onslaught, and many bustling Near Eastern cities and states fell in its wake. Occasionally, the Egyptians scored short-lived victories against their formidable opponents. One such triumph during a naval battle in the Nile Delta is described on the wall of the Medinet Habu Temple of Ramesses III (ca. 1186–1154 B.C.E.) at Thebes. According to the Egyptian documents—certainly not an impartial source—the Egyptians squelched the Sea Peoples and pushed them

---

[56] The introduction of iron is generally viewed as a major advance, one that ultimately led to the production of steel around the first millennium B.C.E. However, one should not forget that before this time, iron was porous, brittle, and impractical compared to bronze. Items made of iron were certainly not unknown before the end of the Late Bronze Age. Before the Iron Age, smiths knew how to handle this metal. This is hardly surprising since iron ores could be found almost anywhere. Consequently, iron production did not blossom as a result of consumer demand for new metals; rather, dwindling copper and bronze supplies made the search for alternative metals acute.

back into Palestine. Several intriguing participants are mentioned in this account, including the *Peleset*, who should most likely be identified with the Philistines of the Old Testament and who gave their name—Palestine—to this part of the world. After their unsuccessful attack on Egypt, the Philistines settled in city-states along the coastal plain and survived into the Assyrian period of the first millennium B.C.E.

The Sea Peoples undoubtedly played an active role in the political and economic decay of the Late Bronze Age; however, we can easily overestimate their role in this process. Egypt's military presence in Palestine survived the struggle with the Sea Peoples for at least another fifty years. The last official, solid evidence for an Egyptian presence in Palestine dates from around the time of Ramesses VI (ca. 1144–1136 B.C.E.), and traces of that presence continue into the tenth century. The Philistines and other Sea Peoples soon settled in Palestine and established their own network of small city-states throughout the region. In this way they helped stabilize, rather than destabilize, the political situation in Palestine.

The widespread retribalization of the local population within Syria and Palestine had a much more profound, deleterious effect on the Bronze Age political landscape in that region. This process did not happen at exactly the same time and in the same way in every corner of the territory. Circumstances varied according to local conditions. Thus the former Hittite center at Carchemish remained northern Syria's political hub. Apart from that, substantial demographic changes occurred that transformed the social fabric of the Syrian countryside for the next two hundred to three hundred years—a period of marginalization that swung the balance of power to the periphery.

In Palestine, a concomitant marginalization occurred around 1200 B.C.E., a period noteworthy for the resurgence of village culture. Again, the periphery became the center. Urban societies disintegrated because they could not remain self-sufficient. Centralized urban politics yielded to the small village social systems that also included a certain nomadic element. Among these villagers should probably also be found the predecessors of the early Israelite tribes known only from the Old Testament, but the Early Iron Age society of Palestine was not identical with early Israel as described in the Old Testament. Many other ethnic groups also participated in the development of Iron Age society, for example, the tribal units who were active around Beth-shan in the thirteenth century B.C.E. and who are mentioned in an Egyptian inscription from this site.

At this point, we return to the *habiru* question. Clearly, the Old Testament Hebrews cannot be connected directly with the *habiru*—a term that eventually became an ethnic designation for the Israelites of the Old Testament. Although it appears that the Amarna period's *habiru* are not directly related to the Iron Age Israelites, there is reason to suspect that elements of these earlier groups ultimately naturalized into later Israelite society. Unfortunately, we possess no evidence to support such a claim. The close linguistic proximity between the terms *habiru* and Hebrews suggests a possible social continuity between Bronze Age and Iron Age societies. A thoughtful consideration of these two groups could shed light on the origin and history of later Israelite tribes in Palestine.

Most likely Syrian and Palestinian nomadic tribes contributed to social reconstruction. This process, which exceeds the boundaries of this volume and belongs mainly to the subsequent periods in the Early Iron Age, resulted in the establishment of a series of Aramaic-speaking states in Syria in the early part of the first millennium B.C.E. The origin of these states should be sought in the periphery of the Syrian society of the Late Bronze Age.[57] The Aramean takeover of Syria and parts of Mesopotamia involved the extensive participation of tribesmen and in this way mirrors the Amorite takeover more than a thousand years before. One might say that with the rise of the Arameans history repeated itself; that is, many parallels can be drawn between the Near Eastern political landscapes of 2000 and 1000 B.C.E. For example, the Arameans spoke a language that originally sounded very similar to Amorite, more or less as the Amorites during the Middle Bronze Age spoke a language not totally dissimilar from the one used in the urban centers of Syria. The Arameans also continued many Late Bronze Age cultural and religious traditions. Thus, the period between 1200 and 1000 B.C.E. strikingly reflects the political and economic environments in the Near East one thousand years earlier—periods when the periphery replaced the center. The stage was now set for the next act in the history of Syria and Palestine.

---

[57] For further discussion, see two articles in *Civilizations of the Ancient Near East:* Niels Peter Lemche, "The History of Ancient Syria and Palestine: An Overview," 2:1195–1218; and Paul E. Dion, "Aramaean Tribes and Nations of First-Millennium Western Asia," 2:1281–94.

3

ASPECTS OF THE RELIGIOUS THINKING AND CULTURE

III.1. INTRODUCTION

Kengel, Horst, ed. *Kulturgeschichte des alten Vorderasien.* VZAGA 18. Berlin: Akademie-Verlag, 1989. **Liverani,** Mario. *Prestige and Interest: International Relations in the Near East, ca. 1600–1100 B.C.* Padua: Sargon, 1990. **Moscati,** Sabatino. *L'alba della civiltà: Società, economia e pensiero nel Vicino Oriente antico III.* Turin: UTET, 1976. **Sasson,** Jack M., ed. *Civilizations of the Ancient Near East.* New York: Scribners, 1995. Vols. 3 and 4.

Thirty-four years ago, the North American Assyriologist Leo Oppenheim wrote his well-known book on Mesopotamian culture, in which he planned initially to include a lengthy discussion of Mesopotamian religion.[1] Although he never accomplished that formidable task, Oppenheim wrote an essay in that book entitled, "Why a 'Mesopotamian Religion' Should Not Be Written."[2] The many forms of Mesopotamian religion, the astounding diversity of Mesopotamian civilization, and its long history all contributed to Oppenheim's frustration. Like other scholars, he could not construct a satisfactory appraisal of Mesopotamian religion.[3] It would have been more reasonable and manageable to limit the analysis to only some of this enormous subject's many component parts.

---

[1] A. Leo Oppenheim, *Ancient Mesopotamia: Portrait of a Dead Civilization* (Chicago: University of Chicago Press, 1964), revised by Erica Reiner, 1977.

[2] Oppenheim, *Ancient Mesopotamia,* 172–83.

[3] Only one book approaches Oppenheim's original goal: the late Sumerologist Thorkild Jacobsen's *The Treasures of Darkness: A History of Mesopotamian Religion* (New Haven: Yale University Press, 1976). Despite the title, Jacobsen's book is an

Similar problems arise when we turn our attention to Syria-Palestine in the third and second millennia B.C.E. Although superficially a more homogeneous culture, it was not really uniform. Like Mesopotamia, the civilizations of the many regional centers of Syria and Palestine shared some basic ideas and beliefs. On the other hand, each of them developed its own traditions and ideas. Moreover, Syria-Palestine produced neither the quality nor the quantity of written documents provided by Mesopotamian religious traditions. Most details remain unknown to us. Only sketchy bits of those traditions come from incomplete and randomly found sources: either scarce written documents or various iconographic representations such as seal impressions or divine images and statuettes—materials that are notoriously difficult to understand and interpret. Thus a coherent historical-critical depiction of the Syro-Palestinian religious climate in the Bronze Age remains impossible, whether we speak of a local religion or the religion of the whole region as such.

Before 1929, historians of Syrian and Palestinian religion in the pre-Israelite period had been able to produce only highly insufficient constructions. They accepted most of the information in the Old Testament about Canaanite religion as primary evidence about religion in ancient Western Asia. Greek and Roman authors belonging to the Hellenistic-Roman period were believed to provide additional valuable information, although their evidence obviously had little to do with "Canaanite" religion in the biblical sense but referred to late forms of Phoenician religion. Equally problematic was the date of these sources, all of them from the first millennium B.C.E.—indeed, some of them even more recent than that, from the first centuries of the Christian era. Furthermore, both biblical and Greco-Roman sources represented outsiders' biases. The biblical writers simply dismissed "Canaanite" beliefs as absolutely offensive, and Greco-Roman writers talked disdainfully about Phoenician "mysticism." Nevertheless, in the early part of the twentieth century, scholars began to publish studies of the influence of the Canaanite religion on Israelite religious beliefs. This influence was seen as very important, if not decisive, and even turned up in core ideas of Old Testament religion. These commentators contended that the anthropology of the Old Testament, its view of God, and its description of the God-human relationship all sprang largely from Near Eastern models.

After 1929, scholars unearthed genuine and abundant religious and historical source materials from the second millennium B.C.E.

---

interesting, although idiosyncratic reconstruction of the psychology of Babylonian religion from the fourth to the second millennium B.C.E. However, it falls short of being a proper history of Mesopotamian religion.

Within a few years, extraordinarily intriguing data came from the extensive Ras Shamra/Ugarit excavations in northwestern Syria—the most notable of which were several epic texts that portray the lives of gods and heroes. During the ensuing decades, the discovery of the religious texts from Ugarit produced a large variety of specialized studies, many of which were written by biblical scholars. These scholars had already for a long time engaged in the study of ancient Near Eastern religion and now hoped to see their theories confirmed by the recent discovery of genuine Syrian texts from the Bronze Age. In this way the texts from Ugarit served a double purpose. They were, on one hand, seen as confirming the theories of the Canaanite background of several religious ideas in the Old Testament. On the other hand, they also seemed to strengthen the mainly negative view of Canaanite religion that the biblical authors expressed. It was accepted without further discussion that the Ugaritic epic texts provided an authentic picture of religion in all of Bronze Age Syria and Palestine.

Today scholars are more careful when they invoke the Ugaritic texts as evidence of Syro-Palestinian religion in the first millennium B.C.E. Such connections must be made with great caution. It is imperative that scholars recognize the chance nature of the non-Ugaritic source materials that we mentioned above. They should also understand that the religious content of the Ugaritic documents may be less clear than usually believed. After all, Ugarit represented only one of many Syrian cultural centers during the Bronze Age; therefore, Ugarit cannot be used as a universal paradigm for Syria's religious experience. Important differences abounded. First, burial customs varied from one region to the next. Ugarit buried its dead in vaults underneath or close to private homes. This was not the case elsewhere. Second, the great epic tales do not necessarily reflect Ugarit's actual religious experience; rather, they are primarily literary constructs written for their aesthetic rather than their religious value. Their character as literary masterpieces becomes obvious when compared to other texts that better reflect the religious ideas and cultic practices of the Ugaritic citizens: the religious world of the epic literature is seemingly very different from that of the Ugaritic ritual texts. Third, we must consider the vast chronological gap between the Ugaritic and Old Testament text traditions. That great divide precludes any direct links between the Ugaritic and Canaanite religions.

These remarks underscore the difficulty—if not impossibility—of developing a coherent and exhaustive depiction of an "intellectual history" of Bronze (and Iron) Age Syria-Palestine. In the following pages, I will explore only individual elements of this history of ideas. I will consider the direct testimony of authentic source materials and allusions from other secondary sources to arrive at a fuller understanding of this very complex issue.

III.2. THE LITERATURE OF THE PERIOD

III.2.1. Preface: The Official and the Unofficial Traditions

The first stop on our journey through the Syrian and Palestinian intellectual universes takes us to the extant Bronze Age primary sources. Most written documents from that era come to us from palace or temple archives and concern official matters. Without any significant extant private documents, we can only sketch the cultural milieu from which the official documents sprang, that is, the world of state officials and the realm of priests at the major sanctuaries. The private world remains a closed book. Furthermore, because we must depend on the random discoveries of individual, scattered excavations, our interpretation of the available corpus of traditional materials remains haphazard and unreliable.

Ugarit, Alalakh, Emar, and to a lesser extent Mari remain the only significant second-millennium archives that elucidate the intellectual history of Syria and Palestine. Even the third-millennium Ebla archive provides only sketchy data for our understanding of that area's religious experience and history, since most of its documents concern economic matters. Other areas of Syria and Palestine yield even more disappointingly uninformative materials. From Palestine the Amarna letters (which were found in Egypt) remain the only sizable collection, and they tell us little about the intellectual history of their time. They are mostly political documents, although they provide important clues for understanding the mind of Syrian and Palestinian peoples.

These documents' official nature notwithstanding, we can develop a vision of the unofficial tradition from them because their authors occasionally share personal insights. Like all people, they were "multifaceted"; that is, they operated under several psychological "aliases." The modern scientist provides a compelling example of this phenomenon. Scientists are accustomed to employ logic and conceptual thinking in their technical work and experimentation. When technical problems arise, they respond logically and systematically. Ultimately, these researchers articulate solutions to such problems in the common parlance of all scientists. The scientific community can then evaluate objective data using the same universally acknowledged language and reasoning. In other words, scientists "speak the same language." Yet scientists are not always "scientists"; sometimes questions appear that do not demand a "scientific answer." Occasionally, emotion overtakes reason—at which point prelogical thinking can lead to full-scale emotional responses. When the scientific facade begins to unravel, logic, conceptual thinking, and established methodological paradigms fall aside. Like these all-too-human scientists, writers in ancient societies often deviated from their own routine behavioral patterns and cultural standards. In antiquity, scribes or writers had at least two professional personas that defined their philosophical cores: an official, public persona; and an unofficial, private persona. Presumably, even official written documents should betray some portion of their authors' private thoughts.

In antiquity, professional scribes wrote their documents in established formats. All scribes endured long, arduous training in approved institutes that stood at the center of all learning. They studied various political protocols and worked toward becoming sound and erudite officials. Along the way, they also became acquainted with their society's literary tradition as it had already been written down. Most of the teaching consisted of copying all kinds of master documents, including literary texts that were not directly part of their training as future officials. In this way scribes in training contributed to the preservation of the literary tradition for future generations. On the other hand, these students, who went on to become scribes, lived together with other people who had no such education and were not influenced by the literary tradition. It is therefore not surprising, but altogether to be expected, that here and there in the written documents formulations crop up that are foreign to the official tradition, so that thoughts and ideas of the unofficial subculture are mixed in with those of the official culture. In this connection we should remember that, compared with the present, very few people in those days belonged to the intellectual elite from which government officials were drawn, and that written communications played only a minor role among the many tasks of administrators.

States in those days—or better, their officials—did not communicate only in writing. Equally important was the oral exchange which went along with every written communication and which in general was mediated by messengers. One often gets the impression that written documents served more as accompanying paperwork for orally delivered messages than as messages in their own right—even in the case of messages exchanged between persons of differing rank. Thus many Amarna letters include a paragraph instructing the "postman" on how to deliver orally the message contained in the written document. The Abdi-Heba letter we quoted (EA 288) contains one of these.[4] Ostensibly, the king of Jerusalem himself dictated the letter to his scribe, who knew a little Akkadian. Pharaoh, Abdi-Heba's overlord, was not himself the recipient of the letter. An official at the court of the pharaoh, conversant in Akkadian, received the letter and was charged with translating the message into Egyptian. The translated message was then delivered either to the pharaoh or more likely to a high-ranking official, whose job it was to convey the essentials to his lord in a fashion that would follow Egyptian

---

[4] See above section II.5.5.

court etiquette. To make straight the way of the message, Abdi-Heba's scribe addresses his superior colleague at the Egyptian court directly, asking him to attach "nice words" to the message, that is, to put it in words acceptable to the pharaoh's ears. The Akkadian message from Jerusalem never went any further than the initial stage of this delivery process and was soon put away in some state archive, probably never to be read in full.[5]

If members of the upper echelons of ancient Near Eastern society preferred to communicate orally, although capable of writing, it goes without saying that ordinary persons almost exclusively conversed orally. To be sure, the cultural climate in Mesopotamia was different from that in Syria and Palestine. Over the span of two millennia, the large Mesopotamian cities developed substantial literary traditions, ones whose value and popularity survived well into the Hellenistic period. Some of this literature, such as the Epic of Gilgamesh, remains meaningful reading even in the modern age.[6] In Syria and Palestine, nothing like the urban cultural milieu of Mesopotamia developed. Whereas substantial enclaves of cultured literati populated cities such as Nippur and Babylon, in most Syrian cities only a few people could write, and the cultural situation in Palestine was even more extreme. Thus in the small Palestinian cities of the Late Bronze Age, the royal scribe was the only person with a literary education. Most likely such scribes were educated by the Egyptian overlords and placed among the vassals of pharaoh so that he had at least one local person who could read and write and act as the local Egyptian agent.

The situation can be summarized as follows. The large Mesopotamia cities possessed an established, official written tradition. Parts of this tradition also trickled through to Syria (maybe even to Palestine). In Syria-Palestine, oral tradition dominated the literary scene in both the cities and rural settlements. Most small towns and villages in rural Palestine depended solely on oral traditions.

We must consider one more facet of this intriguing topic; that is, occasionally, oral traditions survived beneath the surface of the official

---

[5] For a thorough overview of the history of the Amarna letters and their publication, see Anson F. Rainey, *El Amarna Tablets, 359–379: Supplement to J. A. Knudtzon,* Die El-Amarna-Tafeln (2d revised ed.; AOAT 8; Kevelaer: Butzon & Bercker; Neukirchen-Vluyn: Neukirchener, 1978); cf. also William L. Moran's introduction to the corpus in *Amarna Letters,* xiii–xxxix. For the letters' disposition, see J. A. Knudtzon, *Die El-Amarna-Tafeln* (Vorderasiatische Bibliotek 2; 2 vols.; Leipzig: J. C. Hinrichs, 1908–1915; reprint, Aalen: O. Zeller, 1964).

[6] The tradition of Gilgamesh goes back to Sumerian times in the third millennium B.C.E. Of course, the poem's main extant version comes from the Neo-Babylonian period (i.e., from the middle of the first millennium B.C.E.). See the English translations by E. A. Speiser in *ANET,* 72–99, and Stephanie Dalley in *Myths from Mesopotamia* (Oxford: Oxford University Press, 1991), 39–153.

heritage's literary garments. Clearly the scribe often employed elements and literary patterns belonging to the oral tradition in order to convey a message that could be understood by people not trained in his own academic tradition.

III.2.2. The Official Forms: Political Treaties, Royal Decrees, Annalistic Inscriptions, and Chronicles

GENERAL: **Cancik,** Hubert. *Grundzüge der hethitischen und alttestamentlichen Geschichtsschreibung.* Abhandlungen des deutschen Palästinavereins. Wiesbaden: Harrassowitz, 1976. **Hoffner,** Harry A. "Propaganda and Political Justification in Hittite Historiography." In *Unity and Diversity.* Edited by Hans Goedicke and J. J. M. Roberts. Pages 49–62. Baltimore: Johns Hopkins University Press, 1975. **Liverani,** Mario. "Memorandum on the Approach to Historiographical Texts." *Or* 42 (1973): 178–84. **Liverani,** Mario. "Storiografia politica Hittita I: Shunashshura, ovvero. Della reciprocità." *OrAnt* 12 (1973): 267–97. **Liverani,** Mario. "Storiografia politica Hittita II: Telipinu, ovvero. Della solidarietà." *OrAnt* 16 (1977): 105–31.

THE MESSENGER: **Greene,** John T. *The Role of the Messenger and Message in the Ancient Near East and Hebrew Scriptures: Communicators and Communiqués in Context.* BJS 169. Atlanta: Scholars Press, 1989. **Meier,** Samuel A. *The Messenger in the Ancient Semitic World.* HSM 45. Atlanta: Scholars Press, 1988.

Great expectations and huge disappointments accompany every new discovery of ancient Near Eastern texts. Scholars feverishly pour over vastly diverse documents from palace archives throughout the region: from commercial records to brief interpersonal or international memoranda. Beyond Ugarit's impressive collection, purely literary texts are rarely unearthed, especially in Syria and Palestine. Of course, the Ugaritic texts belong exclusively to the Late Bronze Age; therefore, any conclusions derived from them about prior epochs are tenuous at best.

Ebla remains ancient Syria's oldest extant palace archive, dating from the third millennium B.C.E. Twenty years of intense excavation began bombastically: with each new find, sensational headlines ran in major newspapers and magazines, suggesting that the Bible's many mysteries were either clarified or debunked. For some, Ebla became "the missing link" between the Bible and the world from which it sprang. The archive's holdings contained mostly the state's administrative documents and, predictably, almost no literary texts per se. Our earlier discussion clarifies this point; that is, Syrian and Palestinian societies concerned themselves mainly with the vicissitudes of everyday life. Consequently, writing was almost exclusively utilitarian. Few people could afford the luxury of literature. Consequently, the traditions in question were transmitted primarily in oral form: even at royal courts only a few people could read or write—and the few who mastered the art hardly had the time to pursue literary interests.

Characteristically, third and second millennia Syria and Palestine have yielded no specimens of the official literary genres comparable to those unearthed throughout Mesopotamia: state treaties, royal decrees, or inscriptions that relate grand tales of mighty kings and their heroism. Nothing of the sort is found in Ebla, nor is anything like the later Assyrian and Babylonian chronicles or eponymic lists that identified years with the names of individuals (cf. the Roman consular lists). Such lists were known in Assyria during the third and second millennia, but this way of distinguishing years was apparently not used in Syria and Palestine. Furthermore, we possess no other official documents from Syria or Palestine—not even the collections of laws such as those known from Mesopotamia as early as the third millennium B.C.E.

It is difficult to say whether the Syrian scribes were acquainted with such literary genres. They may have been part of their education. As long as we do not possess any evidence, however, we have to abstain from far-reaching theories about the literary education of the scribes in the Bronze Age Syrian administrative centers. We only have one indication of the borrowing of a Mesopotamian literary and administrative genre. This goes back to the archives from Alalakh in the eighteenth century B.C.E. and might be related to royal enactments from Mesopotamia in the first part of the second millennium. In an Alalakh document, we find the month name *mīšarum*, a word that derives from the West Semitic stem *y-š-r*, meaning "to be equal" or "to be just/correct." In Mesopotamian documents from the Old Babylonian period, *mīšarum* was a technical designation for a special category of royal enactment that concerned the administration of social reforms. In most instances, the reform concerned the release of an enslaved debtor's liability and the restoration of his former land holdings.[7] Such decrees appear to have been enacted extensively only during the Old Babylonian period (that is, during the dynasty of King Hammurabi), but later decrees also used the same terminology, although they were not so comprehensive as the Babylonian ones. Consequently, the ideology of "liberation" survives well into the first millennium when it appears in Assyrian and Babylonian documents, as well as in West Semitic inscriptions. We also find examples of this principle in the Old Testament—especially the mandates of debt remission and slave release in Deuteronomy 15 and Exod 21:2–11, which are late echoes of this Oriental tradition. Of course, in Alalakh, the term *mīšarum* may carry none of this baggage. Perhaps it is nothing more than a term for the month to which it directly refers.

---

[7] See also below section III.3.2.

Excerpt from the Story of Idrimi, King of Alalakh

I am Idrimi, the son of Ilimilimma, the servant of Adad, of Hepat and of Ishtar, the Lady of Alalakh, my lady.

An evil deed happened in Halab, the seat of my family, and we fled to the people of Emar, brothers of my mother, and we lived (then) in Emar. My brothers, who were older than I, stayed with me but none of them had the plans I had. I (said to) myself: "Whoever owns the seat of his family is a . . . (while) who does not is but a slave in the eyes of the people of Emar!" (So) I took with me my horse, my chariot, and my groom, went away and crossed over the desert country and even entered into the region of the Sutian warriors. I stayed with them (once) overnight in my . . . chariot, but the next day I moved on and went to the land of Canaan. I stayed in Ammia in the land of Canaan; in Ammia lived (also) natives of Halab, of the country Mukishkhi, of the country Ni' and also warriors from the country Ama'e. They discovered that I was the son of their overlord and gathered around me. There I grew up and stayed for a long time. For seven years I lived among the Hapiru-people. (Then) I released birds (to observe their flight) and looked into (the entrails of) lambs (and found) that after seven years Adad had become favorable to me. So I built boats, made . . . soldiers board them, approached the country Mukishkhi via the sea and reached shore below Mt. Casius. I went ashore and when my country heard of me they brought me cattle and sheep. And in one day, and as one man, the countries Ni', Ama'e, Mukishkhi and my city Alalakh turned to me. My brothers heard (about this) and the came into my presence.[8]

Several Late Bronze Age documents and inscriptions provide marvelous examples the period's "official" literary genres—the most notable (and ancient) of which is the story of Idrimi of Alalakh (ca. 1500 B.C.E.). Idrimi's "career" appears on the face of a statue depicting the king seated on his throne. It is the only so-called monumental inscription from Syria during this period, although Idrimi's story is "monumental" only in the technical sense of the word; it is inscribed on a royal monument. First, it is transparently a piece of official propaganda. Second, it completely ignores concrete historical facts about his life. Consequently, it may be concluded that its author was more concerned about the literary design of the king of Alalakh's biographical sketch than about the historical facts upon which it depends.

---

[8] From A. Leo Oppenheim's translation in *ANET,* 557. See also Tremper Longman III's translation in *COS* 1.148, 479–80.

In an important essay, Mario Liverani analyzes individual, structural components of the Idrimi inscription.[9] Later we will discuss unofficial Syrian and Palestinian narrative traditions during the Late Bronze Age. For now, we concern ourselves only with the Idrimi inscription's stereotypical elements. Apparently, Idrimi, the youngest son of a large family, yearned to flee his civilized existence and seek adventure in the desert. He eventually wins the princess and the kingdom—not, however, his father's kingdom but a neighboring one. Idrimi was clearly a usurper of the throne of Alalakh. The inscription describes a mythical, disjointed, seven-year flight that obviously does not conform to any verifiable incidents in Idrimi's career. If anything, this chronological vignette represents an artificial, literary demarcation between scenes.

Unfortunately, although it demonstrates prototypical techniques of Ugaritic epic literature, the Idrimi inscription remains the only extant Bronze Age story of its kind from Syria and Palestine. Consequently, we cannot determine whether this unhistorical mode of narrative might have been common in historical inscriptions or the Idrimi inscription was a special case in this respect. Apparently popular tradition, which may have been transmitted orally, was more important in the composition of the Idrimi inscription than the actual facts of Idrimi's life.

Further examples of this narrative tradition are found not in Syria or Palestine but rather among the Hittite documents from the Hattusas archive. One such text is the so-called Edict of Telepinus. As its title implies, this document records the efforts of Telepinus to seize the government along with several reflections on early Hittite history.[10] Furthermore, it dates from roughly the same period as the aforementioned Idrimi inscription. Another significant text of this genre is the so-called Apology of Hattusilis III (ca. 1275–1260 B.C.E.), in which the Hittite king rationalizes the usurpation of the throne upon which his nephew Urkhi-Teshup (ca. 1280–1275 B.C.E.) already sat.[11]

---

[9] See Mario Liverani, "Partire sul carro, per il deserto," *Annali dell'Istituto orientale di Napoli*, NS 22 (1972): 403–15. Sidney Smith originally published the text in *The Statue of Idri-mi* (London: British Institute of Archaeology in Ankara, 1949). Important newer investigations of this text can be found in Manfried Dietrich, Oswald Loretz, Horst Klengel, and Rudolph Mayer, "Opificius, Untersuchungen zu Statue und Inschrift des Königs Idrimi von Alalakh," *UF* 13 (1981): 199–290. Manfried Dietrich and Oswald Loretz have also produced significant philological insights in "Die Inschrift des Königs Idrimi von Alalakh" (ibid., 210–69).

[10] For an English translation, see Th. P. J. van den Hout, "The Proclamation of Telipinu," in *COS* 1.76, 194–98. For a discussion of the historical depiction in this inscription, see Mario Liverani, "Storiografia politica Hittita II: Telipinu, ovvero: Della solidarietà," *OrAnt* 16 (1977): 105–31.

[11] For an English translation, see Th. P. J. van den Hout, "Apology of Hattušili III," *COS* 1.77, 199–204. Other ancient Near Eastern texts also employ this custom of listing significant historical events. One such example is the biblical story of David's

Some scholars have drawn direct connections between Hittite, Old Testament, and modern historiography, but such conclusions are rash, because they presuppose a historical consciousness that was unheard-of in antiquity. The ancients had nothing like the modern notion that an author should strive above all to recount the actual facts to the extent that they can be known. In contradistinction to this exaggerated trust in the factuality of Hittite historiography, we want to emphasize here that while the texts in question do transmit historical accounts, they are accounts that are dependent on and even structured in accord with literary patterns. These literary creations may sometimes be absolutely unhistorical. Consequently, we must view them not as history, but as literary depictions of certain events from antiquity (such as the early Hittite "history" in the Edict of Telepinus), or events roughly contemporaneous with that of their authors (such as the Apology of Hattusilis III). In both instances, the author brings to his task clearly defined intentions that may primarily be literarily or ideologically motivated.

Once we eliminate the highly speculative hypotheses about the official literary genres of ancient Syria and Palestine—theories that have as their only basis the Idrimi inscription—we have to admit that the precise literary models employed here remain uncertain. In northern Syria, we can assume a certain knowledge of Hittite official literary genres. Although the scribes of northern Syria might not have been conversant in Hittite and personally acquainted with documents such as the Apology of Hattusilis, they at least knew the types of treaties that were drawn up during the Late Bronze Age between Hittite overlords and their Syrian vassals. These treaties followed very specific literary models. Often they began with historical prologues that explained why the treaty had been drawn up, continued with the actual treaty, and ended with a series of sanctions against treaty breakers and a list of deities who acted as witnesses to the treaty. The historical prologues are particularly interesting because they display many characteristics of other Hittite historical texts, such as those of Telepinus and Hattusilis III, along with various annals, chronicles, etc. No other contemporary culture produced a similar collection of historiography. These texts, however, represent sweeping generalizations of quasi-historical reflection—certainly not historiography in the modern sense. Similarly, each text carried with it a transparent apologetic agenda: to display the Hittite protagonist in the best possible light. The historical prologues in the treaties justified the contractual relationship by outlining and reaffirming the vassal's traditional responsibilities.

---

rise (1 Sam 15–2 Sam 7), whose structure is very close to the story of Idrimi (cf. below, section II.2.3). Another example is the story of Darius I (521–486 B.C.E.) in Herodotus's *History* (III.88). As with Idrimi and Hattusilis, Darius usurped authority, and the so-called Darius inscription carved in the rock at Bisitun in Iran contains a fragmentary reflection of this narrative depiction of his career and intrigues.

Several treaty texts of this variety from the Late Bronze Age are known; however, the oldest among them concern arrangements not between the Hittite empire and small Syrian states, but between the aforementioned King Idrimi of Alalakh/Mukish (Mukishkhi in the above translation) and King Pilliya of Kizzuwatna (in Cilicia). Yet, this text does not include a historical prologue like the later ones between Hittite and Syrian kings of the fourteenth century B.C.E. Thus the prologue of the contract between Suppiluliumas I of Hatti and Mattiwaza of Mitanni contains fifty-five lines. It describes the historical development of relations between Hatti and Mitanni until the moment when Suppiluliumas was "forced" to meddle in Mitanni's political affairs and place Mattiwaza on its throne. Naturally, the treaty is ostensibly only concerned about Mattiwaza's well-being, though the real goal is presumably to establish a faithful vassal on the Mitanni throne.

These historical prologues to the treaties between the Hittite kings and the kings of the Amurru in Syria reveal important insights (from the Hittite perspective) into the history of those relationships stretching over several generations. A notable example is the treaty between Hatti's Mursilis II (ca. 1340–1310 B.C.E.) and Duppi-Tessub of Amurru (ca. 1332–1300 B.C.E.)—the beginning of the association between both states:

> Aziras was the grandfather of you, Duppi-Tessub. He rebelled against my father, but submitted again to my father. When the kings of Nuhasse land and the kings of Kinza rebelled against my father, Aziras did not rebel. As he was bound by treaty, he remained bound by treaty.[12]

Other sources contain information that does not totally agree with this depiction. Aziru's ascension to the throne of Amurru did not concern the Hittites because Amurru at that time belonged to Egypt. Afterward, however, Aziru abandoned his master—the Egyptian pharaoh—and joined the Hittite cause. The Amarna letters—both Aziru's own letters and those of his enemies—chronicle his escapades.

Clearly, we cannot confuse Hittite historiography with present-day scientific historiography. Hittite administrative writers used great finesse to twist every issue, every historical tidbit, to their rhetorical advantage. Yet we should not totally disparage these Hittite writers. After all, they were interested in the past and especially how the past relates to the present. They realized the past's contribution to present circumstances and knew that without this realization the latter would remain hopelessly inexplicable. Consequently, the Hittites developed a "protohistoriography" that, despite all its failings, foreshadows its modern counterpart. Thus, in both its ancient and modern

---

[12] Translation by Albrecht Goetze, *ANET*, 203. The form "Aziras" instead of ordinary "Aziru" may be a Hittite peculiarity.

applications, historiography seeks to harmonize the past with the present in order to reinforce group, societal, or national solidarity.[13]

The only Bronze Age text from Syria or Palestine that exhibits a historical consciousness remains the Idrimi inscription. There are no other indications of a historical consciousness among the Syro-Palestinian population of that time. Thus, we have no indications that other official literary genres or any writings comparable to the Hittite or Mesopotamian annals were known or used in Syria and Palestine. Perhaps they did not exist at all because the local population deemed them unnecessary and uninteresting. Thus it seems that there was little interest in chronological accuracy, and even official documents were almost never dated precisely. To illustrate this point, consider that although many official business documents have survived from the reign of King Niqmepa of Ugarit (ca. 1330 B.C.E.), none of them indicates even the regnal year during which it was drafted. State officials apparently did not see the use in detailing such events. Consequently, it is a daunting task for scholars to date these texts and reconstruct the context from which they sprang without corroborating chronological or historical data.

III.2.3. The Unofficial Forms: Stories, Folktales, and Vignettes

---

FOLK LITERATURE: **Gunkel,** Hermann. *The Folktale in the Old Testament.* Translated by Michael D. Rutter. Historic Texts and Interpreters in Biblical Scholarship 5. Sheffield: Almond Press, 1987. **Lord,** Albert B. *The Singer of Tales.* Harvard Studies in Comparative Literature 24. Cambridge, Mass.: Harvard University Press, 1960. **Milne,** Pamela J. *Vladimir Propp and the Study of Structure in Hebrew Biblical Narrative.* Bible and Literature Series 13. Sheffield: Sheffield Academic Press, 1988. **Niditch,** Susan. *Oral World and Written Word: Ancient Israelite Literature.* Library of Ancient Israel. Louisville, Ky.: Westminster John Knox 1996. **Nielsen,** Eduard. *Oral Tradition.* SBT 11. London: SCM Press, 1954. **Olrik,** Axel. "Epic Laws of Folk Narrative." In *The Study of Folklore.* Edited by A. Dundes, Pages 129–41. Englewood Cliffs, N.J.: Prentice Hall, 1965. **Parry,** Milman, comp. *Serbocroatian Heroic Songs 1.* Translated and edited by Albert B. Lord. Cambridge, Mass.: Harvard University Press, 1954. **Propp,** Vladimir. *Morphology of the Folktale.* Translated by Laurence Scott. 2d ed. Austin, Tex.: University of Texas Press, 1968. **Propp,** Vladimir. *Theory and History of Folklore.* Translated by Ariadna Y. Martin and Richard P. Martin, et al. Theory and History of Literature 5. Minneapolis: University of Minnesota, 1984. **Thompson,** Stith. *The Folktale.* New York: Holt, Rinehart, and Winston, 1946. **Thompson,** Stith. *Motif-Index of Folk Literature.* 6 vols. 2d ed. Bloomington, Ind.: Indiana University Press, 1955–1958.

FOLK LITERATURE AND ANCIENT NEAR EASTERN INSCRIPTIONS: **Alster,** Bendt. *Dumuzi's Dream: Aspects of Oral Poetry in a Sumerian Myth.* Copenhagen: Akademisk Forlag, 1972. **Alster,** Bendt. *Proverbs of Ancient Sumer: The World's Earliest Proverb Collection.* Bethesda, Maryland: CDL, 1997. **Alster,** Bendt. *Studies*

---

[13] I will address this topic in further detail below, in section IV.3.

in Sumerian Proverbs. Copenhagen: Akademisk Forlag, 1975. **Liverani,** Mario. "Partire sul carro, per il deserto." *Annali dell'Instituto universitario orientale di Napoli* NS 22 (1972): 403–15.

The Idrimi inscription allows us to draw certain conclusions regarding the cultivation of Bronze Age Syrian and Palestinian literary traditions by royalty and commoner alike. The inscription's wording indicates that it is not primarily a historical account of the events it portrays. Other interests motivate its author to sacrifice historical accuracy for argumentative effect. The beginning of the inscription reports that Idrimi is the youngest son of Aleppo's exiled king. This information is not necessarily unhistorical; however, the phrase "youngest son" operates as a *topos* in traditional folk literature. It presumably derives from the fact that in traditional societies, the eldest son inherited all or most of his father's estate, while the younger sons had to come up with their own livelihood.

According to Idrimi, his brothers accept the status quo, but he does not. With his horse, chariot, and groom, he sets out to win his princess and his half-kingdom. As Mario Liverani notes correctly, Idrimi's first quest foreshadows the prototypical European fairy tale, except that the ancient warrior descends into the ominous desert wasteland, which in Oriental tradition plays the same role as the wood in German and the mountains in Scandinavian folklore. For heroes, the desert is a place of tribulations where they can prove themselves worthy challengers to the highest positions in society. It is also a crossroads where one encounters strange things and exotic people—potential allies and tools in the hero's royal quest. First, Idrimi meets the nomadic Sutu. After staying only overnight with them, early the next morning he leaves for Canaan to seek refuge among the *habiru* refugees, who in those days were numerous in the Near East. Soon he becomes the leader of the *habiru.* After seven years (the traditional round number in fairy tales), Idrimi reclaims his kingdom with the help of his adopted warrior-comrades.

Everyone is familiar with such adventure stories from childhood, because they are found everywhere in different forms. Students of folk tales have often described the varied *topoi* of the hero tale. For example, in 1928, Vladimir Propp published his thoughtful Russian-language analysis of this type of adventure literature. After World War II, several translations of his original volume gained broad international acceptance. Propp's investigations concentrated on the various literary elements of the male hero in Russian adventure tales, and he created a classification system that identified important individual components and motifs of the heroic persona. He was thus able to show how regularly these motifs appear in such literature, something that also throws light on folk literature from many other places. Although some of the elements of Russian adventure tales differ markedly from those of their ancient Near Eastern counterparts, such divergences are not very important and may be explained as the result of different settings. While Idrimi roams the desert, Propp's heroes traverse the Russian forests. Because the Idrimi inscription contains all the elements of an adventure tale, we can assume that its narrator built his story around that literary skeleton. If so, Idrimi's status as a "usurper of the throne" is nothing more than an individual rendering of a traditional literary model.

The framework of the Idrimi inscription rests on a clearly defined literary model: the youngest son overcomes his brothers' idleness by embarking on a quest. The writer of this authorized version builds a case for his historical protagonist (i.e., Idrimi) around an unhistorical literary model. Consequently, the author must have been acquainted with the narrative even before he sat down to write the Idrimi tale. Otherwise, either he invented the plot himself or Idrimi's career actually followed the pattern of a folktale. Neither is likely. The inscription thus yields the important insight that our modern understanding of "reality" is not commensurate with that of the ancient Near East. What the people of Syria and Palestine had to say about reality often followed narrative conventions, with little respect for the actual course of events.

The most important argument in favor of the hypothesis that the Idrimi inscription is based on a narrative framework derived from traditional adventure tales is the circumstance that such adventure tales were widely current in the Near East at that time. We have not yet found other examples from Syria and Palestine, but from Egypt we have the Tale of the Doomed Prince. This text's narrative structure mirrors that of the Idrimi inscription, although it has nothing to do with the exploits of an actual, historical individual.[14] In view of the close connections between Egypt and the Near East in antiquity, even in the Bronze Age, we might expect to find similar motifs in the tales from ancient Syria and Palestine. That a similar folktale has not yet appeared from these regions may be accidental.

Unlike genuine adventure tales, the Idrimi inscription depicts its hero in a flat and shallow way. Idrimi is simply the hero of the plot, no more, no less. He lacks cunning, he betrays nobody, he obtains nothing through machinations or wisdom—he is, so to speak, too "nice" to act as a real hero of a folktale. When we approach the heroes of, for example, the Grimm brothers' stories, they often show themselves to be less heroic than expected: more or less chosen by accident, unaware of their unique

---

[14] For the Egyptian text, "The Doomed Prince," see Alan H. Gardiner, *Late-Egyptian Stories* (Bibliotheca aegyptiaca 1; Brussels: Fondation égyptologique reine Elisabeth, 1932), 1–9; cf. also the translations of T. Eric Peet in *The Journal of Egyptian Archaeology* 11 (1925): 227–29, and Miriam Lichtheim in *AEL* 2:200–203. Max Pieper discusses the adventure themes of these tales in *Das ägyptische Märchen* (Leipzig: J. C. Hinrichs, 1935), 41–44.

gifts. Only one thing separates the hero from his relatives, namely, his will to act, to abandon the comforts of home and family, and to travel in the world looking for personal success. He is rarely a titanic figure unique among his people—neither a great warrior nor gifted scholar. His contemptuous peers often marvel at his feebleness and youthful inexperience. Yet despite these transparent shortcomings, the apparently unenlightened hero outwits his adversaries, not because he is wiser but because he is more crafty. Hans Christian Andersen's "blundering Hans" may serve as a kind of prototype of this anti-hero. In Andersen's portrayal, the protagonist foils his brothers' intentions by winning the princess's hand through his pure heart and naïveté. Other fairy tales refer to more contentious battles where frustrated (half) brothers or (half) sisters succumb to their bumbling sibling. The Idrimi tale lacks a dialectical tone, almost completely missing are the narrative motifs that would make it dramatic and compelling. Consequently, it betrays itself as a piece of prefabricated political propaganda that employs a traditional story line and narrative design. That the Idrimi tale is propaganda becomes clearer when we compare it with other narratives from the ancient Near East that are structured according to the same narrative pattern—the best parallels of which come from the Old Testament (although these are much later than the Idrimi narrative). We can identify several, analogous biblical narratives.

The first example is the Joseph saga. Like Idrimi, with God's help Joseph overcomes his seemingly inevitable fate. Although, because of his brothers, he is sold to Egypt as a slave, he rises to a high position as the pharaoh's right-hand man. Yet Joseph is too "nice" to count for a real folk hero. He is a "white knight" who rises to prominence without having fought hard for his success. Joseph never consciously envisions a concrete goal or maps a coherent strategy—otherwise, his affair with Potiphar's wife would have taken a quite different turn! His successes reflect amazing good fortune. Perhaps the Joseph saga is more "parlor literature" than folktale: written to an educated audience that stands aloof from the rather crude, gratuitous tones of the more pedestrian adventure tales of ordinary folk.

Jacob is a genuine hero whose career bears an even more striking resemblance to that of Idrimi. First, he is the youngest of two sons. Second, he dupes his older brother. Finally, he wins his princess (Rachel) and his half-kingdom (Laban's flocks). Yet unlike the Idrimi tale, Jacob's success story ends with his return home. In a genuine adventure tale, Jacob and Rachel would remain in Haran, living happily in the manner to which they have become accustomed, and upon his death he would inherit Laban's wealth and property. However, the Jacob story had other intentions as a part of a major cycle of narratives. In this connection some fundamental elements of the plot of such folktales have been relegated to a secondary position: they may elucidate a point in the story line, but they are not decisive for the course of events. Nevertheless, they are there and reveal that the author who composed the Jacob story was well acquainted with the folktale, which had already been in circulation for many centuries.

The next Old Testament parallel to the Idrimi tale also concerns a king who—being crafty—gains and secures his throne through God's assistance: the so-called history of David's rise.[15] The parallels between David's rise and the Idrimi narrative are fundamental elements in portraying either the success or failure of the hero.[16] Prototypically, David is the youngest brother who accompanies his older siblings onto the battlefield, where he battles with the dreadful Goliath, whom nobody else has dared oppose. Although his outward appearance hardly betokens a great warrior-hero (he is too small even to carry Saul's armor), David successfully defeats Goliath. After his amazing triumph, David marries Saul's daughter, princess Michal, and rivals even Prince Jonathan, the designated heir to the throne, who ultimately accepts David's succession of Saul. The story could end here; however, other narrative motifs remain that reflect specific instances in the Idrimi tale. At his career's zenith, an unexpected twist seemingly unravels David's victories: his expulsion from the royal court and the concomitant loss of his wife, status, and wealth. Only Goliath's sword rescues him from this ignominy. In scenes that recall Idrimi's fate, David takes the sword, flees into the desert, and becomes the leader of a considerable force of destitute persons, refugees very much like Idrimi's *habiru* attendants. Through cunning and ingenuity, David eventually succeeds in eliminating all his enemies and becoming Israel's king.

Scholars have offered various interpretations of the story of David's rise.[17] Here we will only state the obvious. David's rise is another example of the folktale genre that concerns the life of not very heroic

---

[15] Although its exact narrative parameters remain uncertain, the David saga stretches from approximately 1 Sam 15 to 2 Sam 7.

[16] The first attempt to draw connections between these two stories was made by the Italian Assyriologist Giorgio Buccellati in his article "La 'carriera' di David e quella di Idrimi, re di Alalac," *Bibbia e Oriente* 4 (1962): 95–99.

[17] See particularly Jakob H. Grønbaek, *Die Geschichte vom Aufstieg Davids (1. Sam. 15–2. Sam. 5): Tradition und Komposition* (Acta theologica danica 10; Copenhagen: Munksgaard, 1971). Cf. also my essay, "David's Rise," *JSOT* 10 (1978): 2–25, in which I attempt to show that this tale must be viewed as royal propaganda; that is, David becomes king only because Yahweh chooses him and manages his career. Of course, even divine support could not make David a good politician. Other studies on this subject include P. Kyle McCarter, "The Apology of David," *JBL* 99 (1980): 489–504; and James C. VanderKam, "Davidic Complicity in the Deaths of Abner and Eshbaal," *JBL* 99 (1980): 521–39. For a survey of the latest research on this topic, see Walter Dietrich and Thomas Naumann, *Die Samuelbücher* (Erträge der Forschung 287; Darmstadt: Wissenschaftliche Buchgesellschaft, 1995), esp. 64–119.

heroes. Although we must concede that the story describes David as very brave, not to say foolhardy, he snakes his way through every obstacle placed before him. One by one his enemies are eliminated—getting themselves killed in one way or the other—and finally David is able, by the will of God, to ascend the throne that has been waiting for him since the very beginning of the narrative.

David represents a more heroic figure than the colorless Idrimi, and as literature David's story is better and more interesting than its extrabiblical counterpart. Nevertheless, both unmistakably reflect the same narrative style. This indicates the availability at that time of an extensive pool of popular narrative, normally transmitted orally, but eagerly drawn upon by authors who sat down to put heroic stories in writing.

A scarcity of source materials precludes the reconstruction of a history of Syro-Palestinian folk literature. Yet undoubtedly, such folk literature existed and flourished. Thus, despite the lack of documents, we can review the different genres expected in societies that are on a similar cultural level to the ones in ancient Syria and Palestine. Here it is important to understand that this cultural level was also not very different from that found in Central and Northern Europe during the early stages of the Middle Ages. Society's upper echelon was extremely small and centered particularly at the royal courts, where initially only a few could read and write. Here professional artists—either members of the royal entourage or traveling minstrels—provided the entertainment. The common people also provided an audience, for example, when minstrels and comedians appeared during market days, at weddings, or for major public festivals. Ironically, this system was relatively "democratic," that is, because few could read or write, they all—high and low—had the same access to such folk traditions. Of course, without widespread literacy, societies (whether in medieval Europe or ancient Syria-Palestine) produced little in the way of written literature. Furthermore, both Syria and Palestine lacked an extensive, educated middle class that would have paid for written literary works. In short, there was no market for books. Only very few administrators rose above the illiterate masses. Still, ordinary people should not be seen as literarily unaware, since they readily enjoyed orally performed literature.

Today we possess many important studies of folk literature, including literature that appears in the Old Testament.[18] Since the days of the

---

[18] The classic contribution to this study comes from Hermann Gunkel's landmark study, *The Folktale in the Old Testament* (trans. Michael D. Rutter; Sheffield: Almond, 1987); originally published as *Das Märchen im Alten Testament* (Tübingen: J.C.B. Mohr [P. Siebeck], 1921). Patricia G. Kirkpatrick provides a contemporary assessment of Gunkel's original study in her previously mentioned work, *The Old Testament and Folklore Study*.

Grimm brothers, students of folk literature have gathered extensive collections of folktales and poetry. From Scandinavia, we possess many heroic legends, fairy tales, and folk songs. Moreover, popular tradition has also survived in the form of short anecdotes. Finally, we should mention the great oral epics collected by scholars of the twentieth century C.E. and made available to the general public. Such epics are especially related to classical literature, especially the Homeric epics. The modern parallels show that, although this ancient literature has almost exclusively survived in a written form,[19] it was founded on orally transmitted paradigms and plots.

The above-mentioned material and our general knowledge of ancient Syro-Palestinian society allow us to review the unofficial oral traditions and the literary genres generated from them. To be sure, our conclusions remain hypothetical, although supported by many circumstantial arguments. The main problem can be summarized quite simply: nothing has survived from the oral literature (how could it?); what we can know is available only from the written versions originally based on the oral traditions.

Folk literature, like any written literature, can be divided into two main categories: prose narratives and poetic literature. Of course, we know that prose can be used for complex discourse, but especially in ancient contexts it was an ideal medium to communicate shorter, precise messages. In traditional literature, poetry is often preferable for long, narrative plots. The reason lies in the power of mnemonics. Poetry—whether short or long—encourages repetition: a grand pastiche of ornamentation, embellishment, and recurring phrases that enhance its overall literary structure. Such repetitive passages allow the minstrel to pause mentally and concentrate on phrasing the next passage. In a prose narrative, such repetitions seem unnecessary and redundant and create obstacles to the flow of the narrative. In poetry they create aesthetic moments that can be enjoyed by the public, who will expect such intermissions and appreciate them.

Undoubtedly, the fullest folk-literary form is the epic. Since antiquity, epics such as Homer's have survived in written form. Orally transmitted epics were constantly feeding the written tradition with motifs and imagination. From Bronze Age Syria, three such epics have survived: the Ugaritic poetry concerning Aqhat, Kirta, and Baal. In the next section, we will discuss these texts extensively. Here we only mention them to emphasize that such literature existed in ancient Syria and probably also in Palestine. It was most likely not something unique to Ugarit.

---

[19] We say "*almost* exclusively in a written form," because many are the pictorial reflections of this tradition in Greek art.

As an orally transmitted form, epic is always in the process of becoming; that is, it never really attains a definitive final form. This insight comes from studies of modern folk art that show how orally transmitted epic poetry changes in the course of performance. It is never repeated verbatim; new elements are added and older ones dropped. The singer or laureate redirects the tale's rhythm, plot, and phrasing with each successive performance. The minstrel's ability to reformulate the tale and the audience's ability to listen and understand are the only limiting factors for the amount and quality of improvisation. Therefore, even so-called primitive societies may possess an extensive and diverse folk literature, and their epics may extend as much as ten thousand lines or more.

Thanks to the work of the American scholars Milman Parry and Albert Bates Lord, we possess impressive insights into similar epic poetry from Serbo-Croatia (formerly Yugoslavia) that they collected between the two world wars. Intriguingly, they discovered a major literary tradition within that population, which at that time was almost exclusively illiterate and living in very primitive conditions. This heritage thus depended solely on oral tradition. Parry and Lord dispelled certain "myths" regarding folk literature's developmental process. Although Parry died before the publication of his initial findings, Lord ultimately published a popular version of them. In it, Lord debunks the notion that oral literature remains virtually unchanged over centuries of recitation. The singer or laureate who reinterprets a piece during each successive performance can quadruple the variations on the original theme and still maintain that the final rendition is a copy of the original. Indeed, at that juncture, the singer or laureate really believes that the lyrics remain pristine!

Generally, we can draw several conclusions from such scholarly observations. First, "illiterate" societies create substantial literary traditions. Second, exclusively oral traditions, as opposed to written literature, are dynamic in nature. Third, folk poetry is not able to portray the world of the past as it really was, because each performance reconfigures its content. The presence of an oral literature is no guarantee that its original content has been preserved. Within even a few generations of the original oral composition, many creative anomalies appear. This is particularly significant when dealing with "historical" events recorded in such literature. Such historical events can only be verified by other extant evidence.

Epic literature knows no social barriers. As long as listeners remain interested, people recite poetry. Yet poetry lovers must possess certain rudimentary skills to interact with the text. Conversely, the singer or minstrel admits certain freedoms and embellishments into every performance. The listener will not object as long as the poem is meaningful and preserves its imaginative force. Such singers should be compared to gypsies who travel the roads of Europe, earning a living by offering their skills. One might say they belong among the descendants of Jubal, Cain's offspring, who, according to Gen 4:21, is "the father of all those who play the lyre and the pipe."

In Syria and Palestine, poetic forms also developed outside the narrow circle of literary specialists. Such poems—better to call them songs—were so short and uncomplicated that everyone could easily recite them. Unfortunately, we cannot say much about this literary tradition since very few and incomplete examples have survived. Nor have the documents from the major ancient cultural centers been informative in this respect. Most extant examples come from Egyptian sources, mainly in the form of work songs and love poems. Some scholars are inclined to count various Old Testament texts as examples of this genre, especially in the Song of Songs. Yet in its present form the Song of Songs surely is one of the latest writings within the Hebrew Bible and thus can provide only very indirect evidence regarding ancient private poetry. At most, it shows that short poems flourished and were sung in antiquity. Their form and content—not to mention the music that accompanied them—are lost to us.[20]

Indeed, it seems paradoxical to use the Old Testament as a source for studying unofficial folk literature of the second millennium B.C.E. While, the biblical literature dates from the first millennium B.C.E. Nevertheless, we can confidently defend this use after investigating the collection's character. Despite their polished, final form, the Old Testament narratives developed from unofficial folk literature rather than official state compositions. Conversely, we find few examples of poetic genres, such as proverbs, instructions, victory songs, and laments, among the extant Bronze Age Syrian and Palestinian documents. We can only approach such genres through the analogies provided by the Old Testament. This procedure is not without justification. After all, hints of such literary genres can be found, for example, in letters from that period. As far as social and economic structures are concerned, Near Eastern

---

[20] Gillis Gerleman compares the Song of Songs with Old Egyptian songs in *Ruth: Das Hohelied* (BKAT 18; Neukirchen-Vluyn: Neukirchener Verlag des Erziehungsvereins, 1965). The Egyptian songs have been collected and edited by Siegfried Schott in *Altägyptische Liebeslieder* (2d ed.; Zurich: Artemis-Verlag, 1950). Many other scholars have compared the Song of Songs with later Syro-Palestinian love poems—especially wedding songs. See especially Helmer Ringgren, "Die Volksdichtung und das Hohe Lied," in Sven Linder's *Palästinische Volksgesänge* (2 vols.; Uppsala: Lundequistska bokhandeln, 1952–1955), 1:82–114. Of course, the songs collected by Linder and others do not prove the existence of this type of literature in the second-millennium Near East, but they do make it seem probable, because they make it possible to show an amazing continuity on the one hand between the Song of Songs and the Egyptian songs, and on the other hand between the Song of Songs and the Arabic poems from Palestine.

society did not change much through these periods. This is especially true when it comes to the life and living conditions of ordinary people. Circumstances under which cultural manifestations developed remained nearly constant for centuries. Thus, with careful methodology, we can draw analogies and propose conclusions based on evidence from different periods, although we would emphasize that it is impossible to do more than generalize.

The situation is similar for ancient Near Eastern prose compositions. The parallels—whether contemporary, earlier, or later—to the literary production in Bronze Age Syria and Palestine that come from comparable societies in Asia Minor, Egypt, and elsewhere in Western Asia that short literary pieces were set forth in prose. Such material may be divided into short stories, anecdotes, and fairy tales, including, for example, the previously discussed genre of male hero stories. Again Egypt provides the best comparative material, whereas prose narratives are almost absent in Syria and Palestine. Thus we cannot say with certainty that such prose literature existed also in Syria and Palestine at that time, or whether on the other hand poetry was not preferred there.

The letter remains the only prose literary genre to which Syrian and Palestinian documents concretely and amply testify. Yet we must use caution when calling these documents "unofficial"; clearly most of them come from "official" state archives in Mari, Ugarit, Hattusas, and El-Amarna. Moreover, these messages were not for publication or performance but were written simply to communicate information.

One cannot confuse the letter genre with great literature. That was not its intent. Yet through these casual documents, we can look into the mind of ancient Syrians and Palestinians. In spite of their casual character, often provoked by specific circumstances, letters illuminate the psychology of people in ancient times. We should not forget, however, that almost every letter was written by and for members of the highest echelon. Often, their letters provide candid, amusing, and even touching insights into life among the elite classes. The correspondence between King Zimri-Lim of Mari (eighteenth century B.C.E.) and Queen Shiptu includes many such glimpses of life at the court of Mari, as when, for example, the queen informs his majesty that she has given birth to twins, one male and one female.[21] Another example from Mari is a letter a servant sends to King Yasmakh-Adad informing him that Beltum, the daughter of the king of Qatna, is recovering from a sun-

[21] "Say to my master: Thus Shiptu, your maidservant: I have given birth to twins: 1 son and 1 daughter. My master must rejoice!" (published in George Dossin, *Correspondance féminine* (Archives royales de Mari 10; Paris: Paul Geuthner, 1978), number 26. See also Abraham Malamat's interesting discussion of Shiptu and her letters in "The Correspondence of Šibtu, Queen of Mari in *ARM* X," in his *Mari and the Bible* (Leiden: E. J. Brill, 1998), 175–91.

stroke, which she probably suffered during a dancing ceremony—an incident he blames on her foolish old nanny![22]

The Amarna letters also occasionally reveal (sometimes unintentionally) a writer's intentions or a recipient's sentiments. Over a period of time, the Amurru king Aziru and his Egyptian overlord exchange correspondences. Initially, Pharaoh demands Aziru's appearance before him to verify his loyalty. Aziru unenthusiastically responds by constantly postponing his departure date. Concurrently, he defends himself against his adversaries' energetically slanderous remarks—especially those of King Rib-Adda of Byblos, who for years has referred to him as a traitor in many letters to the pharaoh.[23] Such letters clearly reveal Aziru's frame of mind, especially in light of his subsequent treason against his Egyptian overlord.[24] On the other hand, Pharaoh reproaches Rib-Adda for his many complaints, insinuating that Rib-Adda has obviously overreacted in his self-appointed role as Egypt's watchdog in Syria: "You write more than all other mayors."[25] This did not dissuade Rib-Addi from writing still more complaints to Egypt.

The discussion in this section can be summarized as follows. During the Bronze Age, folk literature flourished in Syria and Palestine. Even when the sources do not provide fully worked-out examples, significant traces remain available for study. The continuity of the general culture, on the one hand, and literary echoes in later literature, on the other hand, indicate that an orally transmitted popular literature was an important part of life in ancient Syria and Palestine. Until the Hellenistic period, written literature remained as scarce as the market to which it catered. By the last pre-Christian centuries, with the development of municipal societies, a literate elite class promised new markets and creative possibilities for these ancient tales. In time, as cities grew and prospered, elite entrepreneurial classes emerged that could garner enough wealth to build and sustain the creative arts. Furthermore, people of the Hellenistic-Roman periods had a system of writing—a fully developed alphabet—that greatly enhanced literary activity. With the explosive growth of wealth, a new kind of artist burst upon the scene: the writer. Rather than filling a strictly utilitarian role, writing now existed for public consumption and books were stored in both public and private libraries. The

---

[22] This text is published by Dominique Charpin in *Archives épistolaires de Mari I/2* (Archives royales de Mari 26/2; Paris: Editions recherche sur les civilisations, 1988), number 298 (see the English translation by Jack M. Sasson in *CANE* 2:1204).

[23] EA 67–138 contains the correspondence between Rib-Adda and Pharaoh.

[24] EA 156–171 contains the correspondence between Pharaoh and Aziru. A letter from Pharaoh to Aziru (EA 162) is especially revealing: the Egyptians understand very well what is going on in Amurru and plainly explain to Aziru that he should stop his tricks and excuses (for a translation, see Moran, *Amarna Letters*, 248–50).

[25] EA 124:35–40.

character of the earlier documentary archives from Syria and Palestine indicates that never before had there been that kind of professionally written literature. In antiquity, writing served almost exclusively practical purposes. People wrote bills, not novels.

III.2.4. The Epic Texts from Ugarit

PRIMARY TEXTS: See above, section II.1.1.

SECONDARY RESOURCES: **Aitken,** Kenneth T. *The Aqhat Narrative: A Study in the Narrative Structure and Composition of an Ugaritic Tale.* Manchester: University of Manchester, 1990. **Loretz,** Oswald. *Ugarit und die Bibel: Kanaanäische Götter und Religion im Alten Testament.* Darmstadt: Wissenschaftliche Buchgesellschaft, 1990. **Margalit,** Baruch. *A Matter of "Life" and "Death": A Study of the Baal-Mot Epic.* Alter Orient und Altes Testament 206. Neukirchen-Vluyn: Neukirchener Verlag, 1980. **Margalit,** Baruch. *The Ugaritic Poem of AQHT.* BZAW 182. Berlin: Walter de Gruyter, 1989. **de Moor,** Johannes Cornelis. *The Seasonal Pattern in the Ugaritic Myth of Balu, according to the Version of Ilumilku.* Alter Orient und Altes Testament 16. Kevelaer: Butzon and Bercker, 1971. **del Olmo Lete,** Gregorio. *Interpretación de la mitología cananea: Estudios de semántica ugarítica.* Valencia: Institucion San Jeronimo, 1984. **Parker,** Simon B. *The Pre-Biblical Narrative Tradition: Essays on the Ugaritic Poems Keret and Aqhat.* Atlanta: Scholars Press, 1989. **Smith,** Mark S. *The Ugaritic Baal Cycle I.* VTSup 55. Leiden: E. J. Brill, 1994.

The Ugaritic epic poetry discovered by French excavators in 1930 represents the sole exception to the rule that we have no literary remains from Bronze Age Syria and Palestine; but it is a rather important exception, since in Ugarit a whole series of literary texts of mythic and epic character have come to light. All of them come from the Late Bronze Age; most were found in the so called library of the high priest and can be dated to the reign of King Niqmaddu II (ca. 1370–1335 B.C.E.). Unfortunately, missing archaeological reports make it impossible to identify the location of each text more exactly within the archival complex. Perhaps this library contained two sections—one that housed actual religious documents and another that contained all or large portions of epic texts.[26] If so, this separation might reflect a distinction between literary and religious texts.

Each text is written in Ugaritic, a member of the Northwest Semitic language family, related to Amorite and fairly easy to understand for anyone who knows Hebrew. The texts bear unmistakable local trademarks: cuneiform letters etched on clay tablets that are easy to distinguish from Akkadian cuneiform signs. Akkadian was well known in Ugarit because it was a language of international diplomatic correspon-

[26] See Allan R. Petersen, "Where Did Schaeffer Find the Clay Tablets of the Ugaritic Baal-Cycle?" *SJOT* 8 (1994): 43–58.

dence. It is written with syllabic signs, each representing consonant + vowel, or vowel + consonant, or consonant + vowel + consonant. Ugaritic, on the other hand, was written in an alphabetic script. Like Hebrew and Arabic, it only indicated consonants—in contrast to later Indo-European alphabets. Yet as with other alphabets that are primarily consonantal, some phonetic elements crept into Ugaritic to indicate vowels. Although it contains several additional letters at the end of its thirty-letter alphabet, the Ugarit writing system is very similar to Hebrew. Thus, virtually anyone could learn the language; however, its lack of vowels poses problems for the modern linguist, who has troubles reconstructing the language phonetically. Accordingly, its exact pronunciation remains problematic.

When we refer to Ugaritic epic poetry, our attention turns to three important texts: the poems concerning King Kirta (or Keret, as he was first called by scholars), the heroic Aqhat, and the god Baal. None of these texts survives fully and many clay tablets have huge gaps—especially at the beginning and at the end. Furthermore, other tablets are missing altogether—unless they never existed, which seems less likely. If we compare the three poems, clearly the Aqhat and Kirta texts lack conclusions. The Baal poem contains a colophon that identifies the tablet's scribe—perhaps the author himself. Indeed, the same name, Ilumilku (or Ilimilku) also appears in the margins of both the Kirta and Aqhat texts. His full title appears in the aforementioned colophon of the Baal poem:

> The scribe: ʾIlīmilku the Šubbanite, disciple of ʾAttānu-purulini, (who is) chief of the priests (and) chief of the cultic herdsmen; *t̠āʿiyu*-official of Niqmaddu, (who is) king of Ugarit, lord (of) YRGB, (and) master (of) T̠RMN.[27]

Ilumilku's role remains unclear. Was he the actual high priest or a distinguished official in the high priest's service? In another text, he is referred to as a scribe who translates cuneiform texts for the queen. A question commands our attention: Was Ilumilku only the scribe or was he also the author of the three poems presently under discussion? If he was only the scribe who wrote down the texts, did he copy other manuscripts, or did someone dictate them to him? If he wrote these poems, surely he employed existing oral traditions. In this case—in contrast to other "singers"—he wrote down his poems and inscribed his own name. If somebody dictated the poems to him, this might have been the *Atn* or *ʾAttānu* mentioned in the colophon text as the master of Ilumilku. If so, to what end? Were his transcriptions intended for later recitation? In a society like the one at Ugarit, this would certainly have been unusual; epics were generally composed

---

[27] *KTU* 1.6, vi.53–57, translated by Dennis Pardee in *COS* 1.86, 273. See also the translations by H. L. Ginsberg in *ANET*, 141, and by Mark S. Smith in *Ugaritic Narrative Poetry* (ed. Simon B. Parker; SBLWAW 9; Atlanta: Scholars Press, 1997), 164.

and passed along in oral form. Nor is it likely that the poems were written down to preserve them for posterity during a period of danger in Ugarit, since the reign of Niqmaddu II was relatively uneventful. Instead of such dramatic explanations, these poems may simply have served as teaching models in scribal academies, as was done in Mesopotamian academies; in this case, these poems are merely a student's class work, which might explain the many mistakes in these texts. Of course, this explanation calls into question the usual dating of the tablets to the reign of Niqmaddu II. The colophon would be part of the original text that was copied later onto the tablets now in our possession.

Excerpts from the Battle between Baal and Yamm

Go, lads, [don't dally],
  head for
  the Great Assembly,
  for [Mount Lalu.
At the feet of ʾIlu] do not fall,
  do not prostrate yourself (to) the Great [Assembly.
Standing, say
(your) speech],
  repeat your information.
Say to the Bull, [my] father [ʾIlu,
  repeat to the Great] Assembly:
Message of Yammu, your master,
  of your lord Ruler [Naharu]:
Give (up), O gods, the one whom you obey,
  the one whom the hordes (of the earth) fear.
Give (up) Baʿlu [and his attendants],
  (give up) the Son of Dagan, that I might take
  possession of his gold.

The lads head off, don't hesitate;
  they head
  for Mount Lalu,
  for the Great Assembly.
The gods have sat down to eat,
  the sons of the Holy One to dine,
  Baʿlu attending on ʾIlu.
The gods see them,
  see Yammu's messengers,
  the embassy of Ruler [Naharu].
The gods lower their heads
  onto their knees,
  onto their princely thrones.

Baʿlu rebukes them:
Why, gods, have you lowered (your) heads
  even to your knees,
  even to your princely thrones?

As one must the gods answer,
the tablet of Yammu's messengers,
the embassy of Ruler Naharu!
Lift, O gods, your heads
off your knees,
off your princely thrones.
And let me answer Yammu's messengers,
the embassy of Ruler Naharu.
The gods then raise their heads
off their knees,
off their princely thrones.

Thereafter the messengers of Yammu arrive
the embassy of Ruler Naharu.
At the feet of ʾIlu they [do not] fall,
they do not prostrate themselves (to) the Great Assembly.
Standing, they [say] (their) speech,
[repeat] their information.
They look like a fire, two fires,
their [tongue] like a sharpened sword.
They say to the Bull, his father ʾIlu:
Message of Yammu, your master,
of your [lord], Ruler Naharu:
Give (up), O gods, the one whom you obey,
the one whom the [hordes (of the earth)] fear.
Give (up) Baʿlu and his attendants,
(give up) the Son of Dagan, that I might take
possession of his gold.

The Bull, his father ʾIlu, [replies]:
Baʿlu (is) your servant, O Yammu,
Baʿlu (is) your servant, [O Naharu],
the Son of Dagan (is) your prisoner.
He will indeed bring you tribute,
like (one) of the gods he will bring [you a gift].
Like one of the sons of the Holy One (he will
bring you) presents.

[A large gap appears between Baal's (translated Baʿlu here) decision to fight and the actual struggle with Yamm (here Yammu). In the following excerpt, Baal's battle preparations are well underway.]

Kôṯaru-wa-Ḫasīsu speaks up:
I hereby announce to you, Prince Baʿlu,
and I repeat, Cloud-Rider:
As for your enemy, O Baʿlu,
as for your enemy, you'll smite (him),
you'll destroy your adversary.
You'll take your eternal kingship,
your sovereignty (that endures) from generation
to generation.

Kôṯaru prepares two maces
  and proclaims their names:
You, your name is Yagrušu;
  Yagrušu, drive out Yammu,
  drive Yammu from his throne,
  Naharu from his seat of sovereignty.
You'll whirl in Baˁlu's hand,
  like a hawk in his fingers,
Strike Prince Yammu on the shoulder,
  Ruler Naharu on the chest.
(So) the mace whirls in Baˁlu's hand,
  like a hawk in his fingers,
Strikes Prince Yammu on the shoulder,
  Ruler Naharu on the chest.
(But) Yammu is strong, he does not collapse,
  his joints do not go slack,
  his body does not slump.

Kôṯaru prepars two maces
  and proclaims their names:
You, your name is ˀAyyamurru;
  ˀAyyamurru, expel Yammu,
  expel Yammu from his throne,
  Naharu from his seat of sovereignty.
You'll whirl in Baˁlu's hand,
  like a hawk in his fingers,
Strike Prince Yammu on the head,
  Ruler Naharu on the forehead.
Yammu will go groggy
  and will fall to the ground.
So the mace whirls in Baˁlu's hand,
  [like] a hawk in his fingers,
Strikes Prince [Yammu] on the head,
  Ruler Naharu on the forehead.
Yammu goes groggy,
  falls to the ground;
His joints go slack,
  his body slumps.
Baˁlu grabs Yammu and sets about dismembering (him),
  sets about finishing Ruler Naharu off.

By name ˁAṯtartu reprimands (him):
Scatter (him), O Mighty [Baˁlu],
  scatter (him), O Cloud-Rider,
For Prince [Yammu] is our captive,
  [for] Ruler Naharu is our captive.[28]

[28] *KTU* 1.2, translated by Dennis Pardee in *COS* 1.86, 246–49. See also the translations by H. L. Ginsberg in *ANET*, 130–31, and by Mark S. Smith in *Ugaritic Narrative Poetry*, 99–105.

We cannot identify concretely the circumstances within which these Ugaritic poems developed. Nonetheless, we must consider them unique compositions. A comparable literary tradition developed only in the large Mesopotamian cities and later in the Greek city-states—in both cases, with entirely different agendas. The Mesopotamians developed their literature in scribal academies under the direction of trained scholars. The Greeks also used written literature for two purposes: as school textbooks and—as in the case of the Homeric epics—to safeguard the correct wording from changes made during oral recitations. Unlike other epic literature in general, the Homeric epics were actually learned by heart—that is, once they had been fixed in writing.[29] Before that, they were transmitted orally in the same way as other epics. Ugaritic poems are "loners," that is, they have no successors. Therefore, we must approach these epics with great caution, since we do not know whether or not they lived on in oral form even after they were put in writing. In subsequent Syrian and Palestinian literary tradition (written and oral) we find no trace of the Aqhat or Kirta epics, while scattered fragments of the plot of the Baal poem—such as the fight between the god and the Sea—appear in later Near Eastern tradition, including the Old Testament.

In the following pages, we will first briefly describe the contents of the three major Ugaritic poems, then briefly discuss their function, especially their meaning for Syro-Palestinian religious history. As we proceed, we will also try to dispel some misinterpretations still current among modern scholars.

Each clay tablet of the Baal poem contains its own scene or its own segment of the god's life. The precise sequence of the segments remains uncertain, because every last tablet has been broken at the beginning and at the end. Thus any reconstruction of the Baal narrative is strictly hypothetical. One hypothesis—still a hypothesis, though it seems likely enough—suggests that all these scenes should be connected as parts of a single, coherent poem. If so, then the most reasonable reconstruction of the poem's story line recognizes four scenes: Baal's conflict with the Sea; Baal and Anath; Baal's temple; and Baal's conflict with Mot.

The first scene unfolds as the sea-god Yamm's envoys appear at the court of the senior god El (ʾIlu in the translation above). Through his agents, Yamm makes two demands: El and Baal must recognize him as the supreme god and lord; and his adversary Baal should surrender to him. The gods tremble as Baal confronts Yamm's envoys, and only the intervention of the goddess Anath protects Yamm's envoys from Baal's

---

[29] They were first put in writing perhaps at the end of the eighth century B.C.E.; some scholars say a little before the end of the sixth century.

anger. Baal defies Yamm, and with the help of weapons provided by the artisan god Kothar wa-Khasis (Kôṯaru-wa-Ḫasīsu above) he ultimately vanquishes his brash foe.

Plans for building Baal's temple occupy the next two sections. Despite his victory over Yamm and his lofty position as the lord of all gods, Baal does not have his own temple. Since the construction project could not begin without El's approval, Baal and Anath join forces, thinking up possible ways to cajole El into supporting the project. First, Baal and Anath win over El's wife, Athirat (ᶜAṯtartu above), to their scheme. El, never very consistent in his attitude, soon concedes and allows them to build a temple, for which Kothar wa-Khasis receives the contract. This section reaches its climax when Baal obtains his temple, but it ends ominously. Baal's enemies, especially the god Mot (whose name means "death"), begin a campaign against him. Baal throws down the gauntlet with these words: "Baal alone is lord of the gods." Initially, Mot retreats.

The epic's final section has several parts. First, Mot returns with harsh, threatening words that humiliate Baal, after which Baal has no other escape than to descend into Mot's realm, into the heart of the earth where he "dies," devoured by the earth. Once he hears of Baal's death, El must recognize Mot as the world's sovereign. While El's reaction to Baal's disappearance is rather blasé, Anath's response is swift: she sets out to find the missing god. She searches out Mot, confronts him, and forces him to release Baal from the earth. After Baal's resuscitation, Mot kneels before him and acknowledges him as the lord of all gods. This section concludes with a victory song to the sun goddess followed by the aforementioned colophon of Ilumilku.

While the characters in the Baal poem are all divine, the characters in the Kirta epic are mortals assisted and favored by the gods.[30] At the start of the poem (unless there was an introduction that has been lost), a Job-like disaster befalls King Kirta. His seven wives die from disease, disaster, and war—effectively jeopardizing his progeny. Understandably, these events overwhelm Kirta. In a dream, Kirta receives a revelation from El, who asks him to fulfill a number of obligations. First, he will have to prepare a magnificent sacrifice for Baal and El. Then, Kirta must assemble a huge army that will journey seven days and descend like a swarm of locusts to besiege the city of Udum. After a seven-day siege, the king of Udum will offer to cede his throne to Kirta in order to save his city from destruction. Kirta must not accept his offer; instead he must ask for the king's daughter—the beautiful Hurrai—in marriage. Hurrai will become the mother of Kirta's children.

---

[30] For translations of Kirta (*KTU* 1.14–16), see Dennis Pardee, "The Kirta Epic," in *COS* 1.102, 333–43; H. L. Ginsberg, "The Legend of King Keret," in *ANET*, 142–49, and Edward L. Greenstein in *Ugaritic Narrative Poetry*, 9–48.

Kirta explicitly obeys the divine instructions and good fortune returns. Hurrai produces seven sons and seven daughters, after which Kirta prepares a mammoth celebration. Here the text becomes incoherent; however, we know that during or after the celebration, Kirta is struck with a deadly disease. With his bleak prognosis, Kirta's daughter prepares a grave and enters his death chamber. Again, El intervenes in the life of his beloved ally. Because the other gods refuse to assist Kirta, El himself devises a solution: he creates a healer who takes the form of a woman and sends her to Kirta. He overcomes his illness and again returns to his throne, an event not appreciated by all: his eldest son Yassib has claimed the throne. The poem ends with Kirta placing a curse on Yassib and urging the gods to execute him.

Most likely, we lack several sections of this poem's original conclusion. The extant conclusion, which includes a brief colophon with the name Ilumilku, cannot be more than a preliminary end to the part of the epic that concentrates on Kirta's illness. We therefore do not know whether Kirta ever reconciled with his son. One possible scenario is supported by a note within the poem mentioning that this story of Kirta's illness and convalescence is only a subsection of a much larger epic that ends when Kirta's youngest son ascends to his father's throne. After Yassib was cursed and removed from the plot, it is imaginable that more sections followed describing how the other sons opposed their youngest sibling and were overcome by their father, their brother, or the gods. However, this highly mutilated text admits of no conclusive reconstruction.

As with the Kirta poem, the third large epic from Ugarit discusses the relationship between humans and their gods. In the Kirta poem, that relationship is relatively favorable: El always comes to Kirta's rescue. In contrast, those connections are universally negative in the Aqhat epic. The poem hinges on the problems thrust upon humans by the malicious goddess Anath. Her indignation arises from Aqhat's refusal to surrender his bow to her.

The poem starts with a revelatory scene in which the devout King Danel prepares to receive an oracle from Baal and El: Danel is told in a dream that he will be granted a son who will be his heir. Like Kirta, Danel follows the instructions to the letter, welcomes Kothar's goddesses (midwives) into his home, and awaits his child's birth. When the text resumes after another gap that covers two tablets, Danel's son Aqhat is already an adult. As a sign of his manliness, Kothar wa-Khasis brings him a bow. With it Aqhat ventures into the world where he subsequently meets Anath, who covets his bow. The goddess entices the young warrior with promises of gold, wealth, eternal life, and a place in the heavenly court, but Aqhat resists Anath's vain attempts to satisfy her desire. In a biting tone, he summarily refuses to be swayed:

"Fib not to me, O Maiden;
  For to a Youth thy fibbing is *loathsome.*
Further life—how can mortal attain it?
  How can mortal attain life enduring?
Glaze will be poured [on] my head,
  Plaster upon my pate;
And I'll die as everyone dies,
  I too shall assuredly die.
Moreover, this will I say:
My bow is *[a weapon for]* warriors.
  Shall now females *[with it]* to the chase?"[31]

Predictably, Anath cannot tolerate his insubordination; however, she initially exchanges vacant pleasantries with Aqhat—perhaps because she is afraid of the bow. This feigned friendliness serves only as a cover for her treacherous intent. Against El's wishes, Anath initiates her plan: her attendant Yatpan turns into an eagle and kills the unsuspecting Aqhat. At this point, the text is seriously damaged and its contents are unclear. What follows, however, suggests that an eagle consumes Aqhat's corpse, and the coveted bow vanishes. In the wake of his death, nature unravels and humanity suffers from a massive drought.

Danel, who does not yet know of his son's death, is puzzled: Why is the land drought-ridden? He leaves his palace to inspect the damage. As he prays for Aqhat's swift return, two messengers inform Danel of his son's death. Now he turns to Baal in prayer, asking him to help him find his son and to give him a proper burial. Danel finds and kills the eagle that ate his son, and after cutting it open recovers and buries his son's remains. Yet Danel remains upset and seeks vengeance on the murderers. This time, rather than eliciting Baal's assistance, Danel calls upon his daughter Pughat. Her scheme is simple: pose as Anath and lull Yatpan into lowering his guard. At this point, the text ends abruptly; however, we can make an educated guess regarding the original conclusion of this tale. Pughat probably succeeds by killing Yatpan and, as a "surrogate Anath," conquers the real goddess. Just as Anath did to Mot in the Baal poem, Pughat probably forces the goddess to release her brother from the realm of death. Consequently, the lively Aqhat saga ends with the fulfillment of the gods' original promise to Danel: his throne and son are now secure.

This survey outlines three highly dramatic epics from Ugarit. Each has at least one exciting climax. In them, characters die, beautiful wives are sought, brave heroes emerge, and humans converse with the gods. As action and dialogue unfold, the gods who first serve as benefactors become enemies. There is no room for detached boredom.

---

[31] *KTU* 1.17, vi.34–40, translated by H. L. Ginsberg in *ANET,* 151 (see also the translations of Aqhat [*KTU* 1.17–19] by Dennis Pardee in *COS* 1.103, 343–56, and by Simon B. Parker in *Ugaritic Narrative Poetry,* 49–80.

Yet one question remains. What are these epics really about? Why were they composed? Most modern commentators point to myth and legend as the primary literary genres represented by the Ugaritic epics—each with its history and agenda. The myths relate to cult and religion, while the legends entertain the layperson. Early analyses concluded that myths dealt with gods, while legends involved mortal heroes of the past. These categories are inappropriate and imprecise, based as they are on a modern definition of genre that has probably little to do with the world of the Ugaritic epic. Of the three great Ugaritic texts, two concern the relationship between gods and humans. Only one is totally devoted to the world of divine beings. Only this last one (the Baal poem) would fulfill the formal requirements to qualify as a myth, while its two companions should be reckoned legends. Certainly, these categories are highly artificial and do little justice to the content of these epic texts. It is preferable to connect myth and legend in one and the same literary genre. The blend of mythology and humanity in epics offered people in societies like Ugarit the opportunity to consider and interpret existential matters. Here the lives of gods and humans are equally important. Together they inhabit the world. From this perspective, the Baal poem is more than a myth. Although its main theme is obviously the vicissitudes of life for Baal and his fellow gods, their world is equally important for human survival. The poem thus exposes the limits of this world for gods and humans.

Similarly, the Kirta epic and the Aqhat poem describe the limitations of human life. Their primary concern is to show that every human dies—even humans like Kirta, who would claim partial divine origins. No god can change that, which is the main thrust of Aqhat's response to Anath.

In many respects, these poems are the products of a systematic theology. Through them, we learn much about that era's idea of theological reflection. Besides explaining the essentials of the divine world to humans, they also contain an anthropology that projects a positive human self-image—one that recognizes the natural connections between rulers (the gods) and subjects (humans). We should not be surprised that in such a milieu, theological treatises took the form of narratives. After all, the value of these narratives lay in their comprehensibility. The worldview current in those days had little to do with our logically structured universe. It was much easier to explain the essentials of the world through a narrative about gods and humans. Although people in the ancient Near East did not produce philosophical treaties, they were certainly able to formulate their ideas about life and death, the world and humanity's place in it. In short, the mythical-legendary-epic narratives of ancient Ugarit provided their audience with existential reflection. Theirs were not systematic explanations or logical conclusions; on the contrary, their understanding was patterned according to the "logic" and meaning of their narratives.

Since the discovery of these Ugaritic texts in 1930, innumerable theories have developed regarding their intent and meaning. On the basis of the above-mentioned incorrect distinction between myth and legend, some have said that the Baal epic differs in character from the Kirta and Aqhat epics. This is hardly accurate. All three poems share similar literary techniques, language, and motifs. Anath's visit to El is portrayed identically in the Baal and Aqhat epics. These facts alone suggest that one author wrote all three poems—perhaps even Ilumilku, who placed his name on all of them. Yet his narratives developed from a rich oral tradition, deeply rooted in its own literary history. Evidence of this oral background is found in the stereotypical language used for certain recurring moments, for example, the reaction when somebody sees a messenger arrive. Orality also frequently involves the repetition of lines and passages, sometimes very artfully executed with minute changes that reveal how the author of the written poem uses oral compositional technique.

Thus we can effectively dismiss the notion that the Baal poem springs from a cultic milieu while the other two poems had a secular background. Those who believe the Baal poem is a cultic text imagine that it was recited during one of Ugarit's major religious festivals—to this day not attested in any genuine cultic text from Ugarit. The hypothesis relies on Mesopotamian analogies, in particular the evidence that the *Enuma Elish* creation epic was regularly recited during the *Akitu* (New Year) celebration.[32] While this may explain why the Baal text was preserved in writing, it does not explain the existence of the Kirta and Aqhat texts. Clearly, such connections between the Babylonian and Ugaritic epics seem weak. The *Enuma Elish* concerns a conflict between the benevolent god Marduk and the sea goddess Tiamat; however, after vanquishing Tiamat, Marduk creates the world from the carcass of the sea goddess and takes his place as chief of the gods. The *Enuma Elish* coincides with the Baal epic in only one respect: the conflict between a god and the sea. If it is a cultic poem, then the Baal epic would reflect several different cultic occasions, since the poem deals with two or three conflicts between the gods as well as the construction and dedication of a temple.

Many scholars contend that the Baal poem presents a literary portrayal of a seasonal myth: Baal's fate is worked out within a calendar year with its changing seasons. Autumn ushers in the New Year with its

---

[32] For translations of the so-called Babylonian Creation Epic *(Enuma Elish)*, see E. A. Speiser, *ANET*, 60–72; Benjamin R. Foster, *COS* 1.111, 390–402; and Stephanie Dalley, *Myths from Mesopotamia*, 233–74.

drenching rains. Because the rain is his responsibility, Baal demands to be accepted as the lord of all gods. Before he can reach this lofty position, he must fight the god Yamm, the Sea. Both Baal and Yamm are "water gods," and consequently both claim the right to rule the world. Baal is the lord of over the life-giving fresh water; Yamm over the salty, and occasionally destructive, sea water. Thus, their dispute can be viewed as the raging of the elements in the annual autumn storms. Although Baal emerges victoriously and gains his temple, his reign quickly unravels. He sinks into the ground, buried in Mot's underworld kingdom. That Baal must die is as inevitable and necessary as his victory over Yamm. Life itself depends upon this recurring scenario. If Baal did not die, the lingering storms and rain would continue indefinitely and wreak destruction because the grain cannot ripen for harvest. Thus, Baal would no longer be the benevolent god but a destructive force. It is in accordance with this interpretation that in the scene that immediately follows Baal's demise, Anath treats Mot with the same caution as one treats the harvest grain. His destructive nature notwithstanding, Mot is also the god of grain and vegetation; therefore, humans depend on his life-giving powers no less than they depend on Baal's rain.

The theory that the Baal poem is rooted in cyclical mythology is attractive and certainly not unfounded. However, each argument for that hypothesis must contend with an equally valid scholarly contradiction. For instance, some internal evidence suggests that the story line describes a seven-year, rather than a one-year, cycle. The seven-year interval is a stereotypical theme in folk literature. It has no precise numeric value but indicates a period lasting for "some years." Thus the incidents detailed in the poem stretch over more than one year. In its present form, the Baal text could not possibly reflect a simple, one-year fertility cycle, although this does not exclude the possibility that the author may have included motifs that originally were part of a one-year cycle.

If the events of the Baal poem only covered one year, then the final scene of the battle between Baal and Mot is incomprehensible. Baal's victory over Mot corresponds to the victory of rain over drought. Yet in the Near East, the period of reaping ends with the wheat harvest in the early summer. Four or five months later, the rainy season arrives. Thus, Baal's victory was premature, since the rains came too early in the planting season. Perhaps the story was set at this time and place to serve a more important literary purpose: Baal's triumph over every adversary.

Rather than viewing this poem as a reflection on cyclic patterns, we prefer another alternative: the poem is a mythological tale of the relationship between life and death. In one sense, life can conquer death; in another sense, death is a necessary result of life. Life cannot last in perpetuity, nor can it always conquer death and chaos. A hyper-extended existence turns life upon itself; it creates its own alter ego. Consequently, life must yield to death's inevitability. Inversely, death is never eternal;

rather, it naturally possesses a kernel of new life—what Baal's resurrection from death's kingdom signifies. The author has not robbed these basic ideas of their importance by presenting them in the form of a story. To the contrary, the dramatic format makes it easier for the audience to get the point.

This quality of the Ugaritic poems is even clearer in Kirta and Aqhat, where humans become directly involved in the drama. Many scholars have nevertheless misunderstood the fundamental questions these poems address. Many hypotheses have attempted to identify the aim of the Kirta epic—more so than the Aqhat poem (perhaps because Kirta seems easier to interpret than Aqhat, which includes a very peculiar and negative portrayal of devious and scheming gods). Scandinavian and Anglo-Saxon scholars in particular have tended to read into this poem all kinds of mythical information about the origin of the kingdom of Ugarit (not to mention ancient Near Eastern kingship, in general). In this connection especially the Swedish scholar Ivan Engnell suggested that Kirta echoes royal-ritual tradition: the royal New Year's and throne-ascension celebrations. According to Engnell, the outline of the epic mirrors the enactment of this cultic drama: the king's illness, his approaching death, and his sudden recovery.[33] Alternatively, Walter Dietrich suggests that the Baal epic mirrors the way a new group came to power at Ugarit and the social changes that followed in its wake.[34] Unfortunately, it is impossible to say anything about the nature and substance of this reform, or to decide who enforced it and how and when it happened. Finally, others contend that both the Aqhat and Kirta epics represent foundation myths of Ugarit's royal house. As foundation myths the two poems can be compared to the patriarchal narratives in the Old Testament, which some say carry the same meaning although they are structured very differently. Although such ideas about the content of the poems cannot be instantly dismissed, we should avoid the unwise assumption that these poems are simple foundation myths. There are too many literary layers to reduce them to one literary motif. Royal families are not the only groups susceptible to the vicissitudes of everyday existence—the heartache of lost children, natural disasters, Job-like suffering, or the gods' capriciousness.

The Ugaritic epics confirm our earlier suspicions, namely, that folk literature blossomed in Bronze Age Syria and Palestine, though only a small fraction of it has survived for archaeologists to uncover. They are

---

[33] See Ivan Engnell, *Studies in Divine Kingship in the Ancient Near East* (2d ed.; Oxford: Blackwell, 1967).

[34] See Walter Dietrich, "Gott als König: Zur Frage nach der theologischen und politischen Legitimität religiöser Begriffsbildung," *ZTK* 77 (1980): 251–68, esp. 255–59.

important literary productions that have rightfully taken prominent places in our literary histories. The Baal, Kirta, and Aqhat poems not only provide clues to an ancient worldview, they are the forerunners of an epic tradition that stretches into our own time.

III.2.5. Ritual Texts

PRIMARY TEXTS: See above, section II.1.1.

SECONDARY LITERATURE: **Herrmann,** Wolfram. *Yarih und Nikkal und der Preis der Kutarat-Göttingen: Ein kultisch-magischer Text aus Ras Schamra.* BZAW 106; Berlin: A. Töpelmann, 1968. **Xella,** Paolo. *Il mito di Shr e Slm: Saggio sulla mitologia ugaritica.* Studi Semitici 44. Rome: Instituto di studi del vicino oriente, Università, 1973.

The Ugaritic poems have no direct relationship to the cult. Consequently, they can provide only indirect insights into religious perceptions from that era. Yet other documents—religious poetry, hymns, and various liturgical texts—provide direct links to the cult.

One of the strangest texts discovered in Ugarit is the so-called Shahar and Shalim poem.[35] It describes the marvelous conception and birth of two deities. Unlike the Baal epic, this is not a complex, mythic drama; rather, it offers a series of hymnic passages, incantations, and invocations to the gods that are occasionally interrupted by unfathomable ritual instructions. No such instructions appear in the Baal epic—evidence that it is not a cultic text. The short, hymnic passages were presumably recited or sung in the cult. Their meaning escapes us.

Another hymnic text concerns the goddess Nikkal's wedding to the moon-god Yarikh.[36] At the beginning and end of the poem, we find hymns to Kotharot (the midwives), whom we met earlier in our analysis of the Aqhat epic. Clearly, this poem is a wedding song rather than a genuine hymn honoring the moon god. In it, we receive invaluable insights into Ugaritic wedding receptions and their various musical embellishments.

Among this group of mostly hymnic texts stands a collection of love poems entitled the Hadad text, a collection of brief poetic snapshots indirectly related to the Baal epic.[37] Hadad, the hero of these poems, is

---

[35] For translations of this text (*KTU* 1.23), see Dennis Pardee, *COS* 1.87, 274–83, and Theodore J. Lewis in *Ugaritic Narrative Poetry*, 205–214.

[36] For a translation of this text (*KTU* 1.24.), see David Marcus in *Ugaritic Narrative Poetry*, 215–18.

[37] For a translation of this text (*KTU* 1.12.), see Simon B. Parker in *Ugaritic Narrative Poetry*, 188–91.

none other than Baal—the Ugaritic Baal is accordingly identified with the storm and meteorological god of Western Asia, mostly known as Hadad, Haddu, or Adad (other forms of the name are also attested). These poems most likely were never a part of the great Baal poem; rather, they represent independent short hymns relating to this deity. Most of these brief, poetic vignettes contain pornographic recollections of the love between Baal/Hadad and Anath—ones that would shock many modern readers. Baal and Anath appear respectively as a bull and heifer. Like other Ugaritic documents, this text relates a extremely important social question: the production of descendants. In the ancient Near East, the birth of offspring—particularly males—was the single most important issue that decided the fate of a marriage. Without children no marriage could prosper.

The widely held view that the Hadad text is a cultic document (namely, an instructional text for cultic practices) is highly problematic. More likely, it is simply love or wedding poetry. A mythological veneer justifies its suggestive content: "forbidden" and obscene gesticulations portrayed cleverly in poetic garb. Because it underscores the archetypal love between Baal and Anath, its earthy songs are packaged in religious accoutrements.

Other Ugarit poems with religious overtones belong to a well-known Old Testament genre: the lament. In Ugaritic literature, the lament never stands alone but normally appears in incantations and ritual texts dealing with various disasters and maladies, including infertility, war, disease, and pestilence. In one such poem or incantation concerning snakebite, the gods are petitioned to remove the poison from snakes; only the god Horon is able to dispose of the venom.[38] The text is very difficult to interpret. Some have seen in it also an invocation of Horon to save his creatures, namely, the snakes, from utter destruction. Others find a sexual symbol at the end of the incantation. If so, then the incantation would be another example of the Ugaritic religious topic: life intertwined with death. The snakes represent death, but they are also phallic symbols, thus representing fertility.

The corpus of religious poems provides exciting insights into ancient Ugaritic culture. In the next section we will explore the worldview and religious outlook of that period. These reflections on Bronze Age literature in Syria and Palestine lead us to a compelling conclusion: Ugarit's many literary genres prove that the people of Syria and Palestine had already developed a rich and vibrant culture. Our insights about them may be sketchy, but their fascinating character is inescapable.

---

[38] See the translations of this text (*KTU* 1.100) by Dennis Pardee, *COS* 1.94, 295–8, and Simon B. Parker in *Ugaritic Narrative Poetry*, 219–23.

III.3. GODS AND HUMANS

III.3.1. Features of West Semitic Religion in the Third and Second Millennia b.c.e.: The Divine Realm, Ritual, Magic, and Prophecy

---

GENERAL: **Haussig,** Hans W. *Götter und Mythen im Vorderen Orient.* Stuttgart: E. Klett, 1965.

SYRIAN/UGARITIC RELIGION: **Caquot,** André. "Problèmes d'histoire religieuse." In *La Siria nel tardo bronzo.* Edited by Mario Liverani. Pages 61–76. Rome: Centro per le antichità e la storia dell'arte del vicino oriente, 1969. **Caquot,** André, and Maurice **Sznycer.** *Ugaritic Religion.* Leiden: E. J. Brill, 1980. **Day,** John. *God's Conflict with the Dragon and the Sea: Echoes of a Canaanite Myth in the Old Testament.* University of Cambridge Oriental Publications 35. Cambridge/New York: Cambridge University Press, 1985. **Eissfeldt,** Otto. *Sanchungjaton von Berut und Ilumilku von Ugarit.* Beiträge zur Religionsgeschichte des Altertums 5. Halle (Saale): M. Niemeyer, 1952. **Hörig,** Monika. *Dea Syria: Studien zur religiösen Tradition der Fruchtbarkeitsgöttin in Vorderasien.* AOAT 208. Neukirchen-Vluyn: Neukirchener Verlag, 1979. **Korpel,** Marjo Christina Annette. *A Rift in the Clouds: Ugaritic and Hebrew Descriptions of the Divine:* Ugaritisch-biblische Literatur 8. Munster: Ugarit-Verlag, 1990. **Lewis,** Theodore J. *Cults of the Dead in Ancient Israel and Ugarit.* HSM 39. Atlanta: Scholars Press, 1989. **Mullen,** E. Theodore. *The Assembly of the Gods: The Divine Council in Canaanite and Early Hebrew Literature.* HSM 24. Missoula: Scholars Press, 1980. **de Tarragon,** Jean-Michel. *Le culte à Ugarit: D'après les textes de la pratique en cunéiformes alphabétiques.* Cahiers de la Revue biblique 19. Paris: J. Gabalda, 1980. **Xella,** Paolo. *Gli antenati di Dio: Divinità e miti della tradizione di Canaan.* Verona: Essedue, 1982.

DEMONS: **Black,** Jeremy, and Anthony **Green.** *Gods, Demons and Symbols of Ancient Mesopotamia: An Illustrated Dictionary.* Austin: University of Texas Press, 1992.

PROPHECY: **Ellermeier,** Friedrich. *Prophetie in Mari und Israel.* AOAT 202. Neukirchen-Vluyn: Neukirchener Verlag, 1977. **Noort,** Edward. *Untersuchungen zum Gottesbescheid in Mari: Die Mariprophetie in der alttestamentlichen Forschung.* AOAT 202. Neukirchen-Vluyn: Neukirchener Verlag, 1977.

DIVINATION: *La Divination en Mésopotamie ancienne et dans les régions voisines.* 14e Rencontre assyriologique internationale, 1965. Paris: Presses universitaires de France, 1966. **Cryer,** Frederick H. *Divination in Ancient Israel and Its Near Eastern Environment: A Socio-historical Investigation.* JSOTSup 142. Sheffield: JSOT Press, 1994. **Dietrich,** Manfried, and Oswald **Loretz.** *Mantik in Ugarit.* Münster: Ugarit-Verlag, 1990. **Tropper,** Josef. *Nekromantie: Totenbefragung im Alten Orient und im Alten Testament.* AOAT 223. Neukirchen-Vluyn: Neukirchener Verlag, 1989.

MAGIC: **Abusch,** I. Tzvi. *Babylonian Witchcraft Literature: Case Studies.* Atlanta: Scholars Press, 1987. **Cryer,** Frederick H. *Divination in Ancient Israel and Its Near Eastern Environment.* JSOTSup 142. Sheffield: JSOT Press, 1994. **Krebernik,** Manfred. *Die Beschwörungen aus Fara und Ebla: Untersuchungen zur ältesten keil-*

schriftlichen Beschwörungsliteratur. Hildesheim: Olms, 1984. **Thomsen,** Marie-Louise. *Zauberdiagnose und schwarze Magie in Mesopotamien.* Copenhagen: Museum Tusculanum Press, 1987.

INDIVIDUAL DEITIES: **Binger,** Tilde. *Asherah: Goddesses in Ugarit, Israel and the Old Testament.* JSOTSup 232. Sheffield: Sheffield Academic Press, 1997. **Fulco,** William J. *The Canaanite God Rešep.* American Oriental Series 8. New Haven: American Oriental Society, 1976. **Kapelrud,** Arvid S. *Baal in the Ras Shamra Texts.* Copenhagen: G.E.C. Gad, 1952. **Kapelrud,** Arvid S. *The Violent Goddess: Anath in the Ras Shamra Texts.* Oslo: Universitetsforlaget, 1969. **Maier,** Walter A. *Ašerah: Extrabiblical Evidence.* HSM 37. Atlanta: Scholars Press, 1986. **Pope,** Marvin H. *El in the Ugaritic Texts.* VTSup 2. Leiden: E. J. Brill, 1955. **Walls,** Neal H. *The Goddess Anath in Ugaritic Myth.* SBL Dissertation Series 135. Atlanta: Scholars Press, 1992. **Wiggins,** Steve A. *A Reassessment of "Asherah": A Study According to the Textual Sources of the First Two Millennia BCE.* AOAT 235. Kevelaer: Butzon & Becker; Neukirchen-Vluyn: Neukirchener Verlag, 1993.

ROYALTY: **Engnell,** Ivan. *Studies in Divine Kingship in the Ancient Near East.* 2d ed. Oxford: Blackwell, 1967. **Frankfort,** Henri. *Kingship and the Gods: A Study of Ancient Near Eastern Religions as the Integration of Society and Nature.* Chicago: University of Chicago Press, 1948.

As we noted previously, one cannot write a totally consistent portrayal of Bronze Age Syrian religious history. One major problem remains the absence or fragmentary nature of the source materials. Similarly, many premature and all too broad hypotheses have grown out of the evidence. Before the discovery of the Ugaritic materials, the corpus of texts consisted of some first-millennium Phoenician inscriptions, the Old Testament, and classical sources—especially Herodotus, Philo of Byblos, Apuleius, and Lucian.

The Greco-Roman texts must be approached with caution. It is problematic to use the information about ancient Near Eastern religion during the last centuries of the first millennium B.C.E. or from the first centuries C.E. to reconstruct the Near Eastern religious environment during the third and second millennia B.C.E. For one thing, the information in the classical sources has been through multiple redactions. Second, most classical authors shared a prejudicial view of the literary, aesthetic, and ethical impulses of Syrian and Palestinian culture. Consequently, these writings may conform to the religious sentiments and ideas of their own time and show little understanding of the past. On the other hand, we have to make allowances for earlier scholars, because the source materials at their disposal were inadequate. They can fairly be accused only of attempting what was for them impossible.

Problems multiply when we examine the Old Testament's description of Canaanite religion—a portrait whose polemical attitude distorts reality. Generally, the Canaanites are portrayed as servants and worshipers of idols. Because their religion did not recognize Israel's God, Yahweh, their religious practices seemed vulgar and abhorrent. On the other hand, biblical scholars are not unaware that Israelite religion was in part taken over from the Canaanites; that is, that the religion putatively practiced in the time of the Israelite kings in the first half of the first millennium B.C.E. was syncretistic. It blended pure Yahwism (ethical maxims, the unwavering faith of the righteous) and Canaanite elements (the divinization of the forces of nature).

Starting from this view of preexilic Israelite religion as syncretistic, scholars have attempted to reconstruct authentic Israelite religion in its presyncretistic form—although the proposition that such a thing ever existed is purely hypothetical.[39] On top of this, scholars constructed a picture of pre-Israelite, Syrian and Palestinian religion. This hypothetical picture was then used as an analytical model for interpreting new archaeological discoveries that bear upon the history of religion. Sigmund Mowinckel's "royal ascension celebration" hypothesis remains one of the classic examples of this methodological wild-goose chase. In it, Mowinckel suggests that this celebration was the focal point of the New Year's festivals in Western Asia. Scandinavian and Anglo-Saxon scholars eagerly gravitated toward Mowinckel's masterwork, which appeared in the second volume of his study of the Psalms.[40] Mowinckel contends that the New Year's celebration reenacts the mythological battle between Yahweh and the powers of chaos, in which Yahweh eventually wins and reclaims the throne. In his treatise, he uses not only the numerous allusions to such mythic conflict in the Psalms but also documents from the history of religions in general, such as classical and ancient Near Eastern sources.

---

[39] The Old Testament's portrayal of the Israelite religion must be viewed as an invention, as something that never was. The same must be said about most modern analyses of ancient Israelite religion. The study of Israelite religion has generally relied on texts from the Old Testament that hardly predate the Babylonian exile. Thus, uncertainty continually dominates the reconstruction of the actual religious relationships in Palestine within the second and first millennia B.C.E. Thus the idea of a preexilic, syncretistic Israelite religion is founded on two different reconstructions: a modern scholarly one from the twentieth century C.E., and an ancient one dating from the postexilic period, already removed from its subject by hundreds of years.

[40] See Sigmund Mowinckel, *Das Thronbesteigungsfest Jahwäs und der Ursprung der Eschatologie* (Psalmenstudien II; Kristiania: J. Dybwad, 1922). This book can be seen as the culmination of his own scholarly work, but it also draws upon the work of other scholars, including those of the German *religiongeschichtliche Schule*—a school closely associated with such names as Hugo Gressman and Hermann Gunkel. Gunkel was in fact Mowinckel's teacher and a special source of inspiration for him. We should not underestimate this relationship. Often German scholars, especially, forget this fact, even as they consider Mowinckel's theories both strange and unfathomable.

Soon other scholars took up Mowinckel's ideas, including the previously mentioned Swede Ivan Engnell, who offered a more expansive hypothesis: in the New Year's celebration, the king replicated the role of the dying and rising god. With the Ugaritic discoveries in 1930, scholars saw Mowinckel's theory vindicated. Thus, according to this interpretation, the Baal poem represents the reinterpretation of an annual cycle, while at the same time the Kirta and Aqhat epics provide a script for the king's role in the cultic drama. The argument was blatantly circular: the theory affected the interpretation of these texts in such a way that the texts tended to confirm the theory.

As we noted previously, this understanding of the Baal poem is very problematic. Many of its literary elements simply do not fit this hypothesis. Clearly, not all of Mowinckel's colleagues shared his view. Some would say that Yahweh had nothing in common with Baal and furthermore was not some mortal god who could be resurrected from the dead. Such objections are not totally unfounded, although they were often formulated by people trying to defend the veracity of the biblical image of God and therefore not likely to accept anything that would in their eyes diminish the lofty majesty of Yahweh. Although Mowinckel's assessment of the Old Testament texts is brilliant and engaging, it is also highly questionable. The same can be said of his interpretation of the Ugaritic texts, which seems far removed from the religious reality reflected in ritual texts from the cult at Ugarit. The only element that may relate to the New Year's festival is the festival of wine that the Dutch scholar Johannes de Moor identified.[41] Yet in that text we find nothing that agrees with Mowinckel's picture of myth and cult within that festival. We should also remember that no Ugaritic text provides even circumstantial evidence for the king's participation in the cultic drama—as Mowinckel and Engnell insist.

We should not discount all early history-of-religions analyses. Clearly, they provide useful and important observations—particularly the many connections between the Old Testament's mythological attestations and ancient Near Eastern religious convictions. Our criticisms refer to those theories that go beyond the extant documentary evidence. Text and interpretation must never be mixed in this irresponsible way. After all, what seems scientifically plausible to the modern scholar does not necessarily reflect the religious perceptions of the ancient Syrian and Palestinian populations.

Current historians of religion must face the same scrutiny. Even the most highly qualified and reasonable scholars of antiquity cannot guarantee that their reconstructions of ancient Near East religions represent

---

[41] *KTU* 1.41, in Johannes de Moor, *An Anthology of Religious Texts from Ugarit* (Leiden: E. J. Brill, 1987), esp. 157–65.

actual religious practice and experience. Every modern assessment depends on a particular system of logic, accepted by scholars as useful and valid, that is defined by the Kantian categories of time and space. This way of thinking greatly distances us from ancient Near Eastern people who had nothing to do with this development of logical thinking. Their notions of the universe, the earth, and their phenomena have precious little in common with ours. Consequently, we will never succeed in presenting religious convictions in the ancient Near East as logically consistent perceptions—at least not according to our standards. The people of antiquity operated under not just two categories of understanding—time and space—but also a third, namely, the mythical dimension. The causal nexus involved not only material phenomena but also the actions of divine beings.

A story told by the English ethnologist Edward E. Evans-Pritchard aptly exemplifies this older worldview. It deals with an episode during his studies of the Nilotic People of Nuer (Sudan). One afternoon, a tribesman fell into a deep sleep underneath a canopy. Suddenly, the post that supported the roof broke. The roof collapsed upon the man and killed him. For the European ethnologist, a thoroughly rotted post caused the accident: an obvious explanation. The victim's relatives tacitly accepted this explanation; however, their lingering dissatisfaction triggered other questions. Why did the roof happen to fall during the man's nap? What did this man do to warrant his death?

Modern and ancient peoples are not totally different. People will always be seeking explanations that best conform to their experiences and answer their existential questions. However, different ages produce different ways of approaching and answering such questions. Ancient people formulated their religious perceptions within a prelogical or protological way of thinking which in its own way aimed at the same goal as modern systems of thought: namely, revealing the connection between cause and effect. Our kinds of explanation were already known and recognized, at least incipiently, but people did not really expect them to explain the *meaning* of everything. For modern people, on the other hand, religious explanations are a bit of a bother; many are inclined to store them away in a kind of curio cabinet and look instead to the natural sciences for explanations. In the ancient Near East, no such distinction was possible, because in that setting world and religion were two sides of the same coin. So when we today set about to deal with religious ideas from those times, we have to be aware of this difference.

Clearly, ancient human beings sought and found meaningful and reasonable answers to their questions in the intellectual categories with which they were familiar. That system affirmed and illuminated their life-experiences. In many ways, their problems mirror ours. Now, as then, questions regarding life and death are critically important, and there are many answers. In antiquity, life was subdivided into several successive phases, each of them carrying its meaning and importance. Each successive crisis ushered in a new phase in the life cycle stamped with its own unique idiosyncrasies. Ancient people viewed these transitions with trepidation. The consequences of such transitions ranged from the horrible to the comforting: on the one hand, hunger, disease, pestilence, natural disasters, infertility, wild animals; on the other hand, the fertility of people, animals, and fields. Death always loomed at the end of the life cycle—a fact that elicited great interest in what followed life. Many thoughts and perceptions circulated about this theme. Generally, people were convinced that the deceased somehow lived on, maybe only as a shadow; under the right conditions, however, they were able to communicate with the living.

Ancient religion affirmed a three-tiered universe. The gods lived on the highest mountains, human beings and demons walked the earth, and daemons (the underworld gods) inhabited the bowels of the earth. Since humans occupied the center—the focal point—they were constantly threatened from above and below. People struggled to maintain the right balance between the different parts of the universe. They had to placate the inhabitants of a densely populated universe: gods, their fellow humans, spirits, ghosts, and daemons. Life was short—only very few people survived past their fortieth year. Most died as children. Consequently, their brief lives put humans at a terrible disadvantage. Only once did they change levels: when they passed away, they plunged into the realm of death to tarry among the shadows. The gods, for their part, lived on mountains in houses constructed by other gods or humans. They ate and drank, loved and hated, and argued with and fought the daemons—almost like the humans below them. Yet, their situation was fundamentally different from that of humans: they enjoyed immortality. Furthermore, they moved freely from their level to that of humans, because the temple doors represented gates where heaven and earth met. On earth, gods assisted humans in their struggles against daemons, but they also judged people for their behavior, dispensing divine justice with rewards and succor or with punishment, condemnation, disease, and death. The underworld or realm of the subterranean gods was a horrific region to which no one traveled voluntarily—but at times there was no choice. Earth served as the place of meeting between the gods of heaven and the subterranean gods. Death was, however, also a harsh master for the gods of heaven, who sometimes had to fight death and always on a battlefield chosen by death. Thus, it sometimes happened that a god from heaven had to take up residence in the nether world, at least temporarily. Of course, unlike humans, gods had the ability to return eventually from the underworld to their own realm.

The highest god was El (or ᵓIlu), literally, "god." This deity served as the lord of the world and the head of the pantheon—and also the creator of the world and its inhabitants, although we possess no Syrian or Palestinian creation myths that narrate this latter work fully. El's role in creation is nevertheless guaranteed by a "Semitic" quotation from a Hittite mythological text where El appears as *El qun Irsa* ("El, who created the world"), a title that survives in later Phoenician and Old Testament traditions.[42] The formula likewise appears in Gen 14:19: *ᵓēl ᶜelyôn qônēh šāmayim wāᵓāreṣ*, "Blessed be Abram by *God Most High, maker of heaven and earth.*"

It is often noted that in the Ugaritic epic poems El plays an incidental role that sometimes appears almost clownish. Because this image seems unsuitable for a major god, some suggest that El, after the creation of the world, was relegated to the "geriatric ward," where he became expendable and was no longer able to aid and support humankind. Younger deities assumed control—not unlike the son of Kirta who attempted to usurp his father's throne and inheritance—a story line reflected in the dedication of Baal's temple and his elevation to lordship of the gods. These religious perceptions are thought to date back to the Middle Bronze Age.

This interpretation of the respective roles of El and Baal has not survived unchallenged. When El finished his role as the god of creation, he no longer needed to interfere directly in the affairs of this world. After all, he recognized that his creation was, in the words of Genesis 1, "very good" (verse 31). Nothing needed improvement; every subsequent change ushered in corruption and degeneration toward primordial chaos. Thus El settles into a status well known in the general history of religions: that of the *dei otiosi*, that is, formerly active gods who entered retirement once the creation of the world was complete. Yet they do not remain totally inactive. Each deviation from the original order threatens creation and calls them back to active duty. Only the creator god guarantees and guards the world's delicate balance. Only the creator god can repeat his creation when necessary (as after the flood). As long as "it is good," the creator god need not deal with it. However, when the creation is threatened, and he is defied by other powers, the creator god faces a dilemma: he cannot really change things, cannot actively eliminate the danger. Richard Wagner's opera *Die Walküre* deals impressively with the same predicament: the god Wotan, who must let things happen contrary to his own will, declares, "I am the least free of all!" ("Ich unfreiester Aller!") However much the creator god desires to help, any action to assist those he

---

[42] On this, see Marvin H. Pope, *El in the Ugaritic Texts* (VTSup 2; Leiden: E. J. Brill, 1955), 51–52.

favors would destroy his creation. From every angle, the god is enchained. He can do nothing more than maintain his creation "as it once was created."

In the Ugaritic poems, El's role is probably much too passive and sometimes even ridiculous. For example, his daughter Anath intimidates him to the point that he must cower within the safety of his palace. Of course, this portrayal of El is dependent on the literary character of the poem. El must not only play the role of a deity, his *persona* must conform to the poem's literary intent. In this sense, the author holds the keys, enriching the story line with aesthetic and dramatic elements. Nevertheless, the author acknowledges that El remains the undisputed and eternal lord of the gods and their realm. The creation stands outside the Baal poem's theme and therefore outside the author's creative horizon. This does not suggest that his readers are indifferent to these questions; to the contrary, the creation played a critical role in the people's consciousness. We shall address this matter shortly from the perspective of the opposition between cosmos and chaos.

El serves his own definite function: in the people's eyes, he guarantees a stable world, although to impinge further on the course of events lies beyond his ability. He reserves that role for lesser gods, including his wife Athirat. The Old Testament refers to her as the goddess Asherah (in some cases, also a cult object or symbol). Among the young gods we should also count Baal, ostensibly El's son (all the younger deities are called sons and daughters of El regardless of whether they are actually his or offspring of other gods). Baal is not the natural son of El. His father was the grain-god Dagon (Dagan in the translation above). All these secondary gods have special duties that cover every aspect of human life. Each god takes on a specific assignment that serves either life or death.

As modern people in an industrialized world, we often forget that throughout history the preservation of life depended on fertility. In antiquity, human beings knew that survival hinged on their own fertility as well as that of animals and the soil. Consequently, different gods represented different aspects of fertility. Again, we must say that the Ugaritic texts provide only a restricted glimpse into the religious convictions of that era; the portrayal of all gods has to submit to the logic of the dramatic plot. Fortunately, we possess other information that further explains and corroborates the roles of the gods. Since ripened grain and productive fields require a sun god, every ancient Near Eastern religion had one. In Ugarit and Asia Minor, the sun deity is a female, while in most other places a male. The suns warms the people and liberates them from the fear of darkness. Without a sun, all people, animals, and plants would perish. Of all the ancient Near Eastern poems devoted to the sun god or goddess, the sun hymn of Pharaoh Akhenaten remains the most beautiful and impressive.

The Sun Hymn of Pharaoh Akhenaten

Splendid you rise in heaven's lightland,
O living Aten, creator of life!
When you have dawned in eastern lightland
You fill every land with your beauty,
You are beauteous, great, radiant,
High over every land;
Your rays embrace the lands,
To the limit of all that you made,
Being Re, you reach their limits,
You bend them <for> the son whom you love;
Though you are far, your rays are on earth,
Though one sees you, your strides are unseen.

. . . .

Earth brightens when you dawn in lightland,
When you shine as Aten of daytime;
As you dispel the dark,
As you cast your rays,
The Two Lands are in festivity.
Awake they stand on their feet,
You have roused them;
Bodies cleansed, clothed,
Their arms adore your appearance.
The entire land sets out to work,
All beasts browse on their herbs;
Trees, herbs are sprouting,
Birds fly from their nests,
Their wings greeting your *ka*.
All flocks frisk on their feet,
All that fly up and alight,
They live when you dawn for them.
Ships fare north, fare south as well,
Roads lie open when you rise;
The fish in the river dart before you,
Your rays are the midst the sea.[43]

Sometimes the sun also appears as a cruel deity, since too much sun brings death, not life. During the interminable Near Eastern summer, the sun rules over a drought-ridden terrain for six to eight months. Everyone knows the sun's destructive capabilities. If it shines relentlessly, disaster strikes. The power of the sun is restrained both daily and yearly. At nightfall, the sun yields its power to the moon: "the greater light (will) rule day, and the lesser light (will) rule the night" (Gen 1:16).

---

[43] Translated by Miriam Lichtheim, "The Great Hymn to the Aten," in *COS* 1.28, 44–46. See also the translation by John A. Wilson, *ANET,* 370.

Not surprisingly, the moon is usually worshiped whenever the sun is worshiped—both sharing similar importance. Although many associated the moon with the darkness of the night and the dark powers of death, it also served as the god who gained the upper hand over this obscure realm. Except during the critical monthly new moon period, it defeats perpetual darkness. Thus, despite its connection with death's minions, the moon remains a beloved god whose myths are always positive. In many places throughout antiquity, the moon reigns as the preeminent deity.

As the year progresses, the moon loses its potency since the summer days become longer; however, soon rain and thunderstorms arrive, quenching the thirst of fields, livestock, and humans. The well-known and admired storm god symbolizes the onslaught of these Near Eastern weather patterns. In Ugarit, he appears as Baal or Hadad (also known as Adad or Adda). The Horites call him Teshup. By any name, this god reigns during the autumn and winter rainy seasons. With the first shower or thunderstorm, autumn ushers in the battle between the storm god and the gods of evil who ruled during the long and mischievous drought and heat, during the "dead" summer months. The Baal poem also reflects these events, though in a way that is conditioned by the narrative structure of the poem, so that what it says cannot be taken as straightforward data for the history of religions. Nonetheless, Baal's fight with and victory over Mot, the god of death, arises from and can be understood only in connection with the onset of autumn.

Baal becomes embroiled in a second struggle: this time with a god whose role is apparently similar to his own, since he is another water god, namely, Yamm, the god of the sea. But Baal himself is the god of the waters from the firmament. So the two water gods Yamm and Baal are by no means identical, for Baal's fresh water brings life and fertility, while Yamm's salt water threatens human and animal life as well as the thriving of fruits and grains. In the epic poems, life is always victorious, and both struggles in the poem ultimately aim at the same thing: the glorification of the triumph of life over death. In reality, on the other hand—that is, in the course of the calendar year—these are two distinct matters that are not fused together before the poem itself fuses them. Apart from the poem's holding them together, each occupied its own space. Thus in various other texts from Ugarit the opponent of the life-giving god is not Yamm (or Mot) but usually Lotan (or Leviathan, as the Old Testament calls him)—often represented as Hydra, a dreadful, many-headed water monster. Again, in other texts other gods take over Baal's function. In the Babylonian version of the mythical tale, Marduk (also known as Bel), Babylon's god, battles the sea dragon, Tiamat ("Sea"), from whose corpse he molds the earth. The militaristic storm god also appears in other second millennium texts—especially the Hittite mythological tales.

Interestingly, the Ugaritic texts refer to Baal as "son of Dagon," rather than "son of El." Is this designation derived from the notion that Dagon belongs to the same generation as El, or was Baal really seen as the "son of Dagon"? This is not known, but we do know from the size of his magnificent temple that Ugarit's populace revered Dagon. In many other parts of the ancient Near East, Dagon was also held in high esteem and worshiped. Even the Old Testament recognizes him among the foreign gods. As a divinity he belongs among the "chthonic," or earthbound, gods, rather than among the members of the "Olympian" pantheon. He oversees the grain, even becomes its symbol. Dagon loomed so large among Ugarit's inhabitants and poets (for without grain, humans perish) that they also knew the names of his sons and daughters.

The relationship between the rain god and the grain god is quite clear, although their relative placement in the hierarchy seems odd: the grain god is the father of the rain god. In the life cycle, the rain god falls to earth, soaks the ground, and sprouts grain. Grain requires moisture. What is less clear to us is the ancient perception that, conversely, without grain, the rains did not fall. Why? Because once the rain(-god) falls, it remains trapped in the ground. The harvest releases the rain from its subterranean prison.

Especially interesting is the connection between Mot and Dagon. In the Baal epic, Mot ("Death") plays the role of the grain god: he lurks below the ground, engulfs Baal, and then releases him. Later, Baal battles and defeats Mot. Thus, in this drama, Mot plays Dagon's role. Why? Because the battle between Baal and Mot serves as a patricidal myth comparable to many other mythical battles between gods of different generations. This mythical theme seems also to have been popular in the ancient Near East. The Ugaritic texts seemingly reflect it in the strange interplay between El and Baal. Admittedly, this hypothesis is not entirely certain; it is clear, however, that at one point in time Baal must be victorious so that life and fertility may proceed, and that at another point he must die in order to provide new opportunities for fertility. Again we emphasize the previously discussed premise, namely, that death is not the definitive end; rather, death and life are two parts of a whole. Rain "dies" to revivify the earth; otherwise there could be no life. But then at the end of the harvest, the process is finished, and Baal must escape so that the process can be repeated the next year.

Consistent food production is not the only necessary condition of the preservation of life. Human and animal fertility is just as important. Survival hinges on healthy children and animals; therefore, a permanently childless marriage is already an invasion of death. Human and animal fertility depends on the positive dispositions of certain gods. Because they guarantee and protect healthy pregnancies, one must maintain a positive relationship with them. The Ugaritic poems especially signal the importance of one category of gods: the Kotharot, the midwives.[44] The people honor them with huge and expensive festivals.

Love plays a critical role in this mythological context, although this love does not conform to the romantic notions of the modern Western world. For ancient Near Eastern people, the unambiguous goal of the coming together of two people was procreation. This notion finds its strongest expression in the love between Baal (Hadad) and Anath, who in the form of a bull and cow, respectively, "make love" and breed descendants. The relationship between lovemaking and procreation is nowhere so straightforward as in the Aqhat and Kirta epics. Thus Aqhat:

> *[With life-breath]* he is *invigorated.*
> Let him mount his bed [. . .].
> In the kissing of his wife [she'll conceive],
> In her embracing become pregnant.
> [By conception] (and) pregnancy she'll bear
> [A man-child to Danel the Ra]pha-[man].[45]

Here the marriage resembles a production line, rather than a love affair—reproducing offspring for the survival of future generations.

Although the predominant theme of sex and marriage was the production of offspring, erotic obsession and love were not absent. Indeed, literary evidence shows that quite the opposite is true, that is, erotic love was well known and appreciated. The story of Baal's sister Anath is a particularly informative example.[46] In the previously mentioned poems of Hadad, Baal (Hadad) and Anath engage in a raucous, stormy, erotic affair. Anath, however, is a character that unites two opposing qualities. On one hand, she is a beautiful and desirable goddess, the virgin protector of love (in spite of her sexual relations with Baal, she is generally described as "the virgin Anath" in the Ugaritic poems). On the other hand, she is also the goddess of war. She revels on the battlefield, walking among the corpses of fallen warriors. Anath both brings life and extinguishes life, although she is not the only threat to

---

[44] For more on this class of gods, see Dennis Pardee, "Koshar, Kosharot," in *Dictionary of Deities and Demons in the Bible* (ed. K. van der Toorn et al.; Leiden: E. J. Brill, 1995), 913–17.

[45] From the Aqhat legend (*KTU* 1.17, i.38–42), translated by H. L. Ginsberg in *ANET*, 150. See also the translations by Dennis Pardee in *COS* 1.103, 344, and Simon Parker in *Ugaritic Narrative Poetry*, 53–54.

[46] Here Anath's sisterhood seems to originate from the literary context within which she appears. On the use of the terms "brother" and "sister" in such ancient Near Eastern literary contexts, see N. H. Walls, *The Goddess Anat in Ugaritic Myth* (SBL Dissertation Series 135; Atlanta: Scholars Press, 1991), 89–93.

life among the Ugaritic gods. However, her dual role as the goddess of love and war is rather exceptional. Most often such attributes belong to two different deities, as in the epics of Homer. There Aphrodite is exclusively the goddess of love, removed from everything that has to do with war, such as killing heroes.[47] The only exception is her love affair with the god of war, Ares.

Gods and daemons also cause other life-threatening perils. They inflict disease and pestilence. As Ugarit's ritual texts clearly demonstrate, humans both fear and respect the disease-god Reshef, a god who certainly played an important role in the life of every person. Consequently, most people tried to maintain a good relationship with him. This conforms to the remarkable logic of their religious thinking. Although the gods were recognized as life-givers, they were also accepted as purveyors of disease and death. At any moment, one indiscretion could unleash the bad in them. It was possible to experience good relations with a god, though the duration of those relations could never be presumed. Humans were obliged always to placate the gods, including the gods of death and fatal disease. It was essential to appease them—although everyone knew that sooner or later these gods would demand their due: human life.

In addition to the gods, another power always threatened humans, namely, the demons. They came in many forms: disease, snakes, or any other malevolent guise. In antiquity, demons never inspired the kind of veneration that their mountain-dwelling counterparts did; however, they never took a back seat to the gods. Insofar as demons were a reality of another kind, humans could not communicate with them. (Humans enjoyed relatively open communication with their gods; for as the Bible says,[48] they were "made in God's image.") Because they could not communicate with demons, humans sought all means available to fight them. One method entailed allying with a merciful god who would assist in the battle against demonic forces. Others used magical spells against their foes to forestall their anger.

From the cradle to the grave, every life change constituted a potential crisis, a moment when demons sought to control the person. Every step from one zone to another could involve danger. Such moments included the transition from night to day (and vice versa) or the

---

[47] Her only entry into the battle, on behalf of her son Aeneas, is simply pathetic. She is wounded and immediately has to leave the field and seek refuge on Olympus.

[48] This idea of Gen 1–2 is not unique among other ancient Near Eastern creation myths. One need only mention Mesopotamia's Marduk, who kills the god Qingu and mixes his blood with clay to form living human figures. Of course, humans resemble the gods in almost every way except life span. Their respective intellects diverge quantitatively, not qualitatively.

passage from inside one's house to the outside world.[49] Other transitions involved the passage from one phase in life to another (for example, marriage) or a change in social or political circumstances. All such transformations brim with danger, and humans stand almost defenseless.

Its belief in daemons marks Bronze Age Syro-Palestine as a magical society. Such cultures do not develop around rational schemes of perception but are occupied by the relations between, on the one hand, gods and humans, and, on the other, daemons and humans.[50] Humans are the weak party in this company, and to transcend their feebleness they must develop behaviors that aid them in their quest to repel a hostile and threatening world. In antiquity, when humans lacked rational scientific reflection that would have helped them understand the world, they sought other means to control their environments.

In antiquity, from private homes to the halls of power, cultures developed complex mechanisms to help humans gain control over their world. Most private homes contained various trinkets and amulets apparently used to repel malevolent forces. Many such remedies have been unearthed by archaeologists. For example, the Old Testament refers to the *t^{e}rāpîm*, normally translated as "household gods," which people used in their homes to repel demons. People carried charms around the house or placed them on walls for protection. Of course, in a world infested with these demonic forces, charms did not always do the job. When disease and disaster struck, one turned to alternative explanations and more potent remedies. Some of these strategies included performing household rituals or seeking refuge in a temple's unique sacred space. The temple provided the ultimate recourse for contact between humans and their gods.

---

[49] Consider, in this context, the traditional Jewish prayer of Ps 121:8: "The Lord will keep your going out and your coming in from this time forth and forevermore." This prayer refers to the transition from one's house or temple to the outside world. Gen 4:7 provides the background for this prayer: "If you do well, will you not be accepted? And if you do not do well, sin is lurking at the door; its desire is for you, but you must master it." The "sin" to which God refers is Abel's murder at Cain's hand; however, the Hebrew verb meaning "to lurk" *(rābaṣ)* relates to an Akkadian word for demon (*rābiṣu;* "he who lies waiting").

[50] The expression "magical society" was developed by Edward E. Evans-Pritchard in his outline of the magical Azande society in *Witchcraft, Oracles, and Magic among the Azande* (Oxford: The Clarendon Press, 1937); Frederick H. Cryer carried the terminology over to the study of Israel in *Divination in Ancient Israel and Its Near Eastern Environment* (JSOTSup 142; Sheffield: JSOT Press, 1994).

Concerning Prophetic Activities in the Mari Kingdom

Speak to my lord: Thus Itur-Asdu your servant. The day I dispatched this tablet of mine to my lord, Malik-Dagan, a man from Shakka, ca<m>e and spoke to me as follows: "In a dream of mine I was set on going in the company of a(nother) man from the fortress of Sagaratum, in the Upper District, to Mari. *On my way* I entered Terqa, and right after entering I entered the temple of Dagan and prostrated myself. As I was prostrate, Dagan opened his mouth and spoke to me as follows: 'Did the kings of the Yaminites[51] and their forces make peace with the forces of Zimri-Lim who moved up here?' I said, 'They did not make peace.' Just before I went out he spoke to me as follows: 'Why are the messengers of Zimri-Lim not in constant attendance upon me, and why does he not lay his full report before me? Had this been done, I would long ago have delivered the kings of the Yaminites into the power of Zimri-Lim. Now go, I send you. Thus shall you speak to Zimri-Lim, saying: "Se[nd] me your messengers and lay your full report before me, and then I will have the kings of the Yaminites *[coo]ked* on a fisherman's *spit*, and I will lay them before you." ' "

This is what this man saw in his dream and then recounted to me. I now hereby write to my lord; my lord should deal with this dream. Furthermore, if my lord so desires, my lord shall lay his full report before Dagan and the messengers of my lord shall be constantly on their way to Dagan. The man who told me this dream was to offer a *pagrum*-sacrifice to Dagan, and so I did not send him on. Moreover, since this man was trustworthy, I did not take any of his hair or the fringe of his ga<r>ment.[52]

The keepers of the temples—the priests—willingly offered their services to those in need of divine counsel and assistance. When an afflicted person turned to a priest, the priest's first and most important duty was to establish connections with the relevant god who might assist the client in fighting the evil forces that afflicted him. The temples created many institutions and procedures to establish such connections, including methods that gave people information about the future: various kinds of omens and oracles, such as haruspicy (examining bird flight) and extispicy (examining animals entrails). Specialists were needed to administer all of this and to interpret the messages of the gods correctly. These specialists—mostly employed by the temple authorities and belonging to the priestly caste—were no charlatans, although modern

---

[51] The *Binu-Yamina* (Akkadian $DUMU^{me\check{s}}$ *yamina*).
[52] Mari Letter A.15, translated by William L. Moran in *ANET*, 623.

scientists might look upon them as such. On the contrary, they were serious scholars who in a systematic way recorded and decoded the divine signs. In this way, over centuries and millennia, huge collections of such omens were collected and placed in a historical context. If something unusual happened, the diviner looked for precedents in his "books" and could thus foretell the future. The diviner also studied models of entrails that might indicate the special abnormalities that he should look for. Such models have been discovered in archaeological excavations from many places, including Ugarit.

A particular group of specialists was the prophets, most of whom had some relationship to the temples, although it is hard to say precisely what their role in society was. We know very little about the function of prophets during the Bronze Age because our materials are primarily limited to the Mari archives (eighteenth century B.C.E.), where they are quite common. Many provincial governors refer to their efforts. Moreover, we know that their activities were not limited to Mari or to the Middle Bronze Age. For example, an eleventh-century B.C.E. Egyptian text offers evidence in a story concerning Wen-Amon's trade expeditions. During his trip to Phoenicia, Wen-Amon confronts an ecstatic prophet in Byblos.[53] Certainly, the predictions of the prophets could be doubted, since, unlike priestly omens and oracles, their predictions did not follow clearly defined, reliable, and recognized methods. No one could evaluate the veracity of their findings. The prophets understood themselves as inspired individuals, mediums between gods and humans. Naturally, false prophets, who were not empowered by the gods, could easily dupe their adherents with unauthorized utterances and false messages. The Mari documents tell us that people were fully aware of this problem. Provincial governors often imprisoned people who acted as prophets, most likely to wait and see if the prophecy occurred in order to decide whether the prophet was a true or false spokesperson of the gods.[54]

---

[53] See John A. Wilson's translation in *ANET,* 25–29; also Miriam Lichtheim's translations in *AEL* 2:224–30 and *COS* 1.41, 89–93. Hans Goedicke translates this text with a full commentary in *The Report of Wenamun* (Baltimore: The Johns Hopkins University Press, 1975). To be sure, it is not clear whether the genre of this story is a historical report or a fairy tale. However, the important point is that this text describes prophetic activity in Byblos. Moreover, the Egyptian scribe identifies the man not with the usual hieroglyphic sign for male person, but with a nonstandard sign showing a raving man.

[54] There is nothing new under the sun! The Old Testament discusses prophets who are arrested and mistreated by the authorities because of their activities. Thus, in 1 Kgs 22, Michaiah ben Imlah is immediately arrested after he gives a gloomy prediction regarding a military campaign. If we turn to the prophet Jeremiah, we find him taking up lodging in a well in the royal courtyard—apparently a place where prisoners were kept.

The "magical society" placed great importance on differentiating real from bogus messages from the divine world. Although different magical practices promised to assuage people's existential dread, the abuse of these methods never stopped. For example, prophets could call upon the services of demons or other malevolent deities to deceive rather than assist. When a false prophet was exposed for his deceit, he would be treated like a criminal, even a demon. Such false prophets belonged to the realm of the dreaded "black magic." They brought agony and death to people rather than assistance and cure. No one could deny the potency of magic, whether it be the healing and helpful "white" magic or its dark and deadly counterpart. Practitioners of white magic were respected and useful specialists. Their opposites were dealt with swiftly. Methods of interrogation were cruel, and the automatic and inevitable sentence was death. Yet by contemporary standards witches and wizards were not condemned randomly or en masse. Specific rules governed the process. As today, rules guarded against dangerous mob rule, although their methods would look arbitrary from a modern point of view. Ironically, in some instances, the state itself resorted to black magic. The so-called Execration texts from Egypt represent examples of "official" black magic. The statuettes inscribed with curses were aimed against Palestinian, Syrian, and Nubian princes. The act of smashing them against the ground presaged the end of the prince cursed in the inscription.

Oracles and prophecies provided an opportunity to determine—but not control—the gods' intentions for the world. Other sources could also provide that information—especially the deceased who now live as shadows in the empire of death. The best-known example comes from the biblical story about King Saul's visit to a female necromancer in Endor to seek advice from the deceased Samuel concerning the outcome of an upcoming battle (1 Sam 28). The witch summons Samuel, who appears before Saul and announces his death. Ancient people loved these stories of incantations or a hero's visit to the underworld. Such stories appear in the Gilgamesh Epic and in Homer's *Odyssey*, although we do not have corresponding tales from Bronze Age Syria or Palestine. Yet traces of death cults appear in extant liturgical texts that outline invocations of the dead. The best example comes from a Ugaritic text in which the ghosts of long-dead Ugaritic kings are invoked (*KTU* 1.161 cited above). This invocation of Ugarit's dead kings leaves the impression that such petitions were accompanied by all sorts of rituals, among them the preparation of a banquet for the assembly of ghosts and living humans. Since, in this case, the invocation is a benediction for Ugaritic royalty, it may have served a purpose different from ordinary oracles and omens; still, it shows that the deceased might intervene on behalf of the living.

Banquet Arrangements for Ugarit's Dead Kings

The written record of the sacred celebration [in honor] of the Patrons:
You have summoned the Rephaim of the netherworld;
You have commanded the Council of the Didanites!
Summon ULKN, Raph[a!
Summon TRMN, Raph[a!
Summon SDN-w-RDN, [Rapha!]
Summon T̲R-ᶜLLMN, [Rapha!]
[All] summon the most ancient Rephaim!
You have summoned the Rephaim of the netherworld!
You have commanded the Council of the Didanites!

Summon Ammishtamru, the King!
Summon, as well, Niqmaddu, the King!

O, throne of Niqmaddu — weep!
Let his footstool shed tears!
In front of it — let the royal table weep;
Let it swallow its tears.
Tears, and [more] tears; many tears!

Shine bright, O Shapash!
Shine bright, O great luminary!
On high Shapash cries out:
After your lord, from the throne;
After your lord, to the netherworld descend!
To the netherworld, descend;
And go down low into the earth.
Below is SDN-w-RDN;
Below is T̲R-KLLMN;
Below are the most ancient Rephaim.
Bellow is Ammishtamru, the King;
Below is Niqmaddu, the King, as well.

Once — offer a benefaction.
A second time — offer a benefaction.
A third time — offer a benefaction.
A fourth time — offer a benefaction.
A fifth time — offer a benefaction.
A sixth time — offer a benefaction.
A seventh time — offer a benefaction.
You shall present a bird.

Hail!
Hail, Ammurapi!
And hail to his household!
Hail, [Tha]ryelli!
Hail to her household!
Hail, Ugarit!
Hail to her gates![55]

---

[55] The translation of this text (*KTU* 1.161) is by Baruch A. Levine, Jean-Michel de Tarragon, and Anne Robertson, in *COS* 1.105, 357–58.

While people normally sought the dead in official places such as sanctuaries or temples, extensive worship of the dead spirits also appeared in other contexts, such as private homes. Thus, in Ugarit, the deceased dwelled in vaults beneath homes, and it does not surprise archaeologists that the residents of these home installed hidden shafts through which they could deliver food and sacrifices to the dead without disturbing the graves below.[56]

The temple was the primary venue at which the gods received sacrifices. Throughout the year, complicated rituals were conducted in temples, including, for example, the cultic cleansing of the king. Generally the Ugaritic sacrificial practices relate directly to those found in the Old Testament. Two types of sacrifices are most common: that of whole animals or individual organs prepared for the pyre; and bloodless sacrifices involving harvested produce. The temples within which they occurred were mostly well-built structures that housed influential priests. In Ugarit, those priests were royal officials in charge of state affairs. Although we lack documentary evidence that verifies similar practices elsewhere in Syria and Palestine, we can safely assume that in the capitals of the states in Syria-Palestine, close ties normally existed between palace and temple—very much like the situation depicted in the Old Testament, where Solomon's temple in Jerusalem is part of the royal palace complex, much smaller than the royal palace itself. Even in Ugarit, the great temples of Baal and Dagon were considerably smaller than the royal palace, and the temple staff lived in private homes rather than the temple or palace; among these was the so-called house of the high priests in the temple precincts, where the epic poems were unearthed.

The role of the king in ancient Syrian and Palestinian religion intrigues many scholars, and various theories have developed. According to traditional Scandinavian scholarship, the king was considered not only an extraordinary person but a god or at least a demigod. In this alleged divine quality, he would participate throughout the year in the great religious festivals, in particular, the cultic dramatization of the battle between good and evil. Most of the information pertaining to this religious festival, however, does not originate in Syria or Palestine, but in other parts of the ancient Near East. From the moment the Ugaritic texts were deciphered, scholars saw links between these poems and earlier sources, mostly Mesopotamian. One such key fact was the reference to

---

[56] This understanding of the Ugaritic cult of the dead is, however, questioned by Wayne T. Pitard in "Libation Installations of the Tombs at Ugarit," *BA* 57 (1994): 20–37. According to Pitard, the original archaeologist at Ugarit (Claude Schaeffer) completely misinterpreted the results of his excavations at the city's burial vaults. For Pitard, the graves have no direct connection with the homes under which they sit.

King Kirta as the "son" of El. However, scholars overreacted, rashly considering information about the legendary founder of Ugarit's royal house as pertinent to his later successors. The invocation of the deceased kings of Ugarit quoted above shows them to be as mortal as other humans. They were certainly not immortals like the gods. The titles of the Ugaritic kings also show no trace of any divine status. Texts describe kings' parents as ordinary persons, not gods and goddesses. The theory about divine kingship also contradicts the accepted understanding of humanity in the ancient Near East, which did not allow divine status for any living creature on earth. There was no room for a god-king on earth. Kings were administrators of their kingdoms on behalf of their masters, the gods.[57]

Although not divine, the kings of Syria and Palestine enjoyed an elevated position in their society: they represented their subjects before the gods and the gods before the people. They instituted cults, built sanctuaries, and participated in the rituals whenever these were not handled by the priestly specialists. The king and the queen functioned as liaisons between the gods and humans, serving as grand marshals during sacrificial events. Because sacrifices appeased the capricious gods, the king guaranteed Ugarit's safety by appealing to the gods for ongoing human, livestock, and agricultural fertility. While they remained the indispensable link between gods and humans, they never obtained the status of gods. That in ancient Near Eastern religions the king was the person who guaranteed fertility and therefore must have been considered divine is only one among many stereotypes that were read into, not out of, the ancient sources.

We can illustrate this discussion with an example of the so-called sacred marriage. This imaginative notion appears through historical-critical analysis of sources from the ancient Near East. It takes concrete form—or so it is believed—in the aforementioned poems about Hadad and Anath in which the preservation of fertility is supposed to be dramatized in a literary context. This text is considered to be the script for the staged intercourse between the king (Hadad) and the queen (Anath)—a symbolic act that guaranteed fertility and survival. Yet, in spite of ample documentation in art and literature, nothing proves that the concept of the sacred marriage was more than another motif belonging to the realm of religion, not in any way related to earthly kings and queens. Ritual texts provide no corroboration that anyone, anywhere, participated in such a dramatic union. The only indication in the Ugaritic texts of the queen's role in religion appears in an administrative memorandum: a specified quantity of wine must be delivered for the queen's sacri-

---

[57] The situation was very different in Egypt, where the pharaoh was considered a god.

fice in a field belonging to the goddess. This amount of wine was certainly destined for a libation sacrifice, in which the queen poured wine over the field to promote its fertility.

This overview of Bronze Age Syrian and Palestinian religion is necessarily limited and hardly exhaustive. The religious history of this region remains sketchy because of the relatively few documents from which to draw. At times, scholars apply inadequate methods to analyze those documents. Particularly troublesome is the inability, in the study of the religious history, to make clear distinctions between epic poetry and ritual texts. Both genres are considered jointly so that the assumption persists that epics reflect rituals. Yet we should be warned against such misconceptions because there is so little that binds the ritual texts to the content of the epics. This should help students of religion handle this material more carefully. It is fortunate that this process has already begun.[58]

III.3.2. Humanity and the World

Albrektson, Bertil. *History and the Gods: An Essay on the Idea of Historical Events as Divine Manifestations in the Ancient Near East and in Israel.* Coniectanea biblica: Old Testament Series 1. Lund: Gleerup, 1967. **Kraus,** Fritz Rudolf. *Ein Edit des Königs Ammisaduqa von Babylon.* Leiden: E. J. Brill, 1956. **Kraus,** Fritz Rudolf. *Königliche Verfügungen in altbabylonischer Zeit.* Leiden: E. J. Brill, 1984. **Schmid,** Hans Heinrich. *Gerechtigkeit als Weltordnung: Hintergrund und Geschichte der alttestamentlichen Gerechtigkeitsbegriffes.* BHT 40. Tübingen: Mohr (Siebeck), 1968. **Whitelam,** Keith W. *The Just King: Monarchical Judicial Authority in Ancient Israel.* JSOTSup 12; Sheffield: Dept. of Biblical Studies, University of Sheffield, 1979.

Like their colleagues in Syria and Palestine, kings in Mesopotamia were not gods; rather, the king was employed by the gods to preserve humanity's happiness and well-being. This is the first impression we receive from the prologue to the renowned eighteenth-century B.C.E. Code of Hammurabi. In his day, Hammurabi vanquished many foes. He subdued the king of the wealthy city of Mari, and during his reign he united most of Mesopotamia under his rule. In the prologue cited below, Hammurabi does not revel in his victory; rather, he celebrates his completed task: he has done his duty. The gods ordered him to rule the kingdom, his people followed the gods' instruction, and thus they prospered. In Hammurabi's view, the king's duty was as established as the earth (or Babylon) itself, part of the very idea of creation. Being a pious king, Hammurabi only

---

[58] In this regard, we applaud the work of Jean-Michel de Tarragon in *Le culte à Ugarit: D'après les textes de la pratique en cunéiformes alphabétiques* (Cahiers de la Revue Biblique; Paris: J. Gabalda, 1980). He abstains from far-fetched hypotheses and limits his study to the actual information contained within the ritual texts.

fulfilled his obligations and thus assisted the gods in promoting their plans for the world. In the following sections of the code, his just rule is exemplified by the "laws" handed to him by the god of justice, and he gives them back to the god as sign of his piety.

Excerpt from the Code of Hammurabi

When lofty Anum, king of the Anunnaki,
(and) Enlil, lord of heaven and earth,
the determiner of the destinies of the land,
determined for Marduk, the first-born of Enki,
the Enlil functions over all mankind,
made him great among the Igigi,
called Babylon by its exalted name,
made it supreme in the world,
established for him in its midst an enduring kingship,
whose foundations are as firm as heaven and earth—
at that time Anum and Enlil named me
to promote the welfare of the people,
me, Hammurabi, the devout, god-fearing prince,
to cause justice to prevail in the land,
to destroy the wicked and the evil,
that the strong might not oppress the weak,
to rise like the sun over the black-headed (people),
and to light up the land.
Hammurabi, the shepherd, called by Enlil, am I.

. . . .

When Marduk commissioned me to guide the people aright,
to direct the land,
I established law and justice in the language of the land,
thereby promoting the welfare of the people.
At that time (I decreed). . . .[59]

The Code of Hammurabi comes from Mesopotamia and depends on its academic law tradition. While law codes have been preserved in Mesopotamia from the third millennium B.C.E., these collections seem to have had little practical use. They belonged in the academic tradition, nourished at the scribal schools—the universities of those days—and did not play any role in the courtroom, where other rules often prevailed.[60] Such collections, however, express the ideological paradigm for a just king. He must prevent evil persons from assuming control of the world and guar-

---

[59] Code of Hammurabi i.1–49; v.14–25, translated by Theophile J. Meek in *ANET*, 164, 165.

[60] On the status of the Mesopotamian law codes, see Martha Roth's introduction in *Law Collections from Mesopotamia and Asia Minor*, (SBLWAW 6; 2d ed.; Atlanta: Scholars Press, 1997), 4–7.

antee that justice will prevail. Thus we return to a subject that we have already mentioned above: the issue of royal enactments that involved social reforms intended to ameliorate the harsh conditions of life for ordinary people. In Hammurabi's own words, "The strong will not harm the weak."

The Care for Enslaved Persons in the Old Babylonian Period

The Edict of King Ammisaduqa

If an obligation has resulted in foreclosure against a citizen of Numhia, a citizen of Emutbalum, a citizen of Idamaras, a citizen of Uruk, a citizen of Isin, a citizen of Kisurra, or a citizen of Malgium (in consequence of which) he [placed] his own person, his wife or his [children] in debt servitude for silver, or as a pledge—because the king has instituted the *misharum* in the land, he is released; his freedom is in effect.

If a house-born slavewoman or male slave of a citizen of Numhia, a citizen of Emutbalum, a citizen of Idamaras, a citizen of Uruk, a citizen of Isin, a citizen of Kisurra, or a citizen of Malgium . . . whose price . . . , has been sold for money, or was given over for debt servitude, or was left as a pledge, his freedom will not be effected.[61]

The Code of Hammurabi

If an obligation is outstanding against a man and he sells or gives into debt service his wife, his son, or his daughter, they shall perform service in the house of their buyer or of the one who holds them in debt service for three years; their release shall be secured in the fourth year.

If he should give a male or female slave into debt service, the merchant may extend the term (beyond the three years), he may sell him; there are no grounds for a claim.

If an obligation is outstanding against a man and he therefore sells his slave woman who has borne him children, the owner of the slave woman shall weigh and deliver the silver which the merchant weighed and delivered (as the loan) and he shall thereby redeem his slave woman.[62]

---

[61] Paragraphs 20–21, translated by J. J. Finkelstein in *ANET*, 528.

[62] Paragraphs 117–119, translated by Martha T. Roth in *Law Collections from Mesopotamia and Asia Minor*, 103–4.

The technical terms used by Hammurabi in these excerpts are *kittum* and *mīšarum*. The Akkadian word *kittum* derives from the Semitic word *kûn*, which is related to two concepts: "to stand firm," and "to remain unchanged." The word *mīšarum* comes from the word root *y-š-r*, meaning "to be equal," or "is balanced with." While the second word appears in the Old Testament and normally means "is just," Hebrew texts and inscriptions from Syria and Palestine (including Phoenicia) employ *ṣedeq*—a West Semitic word—to connote the meaning of *kittum* (or another form of that word). The Bible usually translates *ṣedeq* as "just" or as a substantive "justice" (in its nominal form). In a late Greek rendering of Phoenician sources, Philo of Byblos describes a pair of gods named *Sydyk* and *Misor*.[63] Thus, by the first millennium B.C.E., the now hypostatized concepts of justice and right are transformed into deities.

With these remarks, we proceed to the core of Near Eastern anthropology. The terminology used in the Code of Hammurabi also appears in emancipation edicts of that era. In their decrees, the (Amorite) kings during Hammurabi's dynasty sought to recreate the world's original order. The ideological foundation was that originally the gods created humans equal. Every free person was given the same opportunities (slaves were excluded). Yet the world remained inherently inequitable, and its inhabitants faced a constant struggle with capricious powers and cosmic chaos. Through their edicts, kings sought to correct this situation. Yet every new law was soon followed by new inequity. Consequently, the king—or his son, his successor—was invoked to cope with inequality and issue a new decree. The underlying concept is that human relations might be decisive for the fate of the world.

For the Swiss scholar Hans Heinrich Schmid, the principle of equality underscored the very essence of creation.[64] In that world, the righteous contributed to the maintenance of justice and right and thus helped preserve the world. The righteous upheld the aim of the creator god and acted as his assistants in the struggle against evil forces. The creator god had initially made everything according to a kind of master plan that was rooted in the concept of *kittum* and had to be followed. Cosmos and justice are therefore two sides of the same coin. The survival of the world, therefore, depends on the maintenance of "justice and righteousness," which also means that interpersonal relations are decisive for the fate of the world.

---

[63] See Harold W. Attridge and Robert A. Oden Jr., *Philo of Byblos: The Phoenician History* (CBQMS 9; Washington, D.C.: The Catholic Biblical Association of America, 1981), 45.

[64] See Hans Heinrich Schmid, *Gerechtigkeit als Weltordnung: Hintergrund und Geschichte der alttestamentlichen Gerechtigkeitsbegriffes* (Beiträge zur historischen Theologie 40; Tübingen: Mohr [Siebeck], 1968).

In the ancient Near East, people knew that chaos preceded creation. The creation brought form and stability to the universe. Chaos became cosmos. Injustice damaged the world, and the gods knew that their finest creation (humanity) provided the means through which chaos could reassert itself. In Gen 6:5, the problem emerges: "The Lord saw that the wickedness of humankind was great in the earth, and that every inclination of the thoughts of their hearts was only evil continually." This becomes the prologue to the flood when the chaotic waters burst forth. The gods exact their vengeance upon a violent world. The arrival of the chaotic waters annuls creation and brings destruction upon humanity. Yet the cause of this devastation rests with humanity. Human evil brings the vengeance of the gods.

The lesson is clear. Everything depended on the decision of humans to act according to divine prescription, to conform to the world that the creator god established as both good and bountiful. This not only involved the cooperation of kings and rulers; every person bore responsibility. Wherever one lived, that place was part of the divinely created cosmos. That is why people turned to the gods if they were ready to follow the gods' will and thereby secure their aid in the fight against evil. Alas, often such hopes and expectations were futile; again and again people sensed that the original cosmic balance was lost forever. The ideal order of creation could never be fully reestablished. (Here the ancient Near East accords with classical sentiments of Greece and Rome: in the beginning was the golden age, followed through history by less prosperous periods, the age of silver and then of iron.) Hence the fundamental longing to do everything possible to restore the world, now threatened by chaos and destruction, to its original condition. Because of the rupture of the initial harmony between the gods and humans—never better described than in the biblical tale of the fall—humans live under the constant threat that evil and chaos could take charge of the world and destroy it. This situation demands that harsh measures be taken against evil so that the cosmos, governed by the gods, may survive and stand firm.

When the gods do not prevail, chaos reigns, creating the empire of daemons. The idea of chaos is not purely ideological but also has concrete political aspects. Just as in the realm of cosmos the gods take an active role in ordering everything down to the last geographical and social detail, the daemons do the same in the realm of chaos. If one's own dwelling place, one's own country, belongs to cosmos, then by the same token all other places and lands fall under the heading of chaos. It follows that chaos reigns wherever "we" ourselves, or "our" gods, do not rule. This concept had very concrete consequences, as when in the first millennium B.C.E. the Assyrians believed they fought their wars and created their empire so that their god Ashur might rule the world and create cosmos where chaos hitherto prevailed.

We have already established that such concepts and ideas permeated the literature from Syria in the second millennium B.C.E. Thus the Ugaritic epics express the continuous fight between the powers of evil and the benevolent gods. In them, maintaining life always takes center stage, even if life must sometimes yield to death. Life and death form two parts of one reality, and life must always consider impending death. This crucial balance must remain harmonious and constant. Similarly, chaos is the necessary antipode of cosmos. Chaos represents the cosmos's evil twin, which humans must avoid; ironically, it guarantees that humans will fight for the maintenance of the good life and an orderly world. The texts testify to this dichotomy between life/cosmos and death/chaos. Righteousness—symbolically expressed in the imagery of the king dispensing justice "at the gate"[65]—cannot survive when the forces of chaos assume power. Life is endangered whenever Baal descends into the underworld, when Kirta falls ill, or when Danel loses his son (because a goddess presumed to be the curator of the world brings with her chaos and death). It was inconceivable that justice could prevail if it ultimately transformed life into death. After all, life (i.e., the cosmos, the created world) and justice are one and the same.

In accord with this concept of the world, which saw every change in the original world order as evil, people of the ancient Near East (the same could be said about the inhabitants of the classical world) were understandably conservative. For all their extensive agreement in their portrayals of humanity, ancient and modern people differ fundamentally in their views of human progress. Modern people consider development not only as a challenge but as a necessity, something positive. To ancient people, anything new would only be acceptable if it contributed to the *reestablishment* of the original god-given state. Anything else would endanger the survival of the world. Interestingly and paradoxically, this negative attitude toward progress in the ancient world finds new currency within the so-called postmodern psychology; that is, it provides a way to disengage from modernity's hyperactive thirst for change. Contrary to popular opinion, this "restorationist" mentality is related to romanticism; it represents a return to a classical perception of the world.

This rather systematic portrayal of ancient Near Eastern views of the human condition was necessary because the ancient texts themselves offer only an incomplete and unsystematic elucidation of their re-

---

[65] In this ideological *topos*, the king always sits at the gate where poor people, widows, and orphans can come to plead their cases. This notion appears not only in Ugaritic literature, but also in ancient Mesopotamian and Old Testament (e.g., Deut 25:7; 2 Sam 15:2–6) portrayals. Widows and orphans possessed no legal standing because they did not own any property. Furthermore, only adult males could enjoy full citizenship. Consequently, the king acted as society's supreme arbiter. As the gods' representative, he alone could dispense justice.

ligious and anthropological undergirdings. There were no introductory textbooks in philosophy or theology. Our reconstruction of ancient theological thinking derives from scattered evidence from many sources. There are two uses for the fundamental idea—which we hardly ever find fully spelled out in one place—that the world was originally created good and complete, but then steadily deteriorated. First, it helps people understand the present condition of the world they live in. Second, it provides a motive for struggling against further deformation, and more than that, for realigning the world with the ancient norms, so as to approach once again the original—and better—state of affairs.

Although as we have noted the Bronze Age inhabitants of Syria and Palestine never systematized these ideas and presented them in an orderly fashion, they form the background to much that we find in their texts, and they make it clear that those ancients were certainly not "primitives." To the contrary, they achieved a high level of intellectual and theological reflection, and in spite of very harsh living conditions they sought a reasonable explanation of the way of the world. We can never share their exact perceptions (although we may not be so far removed from them as we think), but we can nevertheless respect these ancient people for what they were, what they believed in, and what they hoped from life.

4

THEOLOGICAL VANTAGE

IV.1. THE OLD TESTAMENT IN THE ANCIENT NEAR EASTERN WORLD

Dietrich, Walter, and Martin A. **Klopfenstein**, eds. *Ein Gott allein?* OBO 139. Göttingen: Vandenhoeck & Ruprecht, 1994. **Gese**, Hartmut. "Geschichtliches Denken im alten Orient und im Alten Testament." *ZTK* 55 (1958): 127–45. **Gese**, Hartmut. "Von Sinai zum Zion." *BEvT* 64 (1974): 81–98. **Niehr**, Herbert. *Der höchste Gott.* BZAW 190. Berlin: de Gruyter, 1990. **Van Seters**, John. *In Search of History: Historiography in the Ancient World and the Origins of Biblical History.* New Haven: Yale University Press, 1983. Reprint, Winona Lake, Ind.: Eisenbrauns, 1997.

In our analysis of the biblical narratives concerning Israel's ancestors, we concluded that the Old Testament represents a purely or at least primarily literary product with its own distinctive understanding of antiquity. The preceding analysis of the intellectual history of Bronze Age Syria and Palestine confirms this point. Consequently, the Bible provides little or no useful information regarding the Bronze Age before Israel's formation.

Some scholars would prefer to retain some historical elements in any biblical portrait of the early history of Israel, dubbing this the "proto-history" of Israel. Such a proto-history will be based on the bits of real historical information that appear here and there in the course of the generally legendary and mythical biblical narrative.[1] The patriarchal

[1] See the discussion between Abraham Malamat and Niels Peter Lemche in their respective studies: "Die Frühgeschichte Israels: Eine methodologische Studie," *TZ* 39 (1983): 1–16; and "On the Problem of Studying Israelite History: Apropos Abraham Malamat's View of Historical Research," *BN* 24 (1984): 94–124.

narratives clearly do not fit into the social milieu of any known Bronze Age society. The patriarchs interact with kings and their highest-ranking ministers as though they stood on the same social level. Thus the Old Testament ignores the vast chasm between sovereign and subject that appears in the political documents of the Bronze Age. The Joseph saga and the book of Exodus could be seen as a better reflection of reality because they allow only representative Israelites to have contact with the king. In these narratives, ordinary people sit on the sideline: the *hoi polloi* play only cameo roles in the hero's portrait. These differences between the patriarchal stories, the Joseph story, and the Exodus narratives do not suggest that the latter are historically more accurate; rather, they are attributable to different topoi and themes in the various circles in which the narratives were formed. The patriarchal narratives revolve around the fate of individuals, while the perspective of the Joseph and Exodus sagas is national. It should not surprise us that the later narratives portray the relations between leaders and subjects more "realistically." The national perspective offers a more "hardheaded" attitude of leaders toward their subjects, something which should not surprise us. The Joseph saga is not a historical report but a novel that has to heed only literary concerns and criteria rather than earlier historical realities. So its perspective is not "realistic" at all; it is a sophisticated literary work that demands a perceptive reading.

From the perspective of the history of religion, sometimes the Pentateuch and other ancient Near Eastern texts exhibit amazing similarities. Some of the details of the Old Testament's view of God, for example, are comparable to those from around the Oriental world. In particular, later Israelite sacrificial practices somewhat mirror those described in Ugaritic sources. Other points of contact include the presence of house gods in private homes and elaborate institutions of divination. However, such similarities owe their existence to ideas involving the place of human beings vis-à-vis the gods, which were shared by most people of the ancient Near East.

Again, from the perspective of the history of religion, we cannot conclude that the patriarchal narratives are historical because they share religious characteristics with Ugaritic epic texts or other ancient Near Eastern literature. First, the language in question simply represents generic Near Eastern terminology and ideas. Second, it appears not only in the Bronze Age but also in the Iron Age. Thus, in the Oriental view of humanity, all men are basically created equal; and this idea was not merely a romantic ideal; rather, it found expression in everyday life.[2]

---

[2]The practical measures taken to rectify injustice have been noted many times. Even the obligation to care for the poor in modern Christianity, Judaism, and Islam is to be understood in light of this background. In fact, this background forms the basis of the social consciousness of the modern Western and Near Eastern world.

This idea of humanity appears in the Old Testament as well as in Old Babylonian royal inscriptions, especially the previously quoted prologue from the Code of Hammurabi. The idea appears in principle even much earlier, in third-millennium Sumerian texts. This human ideal of equality seems sometimes strengthened by concrete historical developments, namely, by the previously mentioned breakdown of the center in favor of the periphery—a situation often caused by severe social inequity. The ideology of the tribes, which at that time took over the center, said that all members were related as descendants of the same patriarch and therefore had equal standing. This self-understanding shaped interpersonal relations in the states that developed from tribal societies—even in cases where the people no longer really belonged to tribes, but the tribal ideology developed further into an intertribal concept.

Over against such similarities between the Old Testament and other Near Eastern documents stands a fundamental difference between the Old Testament and its counterparts of the third and second millennia B.C.E.: the Old Testament is strictly monotheistic. There is only one God, the God of Israel. This one God takes over all the functions of the gods of polytheism, for Yahweh is not only the creator of the world but also the god who brings about everything that happens in the world. He takes care of people and converses with them on occasion (at least on the literary plane)—when they are disinclined to obey, for example. Fertility (of people, livestock, and soil) is a gift from Yahweh, and enemies forbear to attack because Yahweh himself fights for Israel.

Yahweh's Syro-Palestinian "colleague" El sometimes developed a special relationship with human beings, as with Kirta; but the job of interacting with humans usually fell to the "second-class" gods, such as Baal and Anath. El's role differed: he was the creator of the world but could no longer intervene to change anything. Moreover, according to Near Eastern notions, even the act of creating had to conform to a preexisting design. In contrast to this type of creator-god who was not really free to decide anything, Yahweh acted according to his own will, creating the world and implementing his own plan for it. Nevertheless, even the Old Testament may allude to a predetermined plan for the universe. Proverbs 8:27 speaks of the preexisting "Lady Wisdom" as a goddess who stood beside Yahweh "when he established the heavens."[3]

---

[3]This notion that something existed prior to creation shines through the Gen 1 creation narrative. Here the verb *bādal* (in its causative form) is particularly noteworthy. It means "to differentiate between" and appears in several contexts: to distinguish between darkness and light; sea and land; waters above and waters below. These are not created elements; rather, they already existed previously. One could also point to the four elements of the Ionic natural philosophers: the primary element (light); the cold element (darkness); the dry element (earth); and the wet element (water or sea).

The patriarchal narratives, like the rest of the Old Testament, speak of a single God: even Israel's earliest ancestors are made out to be monotheists. Yahweh chooses Abraham, subsequently reveals himself to Jacob, and chooses Moses to release Israel from Egypt. Yahweh appears to Moses at Sinai and personally leads Israel through the desert. Yet traces of earlier religious traditions find their way into these narratives. For instance, Rachel steals the household gods (*tᵉrāpîm*) from her father's home (Gen 31:19): these are the "foreign gods" that Jacob later buries after he takes possession of their land (Gen 35:2–4; cf. also Josh 24:23). These remnants may have survived as a kind of substratum beneath the monotheistic surface of the Old Testament narratives. At any rate, a definite monotheism was something that Bronze Age inhabitants of the ancient Near East would never have understood. To the mind of the people of the ancient Near East, the world—heaven and earth as well as the realm of the dead below the surface of the earth—was populated by all kinds of gods. For example, in the contract between Ramesses II and Hattusilis III, "a thousand gods from the land of Hatti and a thousand gods from the land of Egypt" are called upon to destroy any treaty breakers.

Monotheism did not sweep the field all at once; it did not suddenly burst upon the religious thought-world of the ancient Near East. Rather, a developmental process began at the latest at the end of the Bronze Age, gained momentum during the Iron Age, and finally issued in a practical, and at certain points even theoretical, monotheism. It seems that particular gods (or better, their priesthoods) gobbled up other gods, so to speak, and so took over their functions and identities. Thus eventuated a monopoly on divine worship—a development that certainly also had something to do with economic and political interests. In Egypt's New Kingdom, monopolization took place within the cult of the god Amun of Thebes, who was served by a large priesthood in an influential sanctuary. Akhenaten's reforms included the relocation of the royal residence from Thebes to Akhetaten (Tell el-Amarna) and the introduction of a "new" religion—or rather, in reality, the strengthening of one old branch of Egyptian religion. This religion concentrated on the worship of the sun disc and should be seen as a reaction against the priests of Amun in Thebes and not so much as a genuine monotheistic revolution. Ultimately, the king failed to uproot the power of Amun's priests, and upon Akhenaten's death, Thebes regained its prior religious and political position. Yet the struggle between the king and Amun's priests continued to influence politics. This perpetual battle between religion and the state finally caused the kings to move their residence to Lower Egypt. There they built a new capital, Tanis, close to Heliopolis (On), where the sun-god Reᶜ lived as the new imperial god, although he had already absorbed most of Amun's traditional attributes, if not his identity. Consequently, Egypt split in two, since the priests of Amun resisted pharaoh's "reforms" by establishing an independent "theocratic state" in Upper Egypt that was ruled by Amun's high priest in the name of Amun himself.

In Mesopotamia, we find a comparable, though not quite as spectacular tendency toward a practical monotheism: a city-god (Marduk in Babylonia; Ashur in Assyria) attempts to remove other gods from his domain. Similarly, in West Asia, the Phoenician god Baal (in the form of Baal Shamem—the "Baal of Heaven") almost attains a religious monopoly akin to that of Yahweh's.

In Israel, as portrayed in the Old Testament, monotheism appears to be already fully developed. The Pentateuch leaves no doubt: Yahweh is Israel's God-without-peers. He no longer serves merely as a patron god for certain individuals—the patriarchs—or the national god of Israel: he rules the world. He forbids worship of other gods and condemns those who do so. Other gods that may have been worshiped earlier in the land of Israel are no more than repulsive and revolting idols.

Generally, from the vantage point of the history of religion, the Pentateuch diverges significantly from the Bronze Age texts. The world as depicted by the pentateuchal narratives varies considerably from the ancient Near Eastern one, insofar as history, society, and religion are concerned. This divergence is not a minor matter, easy to resolve or harmonize; it is fundamental and indicates that the narratives of the Old Testament are far removed from the period to which they refer.

Nevertheless, another avenue exists for an investigation that intends to relate the pentateuchal narratives to Bronze Age Syro-Palestinian culture. Many common folk-literature topics and ideas appear in the Old Testament: fairy tales, anecdotes, and literary genres sometimes related to the narrative world of epic poems. Did the authors of the Pentateuch use some of the same sources as other ancient Near Eastern poets, such as the authors of the Ugaritic epics? The answer to this problem is similar to the question of so-called common religion. Although such common elements are certainly present, they do not indicate a direct connection between, for example, the pentateuchal narratives and the Ugaritic epic literature. In this case we should rather speak about a commonly shared world of folk literature that is not confined to a certain period or place.

The main difference between the Pentateuch and Ugaritic epics[4] is a matter more of form than of content. Narrative prose dominates the Pentateuch. Previously, we noted that longer narrative prose demands a higher literacy level, whereas poetic narrative genres flourish in less literate societies. Here we have an example of how the Old Testament dif-

---

[4]Here we should also mention the Homeric epics, which resemble the Ugaritic epic literature in the way that they blend the divine realm with the human world.

fers in genre from its Bronze Age Near Eastern counterparts. Surely the Pentateuch contains elements of genuine Oriental literature and should be considered a piece of ancient Near Eastern literature; however, it is equally true that its literary genres and forms demonstrate that it does not conform to any generic ancient Near Eastern models. Old Testament monotheism and its distinctive narrative prose hover around the border between the Oriental world and later Jewish-Hellenistic culture.

IV.2. THE GOAL OF HISTORIOGRAPHY

Friedman, Richard Elliott. *The Exile and Biblical Narrative: The Formation of the Deuteronomistic and Priestly Works.* HSM 22. Chico: Scholars Press, 1981. **Mullen,** E. Theodore. *Narrative History and Ethnic Boundaries: The Deuteronomistic Historian and the Creation of Israelite National Identity.* SBLSS. Atlanta: Scholars Press, 1993. **Nielsen,** Flemming A. J. *The Tragedy in History: Herodotus and the Deuteronomistic History.* JSOTSup 251/Copenhagen International Seminar 4. Sheffield: Sheffield Academic Press, 1997. **Van Seters,** John. *The Life of Moses: The Yahwist as Historian in Exodus–Numbers.* Louisville: Westminster John Knox Press, 1994. **Van Seters,** John. *Prologue to History: The Yahwist as Historian in Genesis.* Louisville: Westminster John Knox Press, 1992.

The Pentateuch *seems* to reflect historical events, though without any corroborating evidence to support such a claim. This circumstance raises many questions. First, how did such a unique enterprise—foreign to Oriental tradition—come into being? What motivated its author or authors? What did they want to say? What actual circumstances inspired these stories? For whom were they written? Did the authors recite the stories about Abraham and the patriarchs, Moses in Egypt, and the desert sojourn just to entertain an audience that liked stories of the distant past? Or did their intended audience consist of people who were searching for a home and an identity?

The questions never cease. Although we possess some answers to individual questions, generally, we must sift through too many *possible* solutions. Thus, it is difficult but not impossible to bring clarity to the Pentateuch's period of composition and the venue in which it developed. The answers that scholars have proposed cover a broad historical spectrum: from Solomon's reign in Jerusalem, through the Babylonian exile, to the Hellenistic period.[5] If the Pentateuch comes from Solomon's time,

[5]For the dating of the earliest Old Testament historiography to Solomon's era, see Gerhard von Rad, "The Beginning of Historical Writing in Ancient Israel," *The Problem of the Hexateuch and Other Essays* (New York: McGraw-Hill, 1966), 166–204. Here, the so-called Succession History (Solomon's rise to power) takes center stage. For the Yahwist's function during that period, see von Rad's "The Form-Critical Problem of the Hexateuch," *The Problem of the Hexateuch and Other Essays*, 1–78. Van Seters specifically covers the exilic period in *Abraham in*

from the royal court, it might have been read as more casual literature. If, however, it belongs to the exilic or postexilic period, it urgently attempts to solidify the collective memory of the people in exile by recasting the ancient traditions into a national history.

We must investigate the different proposals for dating the Pentateuch to determine its *Sitz im Leben* and the objectives of its authors. To give the discussion some boundaries, we will consider four periods within which this material could have developed: the tenth century B.C.E. (the time of the so-called united monarchy); the end of the seventh century B.C.E.; the sixth century B.C.E. (the time of the Babylonian exile); and the postexilic period.

For many years, scholars considered the tenth century B.C.E. the most likely starting point of the Hebrew historiography of the Pentateuch. At the same time, the redactional process that led to the appearance of the Pentateuch was understood to be a prolonged period lasting until postexilic times. In this way, scholars imagined a piece of collective history that grew and developed over a period of more than five hundred years! This is not the place to discuss in detail the pros and cons of this theory. What is important are the consequences to be drawn from the theory that the earliest part of the Pentateuch—that is, the so-called Yahwist stratum—belonged to the tenth century B.C.E.

The advocates of this early dating assume that Israel was a very young nation: only a few generations earlier the Israelites had traded their tribal existence for citizenship in a state, possibly even an empire. The traditional materials from this period indicate that the new Davidic-Solomonic kingdom suffered from growing pains. A resilient feeling of independence caused tribespeople to resist the leanings of a centralized state. Furthermore, the kingdom consisted of two formerly independent parts with their own history and social cohesion. Internecine conflict between the two components of the state now threatened the infant nation. Thus, the books of Samuel underscore David's dilemma: he had to "conquer" his kingdom, and then repeatedly defend it against domestic as well as foreign enemies.

From this perspective it becomes obvious that early Israel needed a national history to legitimate its existence. In it, the citizens of the king-

---

History and Tradition (New Haven: Yale University Press, 1975), while more than a hundred years ago Maurice Vernes already detailed the Persian-Hellenistic period in *Précis d'histoire juive* (Paris: Hachette, 1889). Scholars such as Bernd Jörg Diebner and Hermann Schult from the so-called Dielheimer circle have also contributed to the postexilic period discussion in "Thesen zu nachexilischen Entwürfen der frühen Geschichte Israels im Alten Testament," *DBAT* 28 (1994): 41–46. Cf. also Niels Peter Lemche, *The Canaanites and Their Land: The Tradition of the Canaanites* (JSOTSup 110; Sheffield: Academic Press, 1991), and idem, "The Old Testament: A Hellenistic Book?" *SJOT* 7 (1993): 163–93.

dom of David and Solomon would find in their own past the reasons for belonging to a new state under the leadership of an exalted king—a difficult assignment, if one recalls the many obstacles and conflicts that befell this young state. The idea of composing such a national history originated in the new capital, Jerusalem. Members of the new royal elite wrote to unite their fellow elitists by portraying them all as representatives of "one and the same nation." For this purpose it did not matter whether the history was factually reliable or pieced together as a collection of historicized myths and legends. The important thing was to unite everyone by presenting a collective chronological and ideological framework. Ultimately, the focal point of their work was Solomon's temple around which their Israelite state was organized.[6]

Placing the first Israelite historiography during Solomon's reign yields reasonable answers to two important questions. Why and for whom was this history written? The history was written in order to establish the identity of the new nation; and the *Sitz im Leben* of its writing was the Solomonic court, because there it was that people lived who were educated and had an international perspective and so would have been open to such literature. Thus the authors of this historical narrative satisfied the expectations of its audience.

This hypothesis of an early composition is problematic, however, because we possess no corroborating evidence to support the world to which it allegedly refers. As has been noted, the oldest parts of the Pentateuch penned by the so-called Yahwist display strong monotheistic predilections: Yahweh alone is Israel's God. Yet this notion of God does not agree with any known tenth-century construct—at least insofar as it demands belief in one God alone. For this we must look to a later stage in Israel's religious history. This fact alone suggests the late origin of Israel's historiography. Furthermore, other scholars have expressed doubt regarding the existence of a large Davidic-Solomonic empire. This makes the presumption of the historicity of Solomon's reign quite problematic.[7] Of course, if there were no Davidic empire or

---

[6] Consider the victory hymns in Exod 15, where the Israelites' journey does not end until Yahweh guides them and appears to them at his holy mountain. In 1 Kgs 6:1, the construction of Solomon's temple begins 480 years after the Israelites first leave Egypt (i.e., twelve forty-year generations). Already in the Pentateuch, the historical bookends of Israel's "history" are the exodus and the temple construction.

[7] Here we note two important studies: David Jamieson-Drake's, *Scribes and Schools in Monarchic Israel* (JSOTSup 109; Sheffield: Sheffield Academic Press, 1991), and Hermann Michael Niemann's *Herrschaft, Königtum, und Staat* (Forschungen zum Alten Testament 6; Tübingen: J.C.B. Mohr, 1993). Both use different methods to arrive at the same conclusion, namely, that no such state existed in Judah before the eighth century. We also recommend the collection of essays edited by Volkmar Fritz and Philip R. Davies in *The Origins of the Ancient Israelite*

an Israelite state comprising all twelve tribes, it is hard to imagine such a national history appearing in the tenth century B.C.E.

King Josiah's reign (639–609 B.C.E.) provides another possible time for the composition of the pentateuchal narratives. Modern researchers often find this dating as compelling as the Davidic-Solomonic period, and the arguments in favor of a Josianic date are very similar to those used to advocate a Solomonic origin. Although it has to be admitted that Josiah's kingdom was only a small one, he tried to restore a Davidic empire—a dream that arose from the political situation during his reign. From 625 to 612 B.C.E., the once-mighty Assyrian empire was crushed by the simultaneous onslaught of several foreign powers: the Babylonians, the Medes, and the Lydians. In southwestern Levant, this situation allowed Josiah a free hand to expand his jurisdiction into the former Assyrian provinces to the north. Since Solomon's days, two small, separate states divided Israel's land: the northern kingdom (Israel), which fell to the Assyrians in 722 B.C.E.; and the southern kingdom (Judah), which operated as a weak Assyrian satellite state. With Assyria's demise, the royal court in Jerusalem saw an opportunity to reunite the people of the former northern kingdom under the reign of the southern king.

Since Josiah's aim was putatively the reconstruction of the Davidic-Solomonic empire, the arguments for assigning the composition of the Pentateuch to this epoch are almost identical to those given above. The whole population of Judah and of the former northern kingdom would have been ready to unite under a shared national ideology. With their national history, the authors managed to fashion a common historical tradition that both legitimated the rule of the Judean kings over a united Palestine and also justified the costs of their military buildup. After all, the military obviously served the national interest, and private interests had to take the back seat. Josiah's untimely death did not undermine this literary project but rather did much to give it the strength to withstand the blows inflicted upon Judah's dreams of dominance by the *really* dominant powers.

Several compelling arguments suggest the pentateuchal narratives arose during the Josianic rather than the Davidic-Solomonic epoch. A strict monotheism fits much better in this time—easily conforming to this king's cult-reform mentality. Furthermore, this date explains why so many traditions from the northern part of the country survived and were incorporated into this new national history. The northern state no longer existed, and the southern kingdom took over its intellectual heritage and used it in its project to annex the north. Moreover, this date ex-

---

States (JSOTS 228; Sheffield: Sheffield Academic Press, 1996), as well as those edited by Lowell K. Handy in *The Age of Solomon: Scholarship at the Turn of the Millennium* (SHANE 11; Leiden: E. J. Brill, 1997).

plains why so many literary genres of Mesopotamian origin survived in the Old Testament, especially the custom of writing annals (as borrowed from the Assyrians). This is especially true for the so-called Deuteronomistic History: the books of Deuteronomy, Joshua, Judges, 1–2 Samuel, and 1–2 Kings, all related in one way or another to Josiah's reforms.

Generally, Josiah's reforms provide a reasonable backdrop for biblical historiography; however, some facts about that period militate against this hypothesis. For example, the Pentateuch narrates the constant migration: from Babylon to Canaan, from Canaan to Egypt, etc. Such migrations are far removed from the ideology and life circumstances of Josiah's reign. By the end of the seventh century B.C.E., Jerusalem could reflect upon a thousand-year history. Although it may have received an influx of refugees from the northern kingdom after the Assyrian conquest of Samaria, most of its population was still of ancient stock. In short, most Jerusalemites did not see themselves as descendants of immigrants from foreign countries. That their forefathers should once have been nomads would have seemed like a very odd idea.

Ultimately, the Babylonian exile may provide a more likely setting for the composition of the Pentateuch. It is especially the theme of migrations to and from the land of the fathers that seems more congenial to this period of deportation and exile.

In exile, the people grasped desperately for hope amid hopelessness. They satisfied their yearnings in Israel's early history. If Israel once flourished, it might rise again. The new historiography foreshadowed Israel's future direction: a return to a golden age for which this literary construct prepared its readers. Through it, Israel could find its roots, define its national identity so as not to be absorbed by the masses of Babylon.[8]

Eventually it is possible to create a synthesis combining the two last mentioned datings of the historical literature in the Old Testament, including the Pentateuch. First, the historiographic framework developed late in the preexilic period. Later, during the Babylonian captivity, the narrative developed around certain themes that now became important, such as the ancestors' migrations to the promised land. As attractive as this theory is, however, it has not been proved. Against this early date speaks the fact that the Pentateuch consists mainly of prose literature. Granted, there are apparent parallels in Assyrian annalistic literature—something which is only relevant, we would emphasize, to parts of the Deuteronomistic literature (Joshua through 2 Kings). But the prose form, which in the Pentateuch covers several different genres of literature, is

---

[8] On history as an answer to national catastrophes, cf. Niels Peter Lemche, *Ancient Israel: A New History of Israelite Society* (The Biblical Seminar 5; Sheffield: Sheffield Academic Press, 1988), 155–56.

certainly unusual for a sixth-century context; it was a form of narrative which the Greeks developed in the sixth and fifth centuries, and which became even more popular in the Hellenistic and Roman periods. In spite of this, the Old Testament scholar John Van Seters continues to hold to the exilic dating of these narratives. On the one hand, he relates the history of the Pentateuch to early Greek historians such as Hecataeus of Miletus, who, however, was active at the beginning of the fifth century B.C.E., that is, after the Babylonian exile (538 B.C.E.), while, on the other hand, he compares it to Babylonian ideas of history.[9]

Unfortunately, the precise character and scope of Greek historiography in the sixth century B.C.E. is almost unknown. Only a few scattered fragments remain, mostly quotations that appear in later Greek authors. On the other hand, we possess much information about subsequent historiography from Herodotus to the Roman historians. It would be difficult to miss the fact that, despite the obvious differences between this Greek and Roman historiography and the historiography we find in the Old Testament, they basically belong to the same genre. Of course, Van Seters may be correct: perhaps the Old Testament historiography depended on Greek inspiration. Nonetheless, it is an unlikely assumption that Jewish authors of the exilic period could have known the work of their Greek colleagues as well as Van Seters suggests. This type of situation better reflects the Persian or Hellenistic periods, when the Greek and Oriental worlds came into close contact, producing a favorable environment for the Old Testament authors to use Greek historiography as a source of inspiration.

Against this late dating it may be objected that the Pentateuch's subject matter probably meant very little to people living in postexilic times. Why should anyone refer to the travels between Babylon and Palestine after the people of Israel had already long ago returned from exile? The answer to this question comes from the actual historical events at the end of the Babylonian exile: namely, no mass migrations from Babylon to Judea took place. True, some Judeans—maybe we should now call them "Jews"—returned home; however, most descendants of the Judeans who were deported from Palestine to Mesopotamia at the start of the sixth century preferred to stay there. Mammoth Jewish homecoming migrations simply did not take place until this century (in 1952 C.E.) when the Babylonian Diaspora finally dissolved.

The journeys from Babylon through Palestine to Egypt which play such a dominant role in the pentateuchal narratives might reflect the travel between the "homeland"—Palestine—and the Jewish Diaspora, at first dispersed over the Persian and the Greek empires. If so, did the

---

[9] *In Search of History* (New Haven: Yale University Press, 1983), pp. 8–54 on early Greek historiography, and pp. 55–99 on Mesopotamian historiography.

Pentateuch's authors develop a "Diaspora literature" that would justify the claims of Diaspora Jews regarding their legitimate lineage and homeland? Such a composition would provide a response to Jews living in Palestine who might not have easily accepted the claims that these people—who did not want to "go home"—should also be considered Jews. Finally, dating the Pentateuch to the fifth, fourth, or even third century B.C.E. would provide a simpler and more reasonable explanation for the connections between the Old Testament and Greek historiography. At that juncture, Greeks had already migrated east over the course of several generations before Alexander the Great's Near Eastern conquests and the subsequent massive spread of Greek influence.

These considerations will not be sufficient to dispel the idea that the Pentateuch is very likely older, at least in part, and that in the postexilic period it was merely supplemented and expanded—as most scholars still believe at present. Nevertheless, the point here was to emphasize that the important themes and distinctives of the Pentateuch fit very well with the postexilic period, characterized as it was by the interaction between the Jews of the Diaspora and their homeland. But here we can only suggest this line of argument; this is not the place to carry it through.[10]

All of the preceding suggestions regarding the dating of the Pentateuch provide compelling arguments. In my opinion, we must take each one seriously. I feel more persuaded by the fourth option, but each theory carries its own internal logic that commands our attention (although the Solomonic age's historicity remains most problematic). At this stage, we need not arrive at any solid conclusions. One fact, however, does remain: the Old Testament's authors did not intend to write history in the modern sense; that is, they did not offer exact historical reconstructions for their readers. Rather, they submitted a literary-historical program, which will have to be evaluated differently depending on the date of composition. In any event, they were striving to set forth the past in such a way that it could speak powerfully to their own present.

IV.3. WHAT DO WE SEEK IN THE BIBLE?

Diebner, Bernd Jörg. "Wider die 'Offenbarungs-Archäologie' in der Wissenschaft vom Alten Testament: Grundsätzliches zum Sinn alttestamentlicher Forschung im Rahmen der Theologie." *Dielheimer Blätter zum Alten Testament* 18 (1984): 30–53. **Herrmann,** Siegfried. "Die Abwertung des Alten Testaments als Geschichtsquelle: Bemerkungen zu einem geistesgeschichtlichen Problem." In *Sola Scriptura: Das reformatorische Schriftprinzip in der säkularen Welt.* Edited by Hans Heinrich Schmid and Joachim Mehlhausen. Pages 156–65. Gütersloh: Gütersloher

[10] For a full-blown discussion of the Pentateuch as postexilic literature, cf. E. Theodore Mullen Jr., *Ethnic Myths and Pentateuchal Foundations* (Semeia Studies; Atlanta: Scholars Press, 1997).

Verlagshaus G. Mohn, 1990. **Knauf,** Ernst Axel. "From History to Interpretation." In *The Fabric of History*. Edited by Diana Edelman. Pages 26–64. JSOTSup 127. Sheffield: JSOT Press, 1991. **Tadmor,** Hayim, and Moshe **Weinfeld,** eds. *History, Historiography, and Interpretation*. Jerusalem: Magnes Press, Hebrew University, 1983. See also the bibliographical references in section I.3 above.

What do we seek in the Bible? The simple answer to this question would be: the truth. But what kind of truth? Again, the simple answer would be: historical truth, at the least. Of course, most modern people know that the narratives have numerous inaccuracies, at least on the surface; but what else should we expect in such old stories? Inevitably, various accretions changed the original narratives; and sometimes even the original traditions may not be historically precise.

But still, many people do not think that they can give up the existence of a historical Abraham and a historical Jacob who accomplished certain things that were important for the later history of Israel. Otherwise, why would later Israelites have claimed them as their ancestors? And people who are convinced of the historicity of Abraham and Jacob easily believe also in the historicity of the traditions of Israel's sojourn in Egypt, the liberation from Egypt, the revelation at Sinai, and the wandering in the wilderness. And of course they accept that all of these accounts were written down long after the fact. Granted, the actual events may have been less grand than their Old Testament depictions; they may have been relatively peripheral developments whose consequences could not have been guessed at the time—although the liberation from Egypt must have been deemed decisive for the establishment of the Israelite people right from the start. Finally, people are also ready to retain the figure of Moses, since he must have been the central character in the early history of Israel, which makes no sense without him; and the establishment of monotheistic Israelite Yahwism seems hard to imagine without him. So think many people right up to the present.

Why do so many people hold the historical dimension of these Old Testament narratives to be so decisive? Does the explanation lie in the character of the texts themselves—or in the habitual historical orientation of modern people? With regard to the texts, at first glance they do meet our expectations for historical reports. They describe a development, a long historical course of events subdivided into distinct phases according to a chronological schema. In this way the pentateuchal narratives appear deceptively akin to modern historical reports. Hardly anyone would deny that appearance. But their shortcomings and imperfections are just as widely recognized. That goes along with the fact that they arose in a time when the criteria of modern historical research were not yet operative.

First impressions must be revised. We must question whether these texts do reflect history. The historical-critical analysis presented here eliminates any possible connection between these texts and the history of the ancient Near East as far as Israel's early history is concerned. In the final analysis, the pentateuchal narratives are of little use for the study of the history of ancient Palestine.

From those analyses, several irrefutable conclusions follow. First, neither Abraham, nor Isaac, nor Jacob ever drifted through Babylon, Canaan, and Egypt searching for wives, refuge, or land. The Israelites never suffered under or fled from Egypt and its oppressive pharaoh. Israel did not travel through the desert for forty years. These stark denials are meant to make a point: it is a mistake through and through to construe the pentateuchal narratives as historical accounts. They are rather literary constructs. These stories develop according to the rules of a dramatic plot—sometimes totally ignoring the pragmatic considerations of real life. One final word will suffice on this matter. The Pentateuch contains no historical reports, but many beautiful (hi)stories. Historical-critical analysis of the ancient Near Eastern world that putatively provides the background for these narratives leads inevitably to this conclusion.

If we keep on looking for a historical core in the narratives that keep on refusing to provide or even allow for any such thing, we might begin to suspect that the problem lies in the modern expectation. Modern historical research is a child of the Romantic Age, from which we inherited our present-day concept of history. Histories were also written before the Romantic Age; however, rather than proper historical depictions, they contained more or less systematic chronicles about the heroic escapades of ancestors. In a sense, history was told, like a story, rather than written; and that kind of storytelling naturally prepared for authentic historiography. Thus, since the beginning of the nineteenth century C.E., the word "history" has changed its meaning in a fundamental way. While the English language allows for a distinction between "history" and "story"—in itself a derivative from "history"—many other languages do not make this distinction. The usual word for "history" in German, for example, is the same one for "story." In such languages the verdict that the biblical narratives belong to the category of "story" will be almost identical with the description of them as "history," but the difference is, as a matter of fact, a major one.

It was no coincidence that modern historical research and writing developed in the Romantic Age—which was not always very "romantic," since people spent most of their time collecting and systematizing the discoveries of the Age of Enlightenment. Enlightenment methods and insights, which originally had to do with the natural sciences, were now extended into new territory, even to the humanistic fields, such as philosophy and history. It became important to achieve results that would be, almost like the laws of nature, so certain as to be unquestionable. It was therefore critically important to know whether an account was absolutely true or was only a good literary construct. At the same time the groundwork for scientific historiography was being prepared in the discovery that a people's national identity was inseparably connected with its history. Because this notion of history developed within the emergent European nation-states, it became an issue of the utmost importance. Historians from that milieu were called upon to write national histories that ideologically legitimized the nation-states in which they lived. More and more, it was forgotten that historiography was also the literary genre of a beautiful story.

Earlier we noted that chroniclers wrote for the intellectual elite. In the Romantic Age, a new social category developed: *the people.* This group included every citizen, each on a level with the others. In earlier literature, this group is present but not allowed to speak. (Thus in the *Iliad,* Homer's Thersites lifts his voice among the great men only to be flogged by the hero Odysseus.) A collective consciousness could not develop before people saw themselves as belonging to particular nations. In the nineteenth century C.E., this idea blossomed under one banner: compulsory education. Through it, history was taught in clear enough terms that even the sons of peasants should know to which nation they belonged.

It is ironic, then, that this period also witnessed the blossoming of romantic nationalistic fiction dressed up as history, although without any intention of describing the past "as it was"—the keynote of modern historiography for any historical context—such as the novels of the Scottish writer Sir Walter Scott.

Many nineteenth-century historical portrayals are really novels under the guise of scientific historiography. These novels do not relate stories akin to Sir Walter Scott's tales of knights or Bernhard Severin Ingemann's novels about Danish kings of the Middle Ages; rather, their authors "improve" historical facts by reworking original materials. French historians were still writing in this way early in this century.[11] The zenith of this process was reached at the turn of the century when the German historian Theodor Mommsen won the Nobel Prize for literature. With his functional and down-to-earth depictions, Mommsen fully lives up to the expectations of a modern historian!

The Protestant Reformers blazed the trail for this evolution. People had to have and read their own Bibles, and soon the Bible was more decisively important than even tradition. Effectively, the Bible played the role of a "proto-history," in that it told a story that somehow became the history of every Christian. At the same time, the Bible was equated with the truth, since it revealed God's plan for humankind. During the Reforma-

---

[11] Here one recalls not only Adolphe Thiers's extensive treatment of Napoleon, but also André Maurois's various historical "recreations."

tion, the idea that the Bible reveals the true meaning of the Christian life carried with it—almost like the nationalistic sentiments of the early nineteenth century—a frenetic intellectual activity which had as its consequence a fundamental change in the perception of the world. Certainly, the Reformation was from a theological perspective a golden age. Inspired theologians managed to make their messages comprehensible for the common folk. Their success, like that of the Romantics, hinged on the ability to convince their contemporaries of their perceptions. Yet the mood changed as the Reformation yielded to Protestant orthodoxy and the Catholic Reformation. Now the Bible was not simply inspired, but inherently true—an unquestionable, absolute truth. Luther himself still questioned the validity of individual biblical texts (his low opinion of the letter of James is well known), but orthodoxy had no room for such thoughts. Theologians now argued no longer about the human system of thought; rather, they contended over the Bible, which they saw as critical ammunition against the authority of the Roman Catholic tradition.

Orthodoxy developed the notion that the Bible represents the absolute and indisputable truth. At the outset, historical accuracy was not the kind of truth that was meant. The concept of historical accuracy was outside the horizon of people of that day. To be sure, if asked, they would certainly have affirmed that the Bible was true in that sense; but they would not really have understood the question! Visual art from between 1500 and 1800 C.E. shows that biblical themes were never treated with historical accuracy during that period. Biblical characters are portrayed wearing either clothing from the artist's own day or outlandish garb with no historical connections. The narratives so depicted were thus understood either as present-day example stories or as belonging to a fantastic kind of never-never land.

Still, the Bible was accepted as the absolute truth. Thus an ominous trend developed: one no longer searched for biblical truth in philosophy, art, or literature, but in history. This new, historically correct Bible led to unavoidable conclusions that Christians defended to the death. Christians already believed that the Christian Church was indeed "the true Israel," that is, the "people of God." In the Romantic Age these views coalesced around nationalistic ideas: the "people of God" was a nation for which the Bible provided the legitimation. Despite the obviously ideological character of such a conviction, people attempted to examine the historical underpinnings of such claims of legitimization—and not with any intention of calling them into question or undermining them, but in order to be able to ground their "truth" deeply in history and in God's will.

Now two competing biblical understandings clashed head-on. On one side stood the notion that biblical truth is completely commensurate with the truth of history. Thus the Bible is absolutely correct and beyond scrutiny. On the other side, the Bible represents an inexact history whose historical reflections are mainly true. Both sides agreed that the Bible provided the constitution for the people of God. For almost two hundred years, the two groups have retained their militancy toward one another. Yet they agreed on one thing: they both thought that biblical truth could be traced using historical methods.

To this very day many people will still resist the idea that the Bible should not be indisputably correct—even its minor details should be infallible. Among us we will still encounter Christian communities and groups who stick to the absolute correctness of the Bible in spite of two hundred years of scholarly analysis. We should, perhaps, look for the reason for this resistance to modern scholarship in a strange mixture of ideas: on the one hand, the sense of being part of the nation of God, and, on the other hand, the concept of being citizens in a modern nation-state. In both contexts—that is, the Christian community and the modern nation-state—history plays a similar role. It creates common identity and a common destiny for every person who accepts this history as his or her own. In the modern nation-state, this trend led to many disagreements, not to mention strife and even war. The sense of national identity sharpened into nationalistic fervor, and citizens who resisted any attempts to undermine that burgeoning corporate identity. These notions are the products of both positive and negative experiences. Nothing brings people together like collective defeats or national catastrophes. They teach us how to stand together during difficult times. It is almost impossible—not to say inadvisable—to question the correctness of retrospection on a collective history. Such questions may destroy community solidarity and endanger a nation's ongoing existence. Among the people of the nation of God, it is just as dangerous to question the truth of the Old Testament's depictions of Israel's ancient history. This leads to insecurity among or damage to God's people so long as we confine our thoughts exclusively to the historical dimension.

But at the same time, we are witnessing the deconstruction of the Israelite history as portrayed in the Old Testament. We can no longer sidestep the questions: what can we do with an unhistorical biblical history? Does this spell the end to the people of God and the church? Where can we find a solution to this problem? First, we must extend a warning that we should not throw out the baby with the bathwater, that is, we should not lose sight of what we were taught. Otherwise, we are likely to forget that people once believed the Bible to be speaking about history.

Today many scholars—especially in North America—cling to the following proposition: since the Old Testament does not represent history as we understand it, it is inappropriate to continue historical investigations. The narrative intention should be the only and true focus of our investigation (i.e., narrative criticism). We can validate this type of research because until a few years ago pure literary analyses of the Old

Testament were few in number (although never as few as those who practiced narrative and literary studies claim). It should at the same time be underscored that the members of this research school do as a matter of fact attempt to create a new basis for the Bible's legitimacy or its larger place in the Christian consciousness. Thus Christians continue to see the Bible as an inspired source of information for themselves as the people of God, although the formerly undisputed historical rationales for their beliefs have been effectively destroyed.

Such views warrant consideration, and they remain within the tradition of historical reading, understood in its broadest sense, though in order to perceive that this is so one must have a broader idea of history than the usual modernistic interpretation. If the narratives of the Pentateuch have nothing to do with history but are no more and no less than what they promise to be—namely, stories—this does not mean that these narratives are not true to their own intention. As long as they do not claim to be history in the modern sense—something their authors obviously never intended—the idea of reading them as literature will cause no serious trouble. As a consequence, the historical-critical study of the Old Testament will have to change its methods if in the future it is still to qualify as historical and critical. In the future, the theme of this study must be no longer the history of the Israelite people, but the history of the ideologies that persuaded the Old Testament authors to describe the past as they did. In itself, the Pentateuch continues to be a historical document, irrespective of the historicity of the events to which it refers. The scholar therefore still has the responsibility to approach this section of the Bible in a strictly "scientific" way, and it is still appropriate subject matter to investigate how the Pentateuch came into being. On the other hand, the scholar should not confuse this reconstruction of the history of the literature with an analysis of the early history of the Israelite people; all we have is the view of this early history entertained by the Old Testament historians. The recovery of several different layers and editions of the biblical texts and the identification of a series of authors and editors is helpful since it enables the scholar to start, so to speak, a dialogue with the text. This dialogue, however, does not concern the relations between the text and the events narrated by the text but is interested in showing how the author composed a text in order to communicate with the audience, which now includes us.

As far as historicity is concerned, critical scientific analyses of the Bible prove that its claims to absolute authority and undeniable truth cannot stand. Yet its dialectic importance remains intact inasmuch as it presents ideas and thoughts that are just as valuable to present-day readers as to the audience for which it was originally written. It only demands that its readers accept its testimony. Not everyone today considers the Bible an unshakable or unassailable authority. As the British Old Testament scholar and theologian James Barr expressed, the Bible may have lost its authority (people can no longer be pressed into believing in the Bible) but it remains authoritative, that is, a valid and respected source of information and guidance for people who accept it as their Bible.[12] The Bible presents a way of understanding itself, God, and the world: we may affirm this view or reject it, for we—like Martin Luther—should not submit slavishly to everything in it.

---

[12] See *The Bible in the Modern World* (1973; repr., London: SCM Press, 1990), esp. pp. 23–30.

INDEX OF NAMES

INDEX OF PLACES

INDEX OF SUBJECTS

INDEX OF BIBLICAL SOURCES

INDEX OF OTHER ANCIENT SOURCES